The
Birth
of the
Modern
Mum

A new mother's no nonsense guide to looking
after herself in baby's first year.

Heather Irvine
CLINICAL PSYCHOLOGIST

The Birth of the Modern Mum

A new mother's no nonsense guide to looking after herself in baby's first year.

by Heather Irvine

Published in 2014 by Jane Curry Publishing

[Wentworth Concepts Pty Ltd]

PO Box 780 Edgecliff NSW 2027 Australia www.janecurrypublishing.com.au

National Library of Australia Cataloguing-in-Publication entry:

Author: Heather Irvine

Title: *The Birth of the Modern Mum*

Subtitle: *A new mother's no nonsense guide to looking after herself in baby's first year*

ISBN 978-1-922190-92-5 (Print edition)

ISBN 978-0-9924532-8-2 (Epub Edition)

ISBN 978-0-9924532-7-5 (Epdf/Mobi Edition)

Cover and internal images: Shutterstock, Bigstock and Fotolia

Cover and internal design: Deborah Parry

Editorial: Amanda Hemmings

Production: Jasmine Standfield

Printed in Australia by McPherson's Printing Group

Praise from the Gidget Foundation

This book has left me moved, inspired and educated. Every day I am asked to recommend a chronicle of wisdom for pregnancy, birth and mothering. Written with warmth, compassion, genuine insight and humour, Heather Irvine has given us just what was needed.
DR VIJAY ROACH, OBSTETRICIAN AND GYNAECOLOGIST, CHAIRMAN GIDGET FOUNDATION

About the Gidget Foundation

The Gidget Foundation is a not-for-profit organisation whose mission is to promote awareness of perinatal anxiety and depression amongst women and their families, their healthcare providers and the wider community to ensure that those in need receive timely, appropriate and supportive care.

 GidgetFoundation   www.gidgetfoundation.com.au

About the R.E.A.D Clinic:

The READ Clinic was originally established 33 years ago and has gradually grown to become a substantial community presence on Australia's Central Coast. Over 5 years ago Heather became Clinical Director of the business which now houses 25 psychologists and other allied health professionals, making it one of Australia's largest private psychology clinics. The Clinic takes care of all members of the community – from women and children to men and the elderly – who present with a range of psychological issues, including depression, anxiety and trauma, using the most up-to-date and best practice therapeutic assessments and techniques.

R.E.A.D. CLINIC
PSYCHOLOGICAL SERVICES

DEDICATION

This book is dedicated to my inspirational mother and to her mother, to my adoring father and to his mother, to my loving husband and to his mother, to my two amazing sisters, to my sensational BFFs and and to every mother that I have known who has touched my heart, inspired my words and given me strength and determination to stand up for mothers around the world. I do not know what I have done to deserve such amazing people in my life. I hope I have done you proud.

CONTENTS

Introduction

The moment a child is born, the mother is also born. She never existed before. The woman existed, but the mother, never. A mother is something absolutely new. RAJNEESH, INDIAN SPIRITUAL TEACHER

Every woman's journey into motherhood is unique. And important. We have come from many different places to be here. Yet here we are. Sometimes united. Sometimes divided. But forever connected by the knowledge that by some miracle we are now the proud owner of the title "MOTHER". And we've all had moments when we've wondered if we'll survive this new journey. If not physically then at times mentally. But surely we didn't go on this journey just to *survive*, did we? Well no, not really. But it is one of my girlfriend's favourite checks to do at the end of the day. At 6pm yesterday she tweeted: "Yep, all still here. Three of us still breathing. That counts as a good day."

So yes. Parts of this book are dedicated to just that. Survival. About getting us through those dark days of mothering when we can't see our sanity for the dirty nappies. When the only thing we feel we've done well all day is carefully wiped vomit off the lounge.

Other parts of this book are dedicated to those rarer times when we feel we've got enough energy left over to dedicate ourselves to trying *new* ideas to be the best mother we can possibly be. You know those fleeting moments, when baby has finally settled, the house looks vaguely inhabitable again and

1

there's a cup of tea and a macaroon on the table in front of us.

There are still other parts of the book which help us to know what is *normal*. Until I had my babies, I thought a "normal" mothering day would be a baby simply entertaining herself all day (with the odd breastfeed and nap times thrown in) while I enjoyed cappuccinos with other mums. Wrong. Crazy. Absurd really. But until I talked to other mums, I didn't know that my baby's tricky behaviour and my world of chaos was normal. Suddenly, even though my situation was still hard and I still struggled at times, I took great comfort knowing other mums were struggling too.

And then there are the other parts of this book. The ones that we probably wouldn't normally read in our first year of mothering, because they're not just about what the *baby* needs, but about what we – the mothers – need. Because this book has been written after working with hundreds of mothers over the years and identifying that unless mothers take care of their needs, ultimately it's not just the mother who suffers, but our babies too.

Mothering is about many things, but it's not about eternal suffering. While I've met some mothers who were determined to disagree (oh yes…nothing worse than the smell of a burning mother martyr!), ultimately commonsense must prevail. Our babies can be calm if we can be calm. Our babies can work through their emotions if we can work through ours. Our babies will grow up to love themselves and forgive their own mistakes, if we have shown them how. Not through telling them, but by doing those things in our own lives.

I am fortunate enough to have worked with, talked with and cried with many, many mothers. Some of these have been clients, some have been friends and others have been family. I have been blessed to have the job where I could learn all about the psychology of mothering and share it with those wanted to hear it, but to also know when it was simply my job to listen or to simply sit together side by side during a baby's marathon crying session.

I am always amazed at how grateful other mothers are when I share a story, some words of advice or suggest a technique. I have had many mothers thank me with such heartfelt words that it's sometimes overwhelming.

These comments are what gave me the motivation to write this book, and to continue writing it during times when I wondered whether anyone would read it. I particularly remember the comment made by Dianne, a lovely mother I worked with, a very clever teacher who had found the transition to parenting very difficult. She'd said, "I was talking with my friend yesterday and we discovered both of us had come to see you in the early months of adjusting to our new babies. We concluded that every new mother needed only two things when her baby came home from hospital: a 'Heather' and a cappuccino machine."

So, this is my attempt to put a "Heather" in your home. I've tried hard to get down on paper what it is I do in person. You'll notice the language isn't über formal and I often use my slightly unconventional sense of humour. And I've shared my own story at times too. Look carefully for quotes from "Erica" (Italian for Heather). I think it's helpful to know that Struggle Street was a place I visited in my own mothering journey too.

I wish you courage, joy and patience on your amazing new journey as a mother.

Happy reading.

Heather Irvine

10 ESSENTIAL TIPS FOR THE NEW MOTHER

1. **Slow down rather than speed up**. Mothering is more of a marathon than a sprint. Frenzied "I can do it all" attempts in the first months and a being a burnt-out mess for the rest of the time isn't ideal for you or your baby. Take it easy when you can: mothering is a life-long journey.

2. **Forgive rather than fight**. Loads of things will now annoy you that you'd never thought of before (Speak quietly! The baby's sleeping!). You can either get so worked up you blow a psychological gasket or realise people will sometimes misunderstand what you and your baby need because basically they're...umm...not you and your baby.

3. **Show assertion rather than aggression**. Stay forgiving, but back yourself enough to know when you need to stand up for yourself. And keep your claws in. No ferocity required. State your case and state your response if people don't support it. The most powerful change agent is within you, not within another.

4. **Health rather than hairspray**. So you and your baby *look* good, but inside you're an emotional wreck. End result? I'm predicting it's your sanity as much as your hair that's gonna get messy. So spend less time searching for surface solutions and dig into the soul-deep dimensions.

5. **Prioritise rather than please**. Your twice-removed third cousin might be in need of company, but not at the expense of your inner circle of prioritised people. Know the "who's who" of the VIPs in your life and always devote your energy in their direction first. Third cousins can wait.

6. **Connect rather than collect**. Pretty prams are, umm, pretty. And not much else. And your baby doesn't care about it anyway. What is important is the connection you have with your baby. Spend less time collecting baby bargains and more time in baby bonding.

4

7. **Care rather than criticise**. Regarding others and yourself. Seen another mother doing it tough? Been in another mother's tornado-trashed house? Look familiar? This is no time to judge. In loosening up on the parent condemnation factor, we can care for all women who have tough times – ourselves included.

8. **Peace not perfection**. In the search for perfection, you'll find peace as elusive as a rainbow's end. Accept your world for what it is, and yourself for who you are, and you'll find peace might just knock you off your feet...hopefully so you can lie down and have a nap!

9. **Breathe deep, not breath-less**. Check you're not breathing at the same rate as a female freedom fighter. High breath rate means low psychological staying power. Slow it down, relax your muscles. Your baby can't be calmed if all your bodily signals suggest you're in some type of war zone.

10. **Celebrate uniqueness rather than compare**. Wow! You've created a totally unique human being. Sleeping, feeding, pooing, and all the other delights will all be one-of-a-kind. Just like you. Wonderwoman Wendy with Blissful Baby next door probably have their own little dramas. So forget about them. For you and your baby to have an extraordinarily special relationship, you only need to know each other.

Reasons to be grateful and take a stand for others. *How we fare in the mother stakes compared to the rest of the world.* *Women and girls – in many roles, including their role as mothers – drive improvements in the human condition. When we invest in them, we invest in a powerful source of global development.*
MELINDA GATES, CO-CHAIR OF THE BILL & MELINDA GATES FOUNDATION

Mothering is tough. I don't need to tell you that – because you're doing it. But for many women across the globe, it's a whole lot tougher than in our Western World. An extraordinarily informative report has recently been published by the Save the Children fund: *Surviving the First Day: State of the World's Mothers 2013, 14th annual report.*

These are some of their findings for the **babies**:

- Every year, nearly three million babies across the world die within the first month of life, most from preventable causes.
- This is still an improvement on previous years. Since 1970, the number of children dying has declined by more than half, even though the population has almost doubled.
- In many individual countries, progress has been even more dramatic. Barely a decade ago, in 1999, one in five Rwandan children died before turning five. In 2011, the child mortality rate in Rwanda had fallen to one in 20.
- But it is still woeful in some countries. A mother in sub-Saharan Africa, for example, is 30 times more likely than a mother in an industrialised country to lose a baby at some point in her life.
- In contrast, only 1% of the world's newborn deaths occur in industrialised countries.
- Without dramatic change in the trajectory for Africa, it is estimated that it will take over 150 years for an African newborn to have the same chance of survival as one born in Europe or North America.

These are the findings for the **mothers**:

- In 2011, 287,000 women died during pregnancy or childbirth.
- This is progress – it reflects a decline of almost 50% since 1990 when up to 543,000 women died per year.
- Healthcare for mothers in sub-Saharan Africa remains woefully insufficient.
- In Ethiopia, Niger and South Sudan, more than half of all women receive absolutely no skilled prenatal care and more than 80% of women are unattended during childbirth.
- In Somalia, 74% of pregnant women go without care during pregnancy – the highest rate in the world.
- In Nigeria, nearly one woman in five has no one – not even a family member or friend – to help her during childbirth.
- In Somalia, one woman in 16 is likely to die in pregnancy or childbirth.
- In Sierra Leone, the odds for death in pregnancy or childbirth are one in 23.
- Every year, about 40 million women give birth without someone present who has any midwifery skills, and more than two million women give birth completely alone, without even a friend or relative to help them.

What *you* can do:

- Citizens everywhere should urge their governments – both recipient and donor governments – to invest in newborns and honour any commitments they've made to improving services for women and their babies.
- Join Save the Children's global newborn and child survival campaign. Visit the website to find the campaign in your country, make your voice heard, and join their movement. To learn more, go to www.savethechildren.net.

- Seize any opportunities now and in the future that support any efforts, large or small, everywhere in the world, to increase the safety of a mother and her baby.

Every night, millions of mothers around the world wish for their children to be safe, happy and healthy. It's what we all want for our children. And it's certainly not too much to ask.

When a child is placed into his mother's arms for the first time, that woman's life is changed forever. The moment is brief and precious. We must seize the opportunity to invest in this most basic, most enduring partnership – between a mother and her child – if we are to change forever the course of history and end preventable child deaths. JASMINE WHITBREAD, CEO, SAVE THE CHILDREN INTERNATIONAL

Chapter 1

We've created a family! What a mother needs to know about herself in the first few months.

How was the birth?
15 hours of excruciating pain...

What a laugh!
Men should try it...

Never before had I understood the extraordinary process of birth. It was like someone had given me some type of primal power. Sure, my pregnancy wasn't always easy and the birth, well, let's just say it wasn't pretty! But the truth was I had just brought another being onto the planet. Wow. Just mind-blowing. Jo, MOTHER OF ONE

You did it. You actually did. The crazy idea that a baby that big could come out an exit *that small* actually worked! And if your "exit" wasn't up for it, then even crazier that some clever clogs with a big knife sorted it out anyway.

And now you're a mother! Exciting. Amazing. Enthralling. Scary. Absolutely overwhelming. Was all of this is in the contract? Did we miss something in the fine print? Man, oh man. How is it that wise and well-informed women have been tricked into breeding for centuries without *really* knowing what we were in for? I was certainly fooled – I blame the Kleenex ads. And since you're reading this book, I guess you were too.

For some mothers, the first few weeks are fun. For others…well, not so much. The overall impact of the first few weeks has variations between mothers around the same level as say…well…the temperature in Africa and the North Pole. Here's what some of the mothers I work with had to say:

I remember walking friends out to their car after they'd visited to welcome the new baby, and I felt this strange panic – I've left my baby alone in the house, I've neglected her – but am I allowed to go outside for a moment without her? I just didn't want to wake her up. Am I trapped here? How come they get to leave? It took ages to figure out what was OK to do. SHARON, MOTHER OF TWO

Me and my partner just doted on our little Gracie from the time she was born. Everything we did, everything we talked about, everything that was important in our lives was now about her. She was the centre of our universe. She was just amazing. We just felt so blessed. MAGGIE, MOTHER OF TWO

I was in pain. My caesarean wound became infected. I couldn't get the hang of breastfeeding and my husband was pressuring me to switch to bottle feeding. I was so tired…all the time. I didn't seem to be able to stop Joel crying. It was just all too much. This wasn't what I thought it would be like. NAME WITHHELD, MOTHER OF ONE

So are all new mothers overwhelmed?

In a word, yes. But not all the time – and it does get easier. Beware those who profess it to be super-sensationally simple 100% of the time though: suspect delusions, delirium or drunkenness (well, maybe not the last one...). For the realists among us, we're prepared to admit that the onset of motherhood heralds more new experiences than we'd ever imagined. New situations (think poo explosions), new emotions (just let me cry...over nothing...again) and new social interactions (did we just talk for three hours about breastfeeding?).

The good bits of mothering are good. Mind-blowing, miraculous and amazing, really. The bad bits are, well, bad. And sometimes horrendously scary too. If someone had tried to warn me about this, I mustn't have heard them over the noise in my ipod speakers (What? Birth can be hard? Or did you say it could be a laugh?). Ah, the old days. Head in the sand, believing birth and first-time motherhood would be almost...well...just like one long holiday in a fantasy theme park of fun...

Are other mothers also stuck on the "surprising" nature of their baby's birth?

At least I knew what they meant by "the miracle of birth". It really was a miracle and I'm grateful for it every day. But I'd never expected it to be like what it was. In my birth plan I was meant to be listening to music and my husband massaging my back while I rocked on a birthing ball. Ha! I was whisked off to have an emergency caesarean and my husband almost passed out with fear. Not what we'd planned! SARAH, MOTHER OF TWO

There's only one word that unites all mothers when it comes to birth – UNIQUE. Because each birth experience will be just that – completely different to every other woman's on the planet. Some of us have the dream birth – where there's pleasure in the pushing, or there's calmness in the contractions, and it's all just, well, peachy. Some of us have the other type officially banned from Kleenex ads – where there's needles being poked and surgical knives doing their, um, "thing", and it's all, well, messy (or scary or both).

If your birth didn't follow your birth plan, I'm guessing this has then left you feeling deflated or annoyed or let down or guilty about what happened. Sometimes I wish I had a dollar for every new mother whose emotional health is derailed by the "failed" birth plan. Just quietly, I'd be a millionaire by now.

I remember one mother coming to me in floods of tears, overwhelmed with extraordinary disappointment at having screamed out in pain during labour. "My birth plan included being silent. You know, a silent birth," she sobbed. "My calm birth teacher said it was achievable if I used my calm breathing and calm thoughts." Yikes! I felt like saying, "I hope your calm birth teacher isn't advertising the 'benefits' of staying silent through all severely painful events like car accidents or broken limbs," but I refrained.

All jokes aside, some women do have silent births, but I have always been deeply annoyed at the significant amount of time, energy and resources utilised in preparing a "birth plan" that fails to take into account that most of them will need to be changed due to:

a. **To give birth safely for the sake of saving us or our baby**. That sounds pretty important to me. Always wise to change tack if it means saving a life!

b. **Because of how we respond to our crippling exhaustion or excruciating pain**. It's the modern world, ladies – we are allowed to have limits on what we can tolerate. There aren't points being handed out for who suffers the most (although there are some women who think so – bizarre!).

c. **Because we were bossed into doing something by someone we considered a powerful medical professional**. The power imbalance between a woman giving birth and the medical staff helping her can look a little like an elephant vs a mouse in proportion. Nearly all mothers (unless of the fierce and ferocious, scary kind) would have done the same. Forgive yourself for being human.

I spent so much time researching natural births and devising my birth plan before my first child. After it ended in an unplanned induction and episiotomy I kept going over and over what I had done wrong and what I could do better next time. I was so determined to get my second birth "right" and so I went back to all my books and researched everything again.

But surprise, surprise – it didn't go to plan either. It was a really, really long and painful labour, followed by an episiotomy, drips and all the things NOT in my birth plan. Never again would I plan a birth or have preconceived ideas of what a good birth should be, or blame myself for things not going right. If I do have any more children my plan will only be to keep an open mind, go with the flow and focus on what's important – having a healthy mum and baby at the end. ROSE, MOTHER OF TWO

What do you do if you feel derailed by your birth plan?

If like so many mothers out there you're disheartened by your birth not going to plan, here are some suggestions that might help.

- **Discuss with other mothers their experiences**. Chances are you'll quickly realise you aren't alone and there are very few mothers who have the "perfect birth". And for those who did, power to them. You never know, their birth plan may have been one of the only things that has gone right in their life for a long time. Mind you, if they gloat too much, feel free to take that photo of their baby vomiting on their best shirt and post it on Facebook when you get home.

- **Remember the statistics**. Twenty per cent of births are induced, around 30% of births end in caesarean section, up to 15% of us will have an episiotomy, around 50% will have epidurals, and many more will have used other forms of pain relief they hadn't intended to use. Be kind to yourself about being part of these statistics. You can bet that for most mothers, these outcomes didn't reflect the original birth plan!

- **Direct your thoughts to what DID go to plan**. Did you stay home for the intended time? Did you have your birth partner with you? Were you able to avoid medical intervention for as long as psychologically or physically possible?

- **Remember what the whole purpose of writing a birth plan was all about**. Birthing pools, massage oils and husbands cutting cords aside, the main aim was to work through the amazing process of producing a child in the healthiest and safest way possible.

- **Remember you haven't failed.** Failure is only possible if we've prioritised passing a test called "sticking with a plan regardless of how unwell, worn out or ravaged by pain I am", rather than the one called "making the best decision I could according to my psychological and physical strength and my baby's health at the time". Beware of any mother trying to arrange and then pass these types of unhelpful "tests" as time goes on too. She'll be the nightmare of your mothers group: treating parenting like a competition rather than actually being physically or psychologically healthy.

- **Nurture yourself if you feel you were less than adequate in the coping stakes.** Our expectation of ourselves to tolerate excruciating pain in childbirth needs to be eradicated. Each woman has a different body (including the size and shape of her cervix). Each baby presents differently during birth (some with foreheads first, others slightly twisted or shoulders high). Each woman also has a different pain tolerance and each birth presents a totally different set of experiences likely to cause pain. Births *cannot* be compared between women.

- **Acknowledge the research.** No matter what our well-meaning, crystal-wearing yoga/spiritual/meditation leader has ever so calmly suggested, there is no evidence that in cases of a healthy birth outcome (i.e. no excessive medications or complications for the child), the type of birth has *any* impact on our baby's long-term temperament. The type of birth may have an impact on our baby's sleep/pain levels/appetite, etc in the first few days, but over a few weeks the birth can't explain these factors. The fact that your gloating mothers group friend experienced the perfect birth doesn't mean she has avoided a colicky, tricky baby. And try not to look too pleased when her world turns a little more pear-shaped.

15

They kept telling me it would have to come out down there.

I said it wouldn't fit. And it didn't.

Proof: child delivered by emergency caesarean.

What if the whole birth thing was overwhelmingly traumatic?

At one point I thought one of us was going to die. Something had gone wrong with my epidural. Breathing was an effort. The room was full of medical professionals, all telling me just to keep breathing. When my baby was born, she was rushed away for resuscitation. My husband went with her. I was surrounded by people but I felt so scared and so alone. It was awful. DONNA, MOTHER OF ONE

Anyone daring to label you as a histrionic weirdo for admitting your birth wasn't "your best experience ever" or failed to be "an amazing spiritual journey" should check their statistics first. As many as one-third of women will describe their birth experience as traumatic. The upside is that two-thirds of women *won't* but if you're one of the ones who do then life in the post-birth period can be tough. And seemingly there's VERY little empathy (other than from a few mums with similar experiences) for those of us

16

traumatised new mothers. Any cuts, tears, pain, scars, stitches, bruising or near-death experiences are dismissed with those few little words "at least you have your baby now".

As the researcher, Cheryl Beck, explained in her investigations into mothers' birth experiences: "What a mother perceives as birth trauma may be seen quite differently through the eyes of obstetric care providers, who may view it as a routine delivery and just another day at the hospital[1]."

Dismissive words to "get over it" don't cut it. Unfeeling medical staff downplaying the severity of what we experience just makes it worse. And none of it's good enough for helping women in our supposed "modern" society deal with the reality of birth. The fact is that somewhere between 1% and perhaps as many as 10% of women's experiences will not only describe the birth as "traumatic" but will actually have symptoms sufficient to be diagnosed with posttraumatic stress disorder (PTSD). Look around your mother friends. There's one in 10 who could well have diagnosable trauma-based disorder as a result of the birth experience.

I'd had a great pregnancy, really fit and healthy. The birth was perfect too. Everything I'd hoped for. Then it all went wrong. I had a major haemorrhage. I was passing out. I remember my mum (my birthing partner) screaming out for help. I'll never forget the look of panic on her face. Nurses were everywhere. But then I don't remember anything else. It was hours later that I came out of it. I'd lost so much blood. I was so weak for the next few days that I hardly had the energy to breastfeed. Bonding with my most cherished daughter was badly affected. It took me months to feel physically well again and properly connect with my little girl.
GEORGIA, MOTHER OF THREE

So if you're wondering whether you've been traumatised by all or part of your baby's birth, see if any of these symptoms match your experience.

SIGNS OF POSTTRAUMATIC STRESS DISORDER AFTER BIRTH

The Symptoms	Words Mothers Use
Do I have nightmares or regular flashbacks about my baby's birth?	*Every time I try to sleep or close my eyes it's like it's happening all over again. I can't get away from the images of all that went wrong.*
Do I blame myself for what happened?	*I just can't help thinking it's all my fault. That I could have done something different or better.*
Do I feel like I have to check on my baby's safety all the time, fearing something else will go wrong?	*I don't trust myself around my baby. I worry all the time that she'll be injured or stop breathing like when I gave birth.*
Do I become distressed when talking about my baby's birth or avoid talking about the birth?	*Whenever I talk about it, I just get overwhelmed with emotion and burst into tears. It's awful so I don't talk about it anymore.*
Do I regularly feel irritable, angry or sad? Does my mood seem to change rapidly from being OK to being overwhelmed?	*It's like there's just this darkness all around my thoughts and feelings. Then the next minute I just feel so angry.*
Do I feel numb, almost as if I can't feel anything?	*I just kind of feel nothing. Like nothing matters.*
Do I avoid my baby or feel disconnected from my baby because of what happened?	*I don't know what I feel about my baby. It's like she's not mine really. This isn't what I thought it would be like.*
Do I avoid child health nurses, doctors, hospitals or other people and places because they remind me of the birth?	*I just can't face anything that looks "medical". It freaks me out and reminds me of the birth.*

What do you do if birth has left you traumatised?

If you found that a number of these symptoms are reflecting your experience, the following suggestions might help.

- **Tell your story**. It seems a little odd to talk about something that distresses us, but research has shown time and time again how important it is to talk about the hard stuff in order to recover from trauma. However you need a person to share your story who is patient, compassionate and non-judgmental. If you're lacking this helpful ear in your personal social circle (or feel that people don't really understand), early research is suggesting the process of writing down the experience of your baby's birth can be helpful. If that's not something you feel able to do, or it's not enough, then seek the listening ear of a professional – perhaps a kind child health nurse, your GP, a counsellor or a psychologist.

- **It's not just the "baby blues"**. Many new mothers talk themselves out of getting help because all emotional experiences are swept under the "it's-just-the-baby-blues" carpet. If your birth was traumatic and you're experiencing many of the symptoms in the checklist above you could well have much more than baby blues. Seek out help and support (see chapter four for further information about finding a therapist who's right for you).

- **Be compassionate with yourself even if others aren't**. Know that what you went through *was* painful and was scary and you did feel out of control or lost or helpless. Birth is a HUGE experience. But, you were the only one who had *your* experience. Nobody else has the knowledge or the right to minimise your pain, distress or fear. It's like trying to talk someone out of how they felt in a car accident – just plain ridiculous.

- **Give yourself time**. After a trauma, the human brain is programmed to reassess how safe our world is, including everyone and everything in it. While this is happening we can see danger in places we never thought possible. I once worked with a mother whose birth experience had resulted in the near death of her baby. As a result she couldn't have ANY plastic bags in her house in case they flew over and suffocated her baby. But just like this mother, over time, we do learn to trust again and we learn to be less afraid. Be gentle to yourself as you slowly regain the confidence to trust in your world and in others.

- **Wherever possible, don't avoid situations, events or places that remind you of the birth**. Again, this may seem peculiar (why on earth would you go somewhere just to get more distressed?) but unless we do, trauma symptoms tend to increase rather than decrease. Try to see that midwife who was there at the birth, or at least write her a card or letter. Return to the hospital where you gave birth and drop in some flowers. Take it day by day and gradually build up to it. Always take a trusted friend or your partner with you if you need support. And be patient; it could take years to rebuild your confidence to return to places that caused you so much distress.

It took me two years to go back to the hospital where I'd given birth to my baby boy. It had been such an awful birth and he'd nearly died. Part of me was still angry at some of the staff, but there was one midwife who I credit with saving his life. I wanted

to take her flowers and leave a note for her. It really helped my
recovery to go in there and do that. ERICA, MOTHER OF TWO BOYS

- **Connect with others who had similar experiences**. Use the internet to find links to women all around the world who need support just like you. Although your own mothers group or friendship group may have all had the "birds chirping perfect birth", remember that one-third of women in the western world didn't. These women with the "no birds chirping traumatic birth" variety are more than willing to welcome you to the fold and exchange their stories with you.
- **Read more about it**. As you search for other mothers with similar experiences, you'll probably come across a few good websites. But quite frankly there should be a whole load more of them. Interesting to note too that the two main websites dedicated to birth trauma were also started by mothers – not professionals. We have a long way to go to truly honour mothers who experienced traumatic births, but in any case, these two websites are a start:
  - Trauma and Birth Stress (www.tabs.org.nz): established in 1998 as a charitable trust by five mothers who had experienced traumatic births.
  - The Birth Trauma Association (www. birthtraumaassociation.org.uk): established in 2004 to support women suffering from post natal post traumatic stress disorder (PTSD) or birth trauma. It was also founded by mothers and has expanded to an impressive group of parents and professionals all advocating for increased awareness and treatment of birth related trauma.

What if the birth was OK, but your brain's gone to mush?

There was food in the fridge. The same stuff we always bought. But for the life of me I could not figure out what to do with it. It just seemed so hard. It was overwhelming. Matt (my partner) took over the cooking after I served him plain pasta for five nights in a row.
OLIVIA, MOTHER OF THREE

I have a friend who regularly jokes that after her baby was born, her brain was delivered with the placenta and she hasn't seen it since. No doubt you and your mother friends also regularly use the "baby brain" excuse to explain all sorts of usual mother mishaps – forgetting names, mixing up dates, arriving at the wrong location and sending thank you cards to the wrong people (or was that just me?), just to name a few.

Actually, research tells us that your brain is likely to be *more* active in the post-birth period than it was before. Huh? Why doesn't it feel that way? Well a closer look at the fine print also tells us that it grows in all those areas related to caring for our baby – or as the researchers suggested – in areas designed to "orchestrate a new and increased repertoire of complex interactive behaviors with infants."[2] Hmm, nothing about managing complex social diaries, catering for masses of visitors, or starting a university degree then? Well, no…

I had to laugh at myself sometimes. The number of times I walked into rooms and had NO idea why I went in there was nothing short of ridiculous. I was glad I could blame the "baby brain" because otherwise I'd have seriously questioned my sanity.
NINA, MOTHER OF TWO

So why is it that straightforward, everyday things seem so hard? Basically because if you're like most new mums you're frantically busy trying to fit everything in, or you're stressed out, or you're short on sleep. Which means:

a. **The "flight or fight" areas of the brain start to take over**. Otherwise known as the subcortical regions, these spring into action because our system perceives some kind of "threat" and hence the need to take action. It therefore focuses on increased heart rate, respiratory rate and muscle tone.

b. **The "higher functioning" areas disengage**. Otherwise known as the prefrontal cortex, these areas are momentarily regarded as less important. Who needs to solve a sudoku puzzle when you're being chased by a lion? Or at least your brain *thinks* that's the level of threat you're under. So you lose capacities such as decision-making, judgment, planning and sense of self.

How very…unhelpful! But that's the way our brain works. So if you want to re-engage the disengaged areas, it's all about reducing the brain's perception of threat – or to put it more fancily – stopping the sympathetic nervous system taking over. It's then about igniting the opposing brain power – in fancy terms again – powering up the parasympathetic nervous system.

The best ways to do this for a new mum are:

a. **Calming yourself down whenever possible** – through self-talk, breathing techniques, diet, exercise and muscle tension reduction. I've only referred to it briefly here but there's a whole calming collection of tips covered in chapter three.

b. **Prioritising getting some zzz's**. Although not easy, there *are* a few ways to prevent sleep deprivation causing brain evacuation. Read further in this chapter and chapter three.

Now your brain's back in shape, what do you do about your body?

I bet when you were pregnant you knew *heaps* about how your body would change over the nine months you were carrying your baby. From how you were supposed to sleep, the impact of diet and exercise on the body, and massaging your perineum (my midwife tried to tell me it could be a "sensual experience"… whatever…), most pregnant mums I know become a walking encyclopaedia on both their own and their baby's biology. But in the post-birth period, it's different. We become the class dunce; well, about our own bodies in any case.

Which means we often are very unaware of what many mothers commonly experience including:

- **What goes out, must come in**. Once your baby is born (and the placenta less excitingly followed) your uterus begins to shrink. While it started at weighing nearly one kilogram, by six weeks it weighs approximately 100 grams. The process of the uterus contracting can cause lower abdominal pain (or "afterbirth pains") in some women. But while the uterus contracts of its own accord, our stretched-out abdominal muscles may need a little more help. Left to their own devices, they're plotting to stay floppy and then head south. Not the look you were hoping for? The only option is exercise with plenty of abdominal work (once your GP has given you the all clear to start).

- **I'm *still* bleeding.** After birth, women experience vaginal blood loss known as lochia. Lochia is like a heavy period for about the first 12 hours after birth and then begins to slow down. For those of you into "colour therapy", try to read some meaning into this evolution: the lochia is usually bright red in colour for the first couple of days, then changes to a pinky, brown colour for up to four weeks after the birth. Excitingly, there is then a cream or white discharge for up to eight weeks after the birth. Guess it's payback for missing all those menstrual cycles during pregnancy.

- **My water works aren't watertight**. For those who gave birth vaginally, your pelvic floor probably took a huge beating, which means that "leakage" in the early days is normal. While these battered bits will gradually regain their strength (after a few weeks or even months!), help yourself out by doing your old pelvic floor exercises. Boring as they are, they're essential.

    No jokes please.

    Martha's pelvic floor was yet to stand firm during any unannounced humour.

- **You cut me from there to where**? If you had an episiotomy, chances are you're still umm… wondering what on earth happened "down below". Same goes if your baby's head/shoulder/other body part actually *tore* you open. Nice. Never saw that in any Kleenex ad. Anyway, most modern day stitches will dissolve in about two weeks and therefore do not need to be removed and the skin heals in about two to three weeks. In the meantime, squeeze your buttocks together before sitting, place your hand firmly over your "bits" and apply pressure during laughter/sneezing/coughing episodes, keep the area as dry as possible, and wear cotton underwear (save the lacy numbers for...umm...next century...).

- **They ain't grapes lady**! Haemorrhoids seem to arrive on cue as soon as we get pregnant or go through labour. About half of us will be graced (!?) by their presence. They're actually just varicose veins caused by the weight and pressure of the baby and the force of pushing. It's a double bonus – of the "you've got to be kidding" kind – if you have both an episiotomy and haemorrhoids. Relieve the discomfort as much as possible with ice packs or other creams or suppositories suggested by your GP. Avoid constipation by including fruits, vegetables and whole grains in your diet, and by drinking lots of fluids. Haemorrhoids will eventually shrink and become less uncomfortable, but always seek medical advice if you're in serious pain (and get second and third opinions, if necessary, to be actually listened to).

- **So *this* is what a boob job would look like**! After birth, to enable milk production, breastfeeding hormone levels rise which cause an increase in blood supply to the breasts. By around day three or four – whoa mama! – breastmilk production starts in a big way and breast size increases accordingly. But hands off boys! When they're big they're usually pretty uncomfortable. Touch them and expect them to fire breastmilk at you in protest (or receive a not-so-gentle slap from your beloved).

Wasn't feeding your baby just meant to be sort of "natural"?

Breastfeeding. Bottle feeding. How much. How often. Burping. Mastitis. Sterilising. Anyone else wanting to close the whole milk bar down again? Wasn't feeding your baby meant to be one of the best parts of being a mother? Hopefully for you, there are times it is. You know, those times when you and your baby seem to agree on the body positions, consumption amounts and timing of this rendezvous. But, get your wires crossed, and your "date" quickly goes downhill. Cue picture of crying, writhing baby and stressed-out tearful mother (add bleeding and cracked nipples if appropriate).

Both the method and the emotional response to baby-feeding is another mummy-experience as predictable and as common between mothers as well…a tornado. Those who thought it would be amaaazing can often loathe it, while others who saw themselves as the "prissy" type fall in love with getting their boobs out and baby latching on regardless of who's watching. Others wish they could but can't. Some mothers can, but don't want to for many valid reasons. Here's a range of experiences mothers have shared with me:

I couldn't breastfeed my third child. We just couldn't make it work, despite all my experience successfully breastfeeding my first two children! When I changed over to the bottle he stopped being so stressed out, his belly was full and he became the contented baby he was meant to be. Although I felt like a failure at times, deep down I knew I'd made the best decision for him. It also made me feel pretty rotten about how in the past I'd judged other mums who didn't breastfeed. KATIE, MOTHER OF THREE

My daughter's birth ended in a C-section – not the natural birth I'd planned. Then she couldn't feed from me. Once again this was supposed to be a "natural" thing we should be able to do. Women all over the world, in countries with far less access to information

than ours do it without any help or guidance. How wrong can we get it? After 48 hours of her not feeding they administered her into special care and were feeding her with expressed milk via a tube in her nose. Finally after about three days she fed from me using a nipple shield. Once again another completely "natural" process... ha! But once she fed from me all my bonding issues went out the window, I was free. NAME WITHHELD ON REQUEST, MOTHER OF THREE

I loved breastfeeding. It was just the most incredible experience. Being so close to my baby and feeling so connected. Smelling her, watching her. Wondering at how this little being came into my world. It was the best part of being a new mum. ROSEMARY, MOTHER OF TWO

No doubt you got heaps of advice on feeding. If you were like most of the mothers I know, you probably endured six different opinions from six different women – ranging from the lactation consultant in the hospital to the nanna in the hallway who ignored your "get lost" look and proceeded to tell you all she *didn't* know about feeding babies.

You'll find more details on the process of feeding in the next chapter, but in this section I just wanted to highlight a couple of important points relating to a mother's right to choose the method of feeding her baby.

- **We live in a democracy ladies**! Which means choice. Choice to breastfeed. Choice not to. If by any chance you think your choice is better, it's better to keep your opinions to yourself. Take a good look in the mirror and ask what your purpose is before you say a word to another mum about *her* choice. Believe in your choice and let all other mothers do the same.
- **Make no assumptions**. Heard of severe allergies, severe

tongue-tie, chemotherapy, or severe illness? Mothers or babies with medical complications sufficient to contraindicate breastfeeding are rare, but not unheard of. So, if you see a mother bottle feeding, smile. If she or her baby is struggling with major medical issues, she needs your support not your disapproving glances. Why not adopt the premise that she is bottle feeding for reasons that are in the best interest of either her or her baby?

- **Remember what's important**. The health benefits of breastfeeding are numerous, but so too are the benefits of a healthy relationship with your baby. Any mother who is breastfeeding while stressed out of her brain because of constant mastitis, failure to thrive, anxiety about her baby's consumption levels, constant thrush or other factors needs support reassessing her priorities. By all means, seek help to continue breastfeeding first, but know this: your baby's psychological health is less about where their milk has come from than whether they feel loved and connected with you while they are being fed.

- **Get help and seek support**. Regardless of which course you choose, there are times when we might have a million questions about whether we're getting the whole feeding thing "right". Seek the support of your local mothers group, talk to a lactation consultant, or call a parenting support line. For those who choose to breastfeed, there are many associations to support you, including the Australian Breastfeeding Association (www.breastfeeding.asn.au) or the Association of Breastfeeding Mothers (www.abm.me.uk). It's harder to find support groups for those who have decided to formula feed, but one that seems to offer a sensible perspective is www.fearlessformulafeeder.com.

Wouldn't it all be fixed by a few zzz's?

Sleep is the golden chain that ties health and
our bodies together.
THOMAS DEKKER, WRITER AND POET, 1572-1632

Shattered. Pooped. Exhausted. Downright dog-tired. Whatever your personal favourite for describing your state of tiredness, every new mum knows there is no feeling quite like that of sleep deprivation. And I'd predict that if you'd collected a dollar for every wise person who advised you to "sleep when your baby sleeps" you'd be close to being a millionaire by now. But you still won't do it, unless you're literally falling asleep on your feet. Like most new mums, I bet you're using your baby's sleep time to get some washing, ironing, sterilising, cleaning, phone calls and other mountains of chores done that were created by your little baby's arrival.

Understandable, but risky. If you are going to be one of those women who ignores the advice to grab sleep whenever you can, then know this: research suggests that as many as one-third of mothers diagnosed with postnatal depression (PND) may not be depressed at all, but are simply sleep-deprived. It seems that the impact of sleep deprivation over long periods mimics many of the symptoms of depression including teariness, difficulties coping, low self-esteem, changes in appetite, difficulty making decisions, difficulty concentrating, etc. But if you're one of the sleep-deprived, you know that already!

I've never been a sportswoman, but there's no way that the first
year of parenting isn't more exhausting than running a major

marathon. My evidence – the runners can still jump for joy when they cross the finish line. After my baby goes to sleep, I fall into a heap. AMY, MOTHER OF TWO

So, I'm going to be one of those *other* people in your life (that takes you to a million and one dollars) who also suggests that you "sleep when your baby sleeps". Perhaps these factors might help.

- **No put-downs necessary**. Sleeping doesn't make you lazy, inefficient, useless or incompetent. It means you're looking after yourself (you're allowed to, you know – no mummy martyrs required here).
- **Check your priorities**. Yes, all the other jobs will be there when you wake up, but check what's most important in this one: are you putting the importance of a clean house above the importance of maintaining your sanity? As one of my favourite sayings goes: "The work will wait while you show the child the rainbow, but the rainbow won't wait till you've finished your work."
- **It's up to you**. Other people can come in and help with your house-cleaning (husbands, mothers, friends, even house-keepers) but there is NO ONE else who can *sleep* for you! Obvious, but easily forgotten.
- **It's a responsibility thing**. Avoiding mental health problems isn't completely within our control but we can certainly reduce the risks, and getting sleep is one big step towards staying on the sane side of parenting.

So decide if your sleep thief is:
a. **Your baby** – due to her not settling, fussing or intense crying – then check you've used the techniques suggested for baby-

31

settling in chapter two. If the land of nod is still elusive even after applying these ideas then contact your local child healthcare centre and consult with a child health nurse to check your settling and sleeping routines and practices.

b. **You** – due to you feeling agitated, "wired" or just suffering from brain overload. In that case you're probably psychologically and physically strained and need to do an all-round health check. Read chapter three and see whether the tips and techniques I've outlined can get you back into a state where sleeping's possible. If you're depriving yourself of sleep because there's "so much to do" then ask yourself again what your overall goal is. A mother who gets enough sleep functions better on every level, including mothering, and isn't that what's motivating you to stay awake in the first place?

Once I'd worked out how to settle my baby, gave myself permission to sleep more often and stopped obsessing about keeping a perfect home, it was like a cloud had lifted from my mind. It was like I could enjoy my baby again. I could connect with her rather than just keep wishing she'd go to sleep. Shame it took me 10 weeks to figure it out, but I was glad I got there in the end. KATHRIN, MOTHER OF TWO

What if you're too busy crying or stressing to even care?

It was day three and I'd just brought my new son home from hospital when my sister rang. She told me she didn't like the name I'd chosen for my son. I know she's overly opinionated and normally I would have just ignored her, but not this time. It

triggered a crying frenzy that lasted for the next few days. I was just so miserable. I felt I couldn't get anything right about being a mum. Then it stopped and I became my normal self. I guess it was the baby blues – at least that's my explanation anyway! HAZEL, MOTHER OF TWO

The emotional rollercoaster in the post-baby period totally trumps anything Luna Park has to offer. Some moments we're on an emotional high, feeling as though nothing compares to the love between our baby – *our miracle* – and us. The next moment, sadness, anxiety and fear creep in and we can want our little miracle to miraculously disappear, or at least turn down the voice box volume.

When there's more feelings of being overwhelmed than elated, when the irritation, anxiety, sadness or distress doesn't seem to stop, when you burst into tears because your partner asks if you want tea or coffee, chances are you have the "baby blues".

But before this potential diagnosis leads you to tears – if you weren't already sobbing that is – keep in mind the following.

- **Remember how enormous the last few weeks have been.** You've probably been in more pain than you've ever imagined possible without resulting in death, your body is still adjusting to huge changes – boobs growing, uterus contracting, hormones flipping around like yo-yos – you're now *soooooper* responsible for another being's life and you're majorly sleep-deprived. I think it's fair to say that feeling emotionally drained would be kind of expected – bet you don't know anyone else who's been through all that you've been through and is clicking their heels together?
- **You're not alone in your state of "blue".** In meeting criteria

for membership to the honourable emotional club of "baby bluers", you'll be joined by as many as 80% of new mums. Because what you're feeling is *normal*. In fact, you've probably quickly calculated, based on the 80% figure, that it's more normal to experience the baby blues than not to.

- **You'll be out again soon**. Don't get too comfy in your new clubhouse because it's also normal to be kicked out of this institution pretty quick. The good majority of us mums somehow rapidly come to terms with all this baby bedlam within the first couple of weeks (how amazing are we!), with only the essential elements of a sound relationship required to send "the blues" packing – love from those around us, support when we need it, a cuddle when we're struggling and the odd Tim Tam and cappuccino for good measure.

On a more serious matter, if your "baby blues" symptoms are severe or do not clear spontaneously within the first two weeks, a medical assessment is required. Read more in chapter four about symptoms of postnatal depression to see if this might be what you're experiencing and for details on where to get help.

How come you're lonely if you and your baby are together 24/7?

I'd never expected to feel so alone as a mother. Feeds that went on for hours on end. Whole mornings spent trying to get my baby to sleep. Then all the cleaning up and washing. All on my own. Every day. Always alone. I longed for weekends so I could be with people.
JENNY, MOTHER OF TWO

34

OK, so here's the irony. The first stage of a new romantic relationship actually looks spookily similar to your first few weeks with baby. Seriously. Think about this – there's very little sleep because you know who (substitute bloke for baby) keeps waking you up for you know what (substitute sex for feeding). There's a lot of time spent half-clothed (substitute lingerie for unbuttoned flannelette PJs). Possibly a bit of "down there" pain (substitute honeymoonitis for episiotomy or stretched bits as appropriate). Your breasts are getting a serious work out. Nothing else seems important and no other tasks are getting done.

Now for the big difference: with our romantic partner we couldn't have been happier in the isolated little bubble of bliss. On the other hand, with our babies, while many of us can be similarly filled with overwhelming love, unless we have other people around us, life can also get *really* lonely, *really* unexpectedly, *really* quickly.

Mothers need strong social support. The old saying "it takes a village to raise a child" is as much about the mother's needs as the child's. Studies have repeatedly shown that while it is virtually impossible to predict the onset of postnatal depression, social isolation remains a big risk factor[3].

Finding your "mummy tribe" is important. It's hard work, but without it we're at risk. So it's all the more reason for making technology a "friend" to catapult you into a world where you can make real ones. Even if you've only got a five-minute window between feeding, washing, cleaning, settling and sleeping, the following uses of technology are great ways to stay connected.

1. **Skype it up**. Want your Mum in New York to see how your baby settles (or doesn't)? Want your BFF in Melbourne to share an evening with you? Skype them. Most computers

can connect via Skype and some newer TVs do the same. So set it up in your lounge room and dial up your pal. You can leave it on all day and just chat when you feel like it. One of the mothers I work with felt lonely after recently moving to Sydney, but she now uses Skype to stay connected with her mum who lives in Melbourne. Her mum can see her interacting with her baby, give support and advice when needed and generally feel part of the whole experience from 500km away! The newer advance of "group skyping" can mean you and all of your BFFs from around the world can catch up at the same time, or perhaps you and your family can too if you're all spread across the globe.

2. **Tweeting's not just for the birds**. Get savvy regarding social media options. Facebook is awesome for just sharing the odd photo, or tweet on your Twitter account a funny moment you experienced in your day. Who wouldn't want to hear about your baby's projectile vomit? On second thought, set up groups specifically for your "mother buddies" so baby stories and pics will be greeted with amusement not boredom or despair!

3. **Blog around the clock**. There are hundreds of mummy blogging sites. Some mothers have made a whole career out of it. Some use it to share their own stories, while others use it to share some pretty serious research about baby safety or baby development issues. Any time of the day or night, mums are sharing their stories of mothering. Join in and have your say. You'll quickly find a community that seems to suit your parenting style and personality. See the resources section below for website links.

4. **Google new friends**. Whoever said Google couldn't answer every search didn't know how to use it properly. There are

other dads out there being totally in love with their baby but kind of hoping their parenting wisdom descends on them either via osmosis or an act of God. If you weren't so frustrated by it all, you could probably laugh. But if times are tough, it's far from funny business in your house.

Here's what many mothers I work with experience:

- **He thought it would just be so "natural".** If we were fooled that birth could almost be a pleasant experience, then our male friends imagined some type of birthing oasis. Which of course has all the "natural" consequences of the reality of birth ending in a "natural" disaster of the traumatised dad variety. Just like us, many dads can have PTSD symptoms so make sure he gets help and point him to the Birth Trauma Association (www.birthtraumaassociation.org.uk) which covers issues related to dads' experiences too.

- **He has no idea what his new role really means.** Adjusting to being a mum is hard work, but it's also hard for dads to know their role. As mums, we can believe in one technique one minute then read something new and want to make the swap to a different technique the next. But we don't always keep our other half informed of the transition. Which means well-meaning dad thinks he's being oh-so-helpful and uses the *old* technique – duh – and subsequently cops from us a mouthful of "What on earth do you think you're doing!" They should learn to keep up by, umm, reading our minds... Well, not really. It's important to communicate about what your expectations of him are and how he can help.

- **He is super confused about what happened to his partner.** You were there one minute – strong, funny, independent, caring and on-top-of-the-world. But since baby came along he's wondering who the emotionally flippy, anxiety-ridden, it's-all-too-much person is that now sobs away in his lounge room. He tried once to comfort you but as you wailed out "*You wouldn't understand!*", he could only silently agree and hope this "imposter" went away. If you're not coping, chances are neither is he. For every mother out there who is struggling with a psychological disorder in the post-birth period, around 50% will have a partner in the same boat. So get help together if you need it. He can also take a look at the website How is Dad Going? (www.howisdadgoing.org.au) for dad-specific information about adjusting to parenting.

There are many other complex relationship issues that arise as you both adjust to your new roles. For the sake of your sanity and your baby's wellbeing, it's always important to prioritise your relationship with your partner and address ongoing niggling issues. Better to put out tiny spot fires than ignore issues and end up with a raging furnace of family friction. So turn to chapter seven for more suggestions for keeping your cool and taking the heat out of problematic relationship matters.

TOP NEW MOTHER TIPS FOR THE FIRST FEW MONTHS WITH BABY

1. I give myself permission to feel a whole range of emotions (other than guilt) about my baby's birth – to know I did all that was under my control to safely bring my baby into this world.
2. I give myself permission to experience a whole range of feelings about my relationship with my baby – from instant love, to overwhelmed, to awe, to shock, to confused.

3. I back my decision to feed my baby in whatever way is best for us, taking both of our physical and psychological needs into account.

4. I acknowledge that the way my body experienced birth and the way my body will physically recover from birth is absolutely unique to me and cannot be compared to anyone else's experiences.

5. I will remind myself that sleep should not be considered a luxury item and will remain an important priority for me.

6. I acknowledge that adjusting to having a baby, and all the hormonal and psychological changes that go with it, is a HUGE deal. I am not crazy for feeling elated one minute and overwhelmed the next. But I will seek help if my symptoms get too intense.

7. I will be aware that the massive adjustment to being a mum means "baby brain behaviour" is normal, but will use calming techniques to reduce the impact.

8. I will know that I need my "tribe" around me to cope with this mothering business and to use support groups, internet groups, professional support and family to reduce the risks of parenting alone.

9. I give myself permission for the relationship with my partner to have many ups and downs as we both adjust to our new parent status, but commit to doing whatever possible (with exhaustion and physical limitations taken into account) to keep our relationship on track.

10. I give myself permission to take care of myself. To nurture myself. To ask for help. To ditch the materialism mayhem and ignore the perfect (looking) parenting pressure and do all that is required to be what my baby really needs – a sane(ish) mother.

Some last comments

No doubt you've realised – double time – that this parenting thing isn't even close to a walk in the park. It's more the manic/panicked/frazzled dash through rough terrain in a vehicle hugely unprepared for the ride.

But somehow we figure it out. If we thought our babies were miracles, the fact that we learn how to parent them so fast – and live to tell the tale – is on par with all other miraculous events.

I hope that you find moments to praise yourself for what you have done right – of the less-than-perfect variety – every day. And if you have the energy, praise any other mothers you see, too. We could all use as much positivity as possible to maintain our momentum on this crazy journey called parenting.

Being a mother is both the best thing that ever happened to me and my toughest of life's tests. I'm glad I didn't know what it would really be like, or I may not have signed up for the job. But I'm learning to adjust…slowly. And when my baby smiled last week it all felt worth it. Who'd have thought that a smile could change my whole perspective on things, but that's what's weird about being a mum: suddenly the things that really matter in your world are just kind of different. MADDY, MOTHER OF TWO

Chapter 2

You mean there's no handbook with this little "miracle"? What you need to know about your baby in the first few months.

Three weeks post-baby summary: Jane confesses she might have had more success with a labradoodle puppy

Nobody told me I'd be this overwhelmed when my baby was born. Overwhelmed with love, with pain, with exhaustion, but also overwhelmed with confusion. I didn't even know how to change a nappy. The basics of breastfeeding were gradually sorting themselves out – after a few cracked and bleeding nipples. But how to deal with the crying and the settling, and knowing when to feed? There was so much guesswork involved. I just wanted someone to tell me exactly what to do and when, but nobody really seemed to know – so how was I supposed to get this right[1]? KRISTY, MOTHER OF TWO

"This can't be right. I can't do this!" Annie spurted out these words as she entered my room then promptly slumped into her chair in a flood of tears. She had just seemed to compose herself when she raised her head and shouted, "And I can't even quit this stupid job!" and the tears erupted all over again.

Ahhhh...The joy of adjusting to parenting. Just like Annie, many of us were convinced that the cycle of sleep, cry, feed, cuddle, cry, poo, change nappy and repeat it all 2000 times was going to be a walk in the park. The reality? More like a military exercise of the unsuspecting parent kind – poo leaked all over the cot, baby crying at a pitch sure to break the family crystal, wee squirted in your face, cracked nipples as painful as a contraction (almost) and the only restful sleep being had in the house is by the family dog.

Don't worry though, the advice can be endless. When it comes to understanding the minute details of every moment of your baby's biological being, your investment in books offering these explanations can equal the investment in your baby's pram, bouncer, car seat and nappies put together. There are some great ones out there for sure .

But this book is about helping out the mumma. You can get all the information you like about your baby, but actually baby's welfare is well and truly boosted by our sanity (of the grass-roots, slightly imperfect variety). So in staying true to the main issues that keep us on the sane side of the parenting tracks, this chapter will touch on the "Big 4" – sleeping, crying, settling and feeding.

Number 1. How to get your baby sleeping soundly

What's normal?

Don't be fooled by the sleeping superstar baby of your parenting group. Mother nature plays a cruel trick of strategically placing one in each group just to make new mums doubt their capacity. Research tells us that the superstar baby who sleeps 18 hours per day is as "normal" as the baby who only sleeps 10 hours per day – in other words, they're *not normal*. The actual average for a one-to-three month old baby is somewhere between 13 and 16 hours. The table below[2] shows how this "average" baby will also change their habits as they develop.

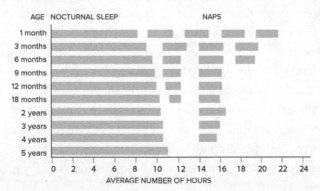

And before you wonder if you have a severe anxiety disorder regarding your baby's capacity to "sleep through the night issue", there isn't a mother I've met who hasn't over-thought the same topic. It's usually the same superstar baby in a mothers group who triggers our panic symptoms. As soon as their Priscilla-Perfect mother announces her baby is "sleeping through" the rest of the group feels like they've just received a big red "F" for failure on their mother report card.

But take heart, because predicting the likely start date of your baby sleeping through the night is as complicated as predicting the exact details of your birth: impossible. This is because:

a. **All babies are different**. There are huge variations in how much babies can consume in a single feed, which influences how long they can go between feeds, which impacts on their capacity to "sleep through". Research suggests that by six months, there'll be a fair majority of babies still taking one-to-two night feeds, so if you're still on night patrol, there are plenty of other mothers reporting for duty too.

b. **All mothers are different**. What one mother thinks is sleeping through isn't the same as another's – and some mothers stretch the truth further than their own perineum during delivery. Some start using the term "sleeping through" when their baby only wakes briefly, or only wakes for one feed, or strings together a total of six hours. You might find that your baby was "sleeping through" long before Gloating Glenda's baby was if you'd used the same definition.

c. **Adjusting to the outside world takes time**. Some babies adjust more quickly to the idea that days are for waking and nights are for sleeping while others "come alive" when the sun goes down (you might have noticed this when you were pregnant).

d. **Maybe your "sleeping baby" is awake**. Most babies wake many times at night, it's just that when they don't cry and go back to sleep without our help: we haven't noticed that they've woken up. It's generally accepted that a baby's sleep cycle looks like the figure below. It helps explain why babies who get used to someone else settling them can't return to the land of nod without being fed, rocked or patted and often need this pattern repeated every 45-60 minutes.

40–50 min
Light sleep, easy to wake up.

0–10 min
Starting to fall asleep.

Baby's sleep cycle every 45 minutes

30–40 min
Coming out of heavy sleep.

10–20 min
Getting into deeper sleep.

20–30 min
Heavily asleep.

Should you be co-sleeping with your baby

Co-sleeping with my baby was one of the most beautiful parts of being a mum. I loved being so close to her, smelling her, watching her. But by the time she was six months old, she couldn't go to sleep without me, and so I knew she was going to struggle when we put her into day care. So we had to work really hard to help her get to sleep without me. It was heartbreaking. I wish I'd helped her to do it earlier and more gradually. NATALIE, MOTHER OF TWO

There's some important insider information you need to know about this co-sleeping business. The baby books and so-called sleep gurus (or sleep whisperers or whatever exotic names they call themselves) aren't all on the same page when it comes to defining what "co-sleeping" even is. Some insist it *only* involves sleeping in the same bed as the child. Others have spread the net a bit wider and included *both* sleeping in the same bed *and* having the baby in a crib/cot right next to the mother's bed.

So? Well, some of these books make you feel like a lousy mother for choosing *not* to co-sleep, when in fact, by having baby's crib right next to you – something you were probably doing already – you're actually ticking that box. Guilt factor reduced by one. Two thousand other guilt-ridden parenting issues left to go…

I often get asked what my position is on this co-sleeping business. Basically it's this: I *am* a fan of co-sleeping if it means the baby sleeps in a cot or crib right next to you. I am not a fan of co-sleeping when it means mother and baby are in the *same* bed. There are two main factors that have influenced my position on this issue:

a. **It can lead to long term issues**. In my experience if it continues over the first year *without ANY opportunity for the baby to sometimes fall asleep or resettle without you* the child can have difficulty getting to sleep and staying asleep *unless they have a parent in bed with them well into their older childhood years*. I treat children as old as 10 who still can't sleep in their own bed. And before I hear how it doesn't matter and that a parent's role should include being there at all times for our children, also remember that our job is to help our kids feel secure. If our baby turns into a school-age child who continues to freak out when we're not next to them to go to sleep, that hasn't made them *more* secure, it's made them *less* secure. School camps are off the agenda! At some point in that first year of life our babies need to learn that getting to sleep without significant help from us is an OK thing to do.

b. **It's dangerous**. I also cannot ignore the abundance of research which says that *co-sleeping significantly increases (in some studies as much as 20-fold) a baby's chances of death*[3]. Now, I have taken a closer look at many of these studies and it does seem that some of the characteristics of both the parent (such as being obese or a drug and alcohol user) and the sleeping environment (such as use of a pillow, or using a lounge rather than a bed) weighed heavily on the research outcomes. I do understand that many parents are aware of these risks (further detailed below) and make the recommended adjustments…But I'm still not a fan.

And I'm not the only one who has yet to sign up to the co-sleeping fan club. In 2011 some of Australia's most well-known and educated child health experts held a one-day scientific consensus forum that reviewed the evidence underpinning the Australian SIDS and Kids Safe Sleeping Health Promotion Programme. At the end of the forum, it was recommended that children were at the *least* risk of SIDS when the focus was on:

a. placing babies on their back to sleep
b. keeping babies' faces uncovered
c. the parents' avoidance of cigarette smoke before and after birth
d. creating a safe sleeping environment (temperature, hard mattress, etc)
e. SHARING A ROOM WITH A PARENT BUT WITH THE BABY SLEEPING IN HIS OWN COT.

My babies both slept in a cot right beside my bed until they were over six months old. Actually, when my first one was born we had a futon type bed which was virtually on the ground and he slept in this tiny little crib next to me on the floor. It was easy to gently rock the crib and stroke him if he needed it. It was also reassuring for me to know he was safe and beside me. It was what I needed as a first-time mum. ERICA, MOTHER OF TWO

BUT…This book is for all mothers, and if you're still determined that co-sleeping in the same bed is OK for you, then there are some extremely important guidelines you *must* follow:

1. Make sure your mattress is firm.
2. Keep bedding light and minimal.
3. Never sleep on a sofa/lounge chair or waterbed.
4. Keep baby warm, not hot.
5. Don't let your baby sleep on a pillow.
6. Never let babies and toddlers sleep next to each other.
7. Don't leave baby alone on the bed.
8. Don't wear lingerie with string ties longer than eight inches and don't wear dangling jewelry to bed.

AND don't even *think* about co-sleeping if:

1. You or your partner smoke.
2. You or your partner have been drinking alcohol, or have taken medication or drugs.
3. You feel extremely tired.
4. Your baby was premature.

Also, if you are going to co-sleep in the same bed as your baby, promise yourself one thing: that as they get older you will help them to settle without you right next to them. You'll both reap the benefits of a relationship where your child can distinguish between needing you and wanting you (and where you can make this distinction about them, too). Plus, I guarantee you'll both sleep better in the long run.

> But *please*, don't just read this list and decide you can co-sleep with your baby. The decision needs to be taken with a **GREAT DEAL** of reading and preparation.

Please go to websites (such as www.babycenter.com.au/baby/sleep/cosleepingsafely) and talk to your child health nurse and GP before you even contemplate co-sleeping with your baby.

Number 2. What do you do about the feeding?

Newborns need to be fed at least every three hours. Within a couple of weeks, they will have grown enough so that as long as they get somewhere between six to eight feeds within a 24-hour time period, it is OK to stretch out feeds longer than three hours (which allows for longer night sleeps).

The best feeding advice to mums has always been to try and get more feeds into the daylight hours so less will be needed during the night. But be aware, newborns differ in sucking strength (eg, the lower birth weight baby and the premature baby will be less strong than others) and this affects both how much they consume and how rapidly they do it.

Whether you're breast or bottle feeding, keep in mind that the sucking motion is comforting to an infant. Don't be tricked into thinking that every time our baby moves their lips into the sucking positions that the milk bar needs to be opened. Advice centres such as Tresillian tell us mothers that sucking signs could also mean that the baby is overfed and has a tummy ache.

As Dr Howard Chilton (baby physician) describes in his wonderful book *Baby on Board*, comfort sucking can result in the following: "From being a culturally acceptable six times a day feeder and sleeper, he rapidly develops into a half-hourly whingeing demander as he tries to use the breast as a soother."

He then goes onto explain how feeding your baby each time he "seeks out the soothing" can result in:

a. **excessive lactose in the system** – which results in gassy, explosive poos, farting and the lactic acid burning the skin on baby's bottom. Result: baby is inaccurately diagnosed with lactose intolerance, mother is told to stop breastfeeding and baby is put on lactose-free formula. Unhelpful...

b. **over-fullness of the stomach** – leading to baby vomiting, vigorously and frequently. Result: baby is diagnosed with gastroesophageal reflux disease (GERD), or what we call "reflux", and numerous unnecessary medications are prescribed. I'm assuming we all agree this is unhelpful too...

So, if you're one of the mothers who is feeding on the hour, every hour, with a baby that seems to be distressed unless engaged in the sucking position, it could be that your baby needs a way to calm down *without* putting him on your breast or on the bottle (see below for suggestions for settling).

By all means, don't feel the need to give up "demand-feeding", but do make sure that feeding is actually what your baby needs. After all, the reason we are choosing to feed on demand is because we've been told it's in the best interest of our baby –not to create problems – so double-check your noble intentions aren't creating digestive dilemmas.

Number 3. How do you handle the crying?

In the first few months of life, babies cry around one to three hours per day. This may not seem like much to those without babies, but we need to take two factors into account:

1. How much of the day is taken up by sleeping and

feeding, which means a great deal of "other time" might be spent listening to a crying baby.

2. How much the ongoing crying of your baby can affect you psychologically and emotionally: nature clearly designed their little high-pitched squeals to be as hard to ignore as contractions during a drug-free labor.

Research also confirms that there are just those babies who seem to have been blessed (!?) with a big set of lungs and a matching predisposition to cry. A paediatrician in Canada, Ronald G. Barr[3], who has done an extraordinary amount of research into this area, calls these babies the "high criers". His research led to the development of the website The Period of Purple Crying (www.purplecrying.info), which provides estimates of three "types" of baby-crying habits.

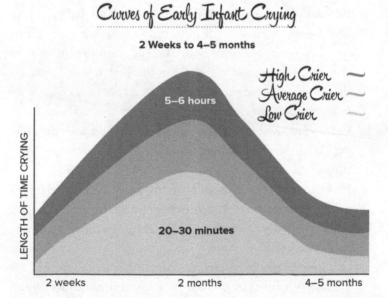

Curves of Early Infant Crying

2 Weeks to 4–5 months

High Crier
Average Crier
Low Crier

5–6 hours

20–30 minutes

LENGTH OF TIME CRYING

2 weeks   2 months   4–5 months

But notice something here. Dr Barr hasn't written "crap mother" next to the "high crier" category, nor "star mother" next to the "low crier" category. That's because he knows, perhaps better than anyone on the planet with all the hundreds of parents he's worked with, that there are some awesome and amazing parents who have "high criers" and some pretty disengaged and disinterested parents who have "low criers".

Even with the best will in the world, Dr Barr suggests that around 10% of the time a baby cries, there quite simply isn't a technique that will work. Quite frankly it's just a case of *some things works some of the time, but nothing works every time*. Which, of course, is the main reason that at times we feel useless, helpless and completely unequipped for the job of mothering...again!

But if it seems like your hit-rate for unsuccessful soothing looks more like 80% than 10% or if you are struggling to cope yourself when your baby cries, you need to:

a. **Remember crying is communication**: Your baby's crying isn't always a sign of distress. Crying is our baby's first language – it's the only way of making any noise (other than the filling-the-nappy variety) for the first few months. As the American Academy of Pediatrics recognises, *crying is an important and natural part of a baby's day*[4].

b. **Calm your own internal crisis**. Read chapter four for more details on how to manage your own emotions when your baby cries.

c. **Have a plan**. The stress of a crying baby hardly finds us at our creative best, so plan ahead for troubled times. See the section below for some helpful hints for proactively calming the crying crisis.

d. **Get help when necessary**. If these ideas aren't enough, see a family-friendly GP, or your local child health nurse about your baby's crying. There may well be some other techniques they can suggest that would be helpful.

Number 4. What settling techniques should you use?

Just like there's not one song that makes us **all** want to launch into air guitar antics or one movie star that makes **all** our hearts skip a beat, the same approach of *vive le différence* needs to be applied to settling techniques for our babies.

The basic premise for settling is this: when the distress is higher, use maximum settling interventions. For *lower* distress, use as minimal intervention as possible. So, if you put your baby into their cot and they fuss, then probably a few rocks and patting will be enough. If they're really distressed, it's time to use more interventions, including picking them up and waiting until they've calmed down before starting the settling routine again.

The techniques below are methods I've found to be effective from a combination of my own work with mothers, as well as Dr Harvey Karp[5], Annie Gethin and Beth Macgregor[6], and a good measure of the sound advice from places like Tresillian and Karitane too.

a. **Have a few regular behaviours that your baby can learn to associate with sleep**. For "day sleeps", this might be the act of swaddling itself, it could also be the reading of a story, the playing of some soothing music or some gentle rocking in a room that is slightly darker than the rest of the house. At night time, you might want to add in a bath time, or you may want to breastfeed in a darkened room as a cue that it's time to get a good night's sleep.

I would put on this Mozart DVD (quietly) and she would know it meant sleep time. I'd play it as I swaddled her and rocked her for a bit before putting her in her cot. Then I'd leave it on 'til she drifted off. It worked a treat and we still use the same music now she's five! ROSLYN, MOTHER OF TWO

b. **Get to know your baby's tired signs**. These could include: weird-looking facial grimacing, yawning, fussing, sucking, staring, inactivity, turning their head away or to the side, jerky movements or becoming more active, clenching fists, rubbing eyes, squirming or crying, (a bit like a politician at a press conference really!). Responding as quickly as possible to your baby's tired signs can stop your baby becoming over-tired and distressed. It prevents your baby getting themselves (and subsequently you too) into a state of distress that requires lots of effort to calm.

If your baby has started to settle into their own routine throughout the day and you can start to predict what time he will get tired, you can start your bed-time routine (sleep association behaviours) before that.

My first baby's tired sign was so obvious. As soon as he rubbed his eyes, I knew I could put him in his cot and he'd be asleep within a minute. It was incredible. My second son's tired signs were less fabulous…He just seemed to get moany and whingey. But at least I knew what it meant and he would happily go off to sleep soon after. ERICA, MOTHER OF TWO

c. **Calm yourself (as much as possible)**. I don't know who wrote the phrase "*How can my baby be calm if I'm not?*" but I love it, and it has always helped both me and all the mothers

I know and work with to get themselves into the right headspace before they even try settling their baby. Heaps of calming methods for mothers are contained in chapters three and four, but here is a quick self-settling technique I give the mothers I assist. Note it's based on a spelling variation of "burps" – BIRPS – for ease of remembering.

(B) Breathing – slow it down and focus on the out breath, saying "calm" to myself as I breath out.

(I) Imagining myself handling the situation in the way I want to – including being calm and patient. It also includes imagining myself putting my baby down if my own distress gets too high.

(R) Relaxing my body – tense it up and then let it loosen again, dropping my shoulders and gently rolling my head backwards and forwards.

(P) Permission to put my baby down and take time out to resettle myself if I get too worked up.

(S) Soothing self-statements such as "we can get through this" or "this crying will end, it might take a little while, but it will. It always does".

d. **Wrap your baby in some type of swaddle**. The gentle pressure of being wrapped is really calming for them (well, most of them – some loathe it – and if they do, skip this step). But when swaddling gets loose, it can also result in maximum baby distress as they engage in ninja warfare with their muslin. In his video Dr Karp models wrapping using traditional swaddling wraps (and believe me, if you use his technique, your baby won't be shimmying out of this one). But if it feels like you need the skills of a Japanese origami expert to master his methods, try some of the more modern takes on this ancient tradition, which mimic a swaddle, but are easier to use.

Remember though that swaddling needs to be gradually reduced over time. We need our babies to steadily adjust to a world where we don't swaddle them (know any adults that still want to be swaddled?). From a safety perspective too, as babies start to roll around and undo their wraps, there is also some chance they might become entangled. For this reason it is recommended by numerous infant specialists (including Karitane) to stop using a wrap at around four to-six months and, instead, tuck your baby into their sheets firmly or use an infant sleeping bag.

Man oh man. Don't even think about settling a baby unless you know how to swaddle. It was the only way my baby would ever get off to sleep. I had the best method down pat by the third week and I showed my whole mothers group how to do it in a way that was safe and effective. I got praise for ages. Shame other areas of parenting weren't so easy to master! JODY, MOTHER OF THREE

e. **Put your baby on their side or stomach**. So many mums have told me that their baby just would not settle on anything other than their side. It's not uncommon and basically it's thought that this position triggers the calming reflex by imitating the position they *loved* when they were in your uterus. In contrast, it's thought that laying a baby on their back can sometimes trigger their falling reflex which can make then feel insecure. But, just remember, lying babies on their side is only a brief method for soothing and settling, and that **once your baby is calm, they need to be rolled onto their back for sleep time**.

58

When my baby was distressed, the only way to calm him down was to roll him onto his side and pat him over and over, with the occasional stroking in between. I'd gradually reduce the frequency of the pats as he settled and then leave my hand resting on him until he went to sleep. Then I'd tiptoe out of the room as quiet as a mouse so I didn't wake him up again! EMMA, MOTHER OF ONE

f. **Use a gentle "shhh" sound**. "Shhh"ing babies kind of reminds them of what they heard in your uterus. Keep in mind that the sounds in utero could have been as loud as a vacuum cleaner for your baby. Dr Karp recommends placing your mouth two to four inches from your baby's ear when you make the "shhh" sound and making sure it's loud enough to match the sound of your baby's crying, or they won't hear it. Remember, while it can look a little strange, this is not saying "shut up" to your baby, it's telling them *in a language they understand* that you're right there with them helping them deal with their distress.

I would say shhh to my baby for ages. It was like I was telling us both to calm down. It sort of came out like a song in the end. I would move about and rock her to the rhythm and the words never varied. Just shhhhhhhh…shhhhhhhh…Boring, but the most effective song and dance routine ever invented for my baby! JANINE, MOTHER OF TWO

g. **Use some form of gentle movement**. Remember that in our uterus, unless we were sitting down, our babies were moving about as we were. So when we use forms of rhythmic moving with our baby, it imitates the jiggling they felt inside the uterus and activates the calming reflex. Keeping the baby in the cot, you can have one hand to hold them on their side while the other gently sways the cot. If you need to, rock them gently in your arms until they settle again, but always try to get them back into the cot (with one hand holding them on their side and the other rocking the cot if you need to) before they go to sleep.

One day I told my husband he needed to take responsibility for settling our baby. I showed him how to rock the cot to help her get off to sleep. He told me there had to be an easier way because it was too heavy (as if I didn't know!). The next day he put wheels on the bottom of each leg. It was great, and within moments she'd be off to sleep, and it didn't require me to have the muscles of Arnold Schwarzenegger any more to rock it. MICHELLE, MOTHER OF TWO

h. **Help the baby to suck on something**. Because the sucking movement also triggers a calming reflex, many mothers get also get "sucked" into feeding the baby every time they cry (see feeding section above for more details). Sometimes it works out OK, but for others it can start a disastrous pattern between a baby and mother which causes a great deal of long term problems for them both. Don't forget, your finger or a real dummy can also help to stimulate the calming reflex and settle your baby. The aim is not to get them to sleep with any of these items (including your breast – unless you want to and unless you are aware of the long-term potential problems this might cause). So if you use dummies, avoid letting your baby go to sleep sucking on them. Only use them to calm the baby and then employ one of the other techniques to get him to sleep.

i. **Distinguish between night and day from the time your baby comes home from hospital.** Remember that your baby has virtually been in the dark for the past 40 weeks. Adjusting to the idea of night and day is as hard for them as making sense of the different types of crying is for us. So the only way they're going to figure out that night is for more sleep and day is for less is if we teach them. Using the sleep/feed/play cycle is essential for this to happen. Always feed somewhere bright in the day and get some activity happening soon after. Conversely, if your baby wakes during the night, keep activity to a minimum. Change or feed your baby in the dark, and don't play with him. Your little one will start to get the message that you're pretty boring during the night, so they might as well just go back to sleep.

Note: some experts warn against making eye contact at night, but this needs to occur on a case-by-case basis. Certainly if bonding is an issue for you I would advise against avoiding eye contact. If you're heavily bonded with your baby, then reducing eye contact is unlikely to be a problem for you both. In any case, keeping the room as dark as possible when feeding/changing normally prevents this really being an issue anyway.

There seem to be so many mothers using "attachment parenting". Is this method best for my baby?

Firstly, let's give a quick run down of what attachment parenting (AP) is. In essence, it's a parenting style supported by American paediatrician, Dr William Sears, which promotes co-sleeping and feeding on demand. Mothers who support this method often "wear" their baby on them (using a baby sling) during the mother's waking hours to promote constant contact and closeness between the baby and the mother for the first few years of the baby's life.

Sound like fun? Well…I think I'm stating the obvious when I say that this may not be every mother's "parenting cup of tea". And do I think this is the best method by which to raise our babies anyway? Quite frankly, my answer is NO – well not the extreme version anyway. So, am I an advocate for the other end of the spectrum where routines and "controlled-crying" practices are followed in an extreme form then? My answer is NO to that one too.

As parents, we need to adopt a responsive and emotionally connected set of behaviours toward our baby. This helps our babies to feel secure and produces what's known as a "secure attachment". But don't believe extreme AP advocates who say that their version of attachment parenting is the only way to achieve this security for your child. It's not. In fact, I have worked in some cases where this method has been used and it has caused what's known as an ambivalent attachment – where the child fears separation from the parent because the parent has feared separation from the child.

Listen to the less extreme AP advocates who allow for the fact that every woman's situation is different and as such can accommodate things such as bottle feeding, working mothers and those mothers who don't enjoy or aren't able to "co-sleep". As the UK attachment parenting website (www. attachmentparenting.co.uk) states: "Attached families may enjoy the benefits of bedsharing, babywearing or breastfeeding but these are not essential; they support the ability to be a highly responsive parent – *tools not rules!*"

And don't worry that in deciding not to be an AP you've also decided to be an "unattached parent"! Read more about the advocates for routines and you'll find that they offer highly responsive, child-centred advice too, like using times to feed, sleep, play, etc, as "tools not rules" (sound familiar?), as well as always responding to a distressed baby and advocating co-sleeping (using a cot next to the bed). But beware, in the same way that the extreme AP approach can create attachment issues, so too can the extreme use of routines and controlled crying, where the child ends up with an avoidant attachment style because he doesn't know how to manage his emotions because no one has ever helped him process them.

There have also been some rather sensible health professionals wade into the whole "attachment parenting" vs "routine parenting" debate. Firstly, there are supporters of attachment parenting principles who make it clear that a strong attachment relationship is not simply a formula of 24/7 togetherness[7]. Others, like Dr Ian St. James-Roberts, on the website Purple Crying (www.purplecrying.info), suggest that rather than one of these parenting approaches being "better", each of them has different benefits at different stages – the more highly responsive being linked to better settled babies in the first 12 weeks, but the movement toward routines and gentle co-settling methods being linked to more settled babies after the first 12 weeks. In fact, he suggests that in not making this gentle transition, the result could well be that a baby's night waking becomes a problem.

And if you want to really know about healthy attachment, then look no further than the Circle of Security (COS). I consider it one of the most well-balanced, well written and sensible parenting programs on the planet. There is a whole load of information about it on-line (see www.circle ofsecurity.net), and there has just been a beautiful book published to explain this further: *The Circle of Security Intervention: Enhancing Attachment in Early Parent-Child Relationships* by Bert Powell, Glenn Cooper, Kent Hoffman, Bob Marvin and Charles Zeanah.

So, my final stance on this whole issue? As far as I'm concerned, sensibly and sensitively applying the appropriate components of each style of parenting actually ends up with many of the parental behaviours looking remarkably similar. So let's stop trying to justify which one is better or worse than the other and get back to being responsive and caring parents in whichever way best suits us and our baby. And what's best should be the style that:

a. makes sense to you as a person

b. reflects your beliefs on how children should be raised

c. reflects your understanding of how to best meet the healthy attachment needs of your baby.

Perhaps I'm struggling to define myself. If someone asks me if I'm an "attachment parent" I'd say yes and no. Do I co-sleep? No, but I'm not against it. I was 100% open to it. And then I realised after over a month that I got exactly two hours of sleep per night because I was a) so worried about hurting my baby and b) my baby wanted to be comforted and nursed ALL NIGHT LONG. Over and over again, I would be awake the next day and so exhausted that I would frequently start crying at the drop of a hat and my patience during the day was almost zero. We moved him into the bassinet in our room. Am I a bad parent who's putting my needs in front of Dax's? Absolutely not.

DARCY, MOTHER OF ONE AND "MUMMY BLOGGER" ON WWW. THREESIXFIVEDEGREES.COM

WORD OF CAUTION

The method you choose and how you do it should **NEVER** be cause to criticise another mother's choice. Hold in the depths of your heart the knowledge that nearly every mother is doing what she thinks is best for her baby, as well as what seems to **WORK**.

Until you have lived another woman's life, known her experience of conception, pregnancy and birth, know what her baby has been like and know all of her environmental influences you simply **CANNOT** know why she has chosen the methods she has chosen. Step back. Unless what the mother is doing is dangerous for the baby then say nothing (unless it's nice). Concentrate on what **YOU** are doing with **YOUR** baby.

If routines are your preference, which ones should you follow?

Routines were absolutely essential for my own sanity in the first year of my babies' lives. Being able to predict when they would sleep, and for how long, allowed me to plan my day and, in particular, plan my own day-time naps! I admire parents who are

able to go with the flow with no regular schedule in place, but for me, having a routine was nothing short of sanity-saving. Now my children are both in primary school and, although our schedule remains important to the smooth functioning of our family life, we have relaxed the rules a bit and I'm more easily able to cope with a bit of spontaneity in our lives! PIPPA, MOTHER OF TWO

The degree of "routine" suited to each mother has as much variation as your hormones during pregnancy: heaps! Some will have routines that only go as far as a loosely-defined sleep preparation and settling routine (outlined below), while others will choose for a full-blown routine with hour-by-hour guidance.

More defined routines *do* suit some parents and their babies. Conversely, there are many parents for whom defined routines *won't* suit. Basically, this is because putting baby on a heavily-defined routine means putting you on the same routine too. So if you can't stand the idea of a highly-routined day, you don't need Einstein's help to figure out you should probably avoid this approach to parenting.

But if you're a "research scientist" mother – determined to know the hard core evidence on whether a defined routine is "the answer" or not – unfortunately there isn't a definitive answer. One of the biggest studies on routines found just what I've already said – for some it worked, for some it didn't and for some it made things worse[8]. The researchers concluded that this was fundamentally because the programmes didn't allow for the fact that we're…umm…*human*. Which means of course is that no two mothers and their babies (as well as the environments they live in) are ever the same. Sometimes it takes a lot of money spent on research to tell us what was blindingly obvious to us anyway.

But if you *are* a bit keen on getting more details on how to use the sleep/feed/play cycle (below), or would like to read a bit more about how routines would suit your little family, you might like to check out the following:

a. **Save our Sleep by Tizzy Hall**. You can also get quite a lot of information on her website (http://saveoursleep.com).

b. **The New Contented Little Baby Book** by Gina Ford. But beware…Gina has MANY critics, and some of your friends won't understand your choice to use her routines, but it does work for many mothers. Gina also does do a fair job of answering her critics on her webpage www.contentedbaby. com/FAQ-Routines.htm if you're brave enough to have a look.

c. **Baby Bliss** by Jo Ryan. Jo has a bunch of baby sleep routines similar to Tizzy's, but they're freely available on her website. Woo hoo! See www.babybliss.com.au/services/babybliss-routines.

d. **What Were We Thinking! (WWWT)**. This supports new parents' use of settling techniques and was found to be effective for some parents (find out more at www. whatwerewethinking.org.au). WWWT also has some useful video footage which helps their suggestions make more sense and seem more user-friendly, too.

e. **Tresillian**. Yes, the tried and tested routines of an Australian mother's institution are well worth a look. You can also access them on their website (see www.tresillian.net).

Some words of caution in using routines.

1. ALWAYS go to a highly distressed baby (even just to pat or stroke them). The only exception is when **you** are so distressed that it's safer for the baby for you to stay away (see chapter four for more details). Don't let any advice on routines tell you otherwise.

2. Controlled crying is not advocated for young babies (ie less than six months old). The Australian Association for Infant Mental Health makes it clear that this is not an option for our little ones. Go to http://www.aaimhi.org/policies.php for more information.

3. Factors such as illness, teething, changes to your baby's environment (such as your return to work or starting day care), and developmental stages can significantly unsettle your baby. At these times, increasing physical closeness and other soothing methods are helpful to calm your baby.

4. And...if you think your baby is hungry, please feed them. The decent books on routines support (as I do) a "top-up feed" for between regular feeding times if your baby seems to need it.

The sleep/feed/play cycle

Knowing about the cycle saved my sanity. It took a couple of days to get it working, but my life has been completely different ever since. I'm just a little angry that I wasn't taught this in the hospital before I took my baby home. It would have made such a difference. I recommend it to any new mother. MANDY, MOTHER OF ONE

One of the most sensible and achievable approaches to a good balance between being a responsive parent and having some control over your environment is the *sleep/feed/play cycle*. I actually estimate that around 80% of most mothers I work with can get nearly all the tips for parenting they need simply by building their mothering repertoire around the cycle.

Sensible and helpful organisations such as Tresillian, Karitane and the website Raising Children Network all support this cycle too. In fact, the Tresillian "routines" tip sheet expressly states: "The feed, play, (prepare for sleep) then sleep routine is the core structure of a baby's day at any age".

The system is fairly self explanatory and it's relatively simple. In a nutshell it means:
- You feed the baby AFTER the baby has slept.
- Playing (well, for babies, watching the dangly bits of a play mobile!) comes AFTER a feed.
- Preparing for sleep will come AFTER a bit of a play – which means baby is put to bed AWAKE.
- Sleeping comes AFTER the "preparing for sleep" stage (not after feeding).

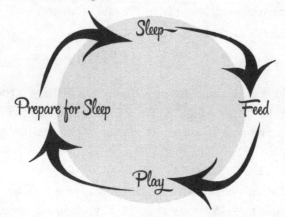

My experience as well as research outcome data shows that babies placed in bed *awake* rather than *asleep* are more likely to learn to settle without our help and to have longer continuous sleep periods. And no – this doesn't mean leaving baby to cry himself to sleep, it just means trying to put him to bed when he's in the "preparing for sleep" rather than "asleep" part of his cycle.

There are some exceptions to this though:

a. **During the night**: baby should be only awake enough to feed, the lights should be kept dark, and after the feed he should be placed straight back into the cot to sleep.

b. **In the very early weeks**: if you have a sleepy baby and you're struggling to work out any routine at all, it doesn't really matter if baby goes to sleep straight after a feed. I do recommend, however, that by around four weeks you try to start using the cycle above.

c. **When your baby has just got himself super worked-up in a ferocious frenz**y: and seems to only settle to sleep after a bit of a feed. It's not a pattern that's helpful in the long run, but if a quick feed settles the baby – and they aren't insisting on a feed *every time* to be able to get back to sleep – don't worry too much about it on the odd occasion.

One last comment.

Chances are, if you're doing OK on the "BIG 4" (sleeping, settling, feeding, crying), you're generally in a good emotional space as a mother. If you're just starting to get a handle on these tricky baby behaviours, then I hope this chapter has helped you in three ways:

1. Reducing unrealistic expectations about your baby's behaviour – like letting go of any idealistic thoughts of baby sleeping through the night at four weeks of age. Nice thought, just not very likely…

2. Reassuring you that you're not a failure if your settling techniques aren't 100% successful 100% of the time; that every mother out there has struggled at some point – perhaps at many points – with settling her baby. There simply isn't a technique that works all the time every time.
3. Providing some tried-and-true practical tips to reduce the confusion by the baby bedlam that is part-and-parcel of first-time parenting.

BUT – and this is a big "but" – NEVER forget that how you manage *your own* feeding (diet), sleeping (eight hours per day minimum), settling (comfort activities) and crying (emotional support) has a huge impact on your ability to care for these needs in your baby. Pretending that you're superwoman and ignoring your own needs will just end up in you needing to be rescued down the track. Looking after yourself *is* looking after your baby. And let's raise another wine (oops…decaf cappuccino) to that!

It wasn't until about week four after Mia's birth that I felt I knew what I was doing with her. I'd come up with a basic routine that worked well for us both.

I recommend that any new mother gets help for these things if she feels her days are out of control. They don't need to be. There are other options which can change your whole experience of parenting. Now I feel I can be the loving, positive mother I was meant to be. Not just some exhausted emotional wreck. JODY, MOTHER OF TWO

Chapter 3

I want to ENJOY my baby, not feel run down and wrung out.

Essential tips and techniques to boost your feel-good factor.

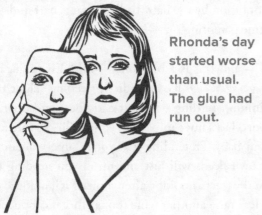

Rhonda's day started worse than usual. The glue had run out.

There were a number of times I hated being a mother. If I knew the job description before I had my babies I wouldn't have applied. I loved and wanted my children, but I never realised how crap the reality could be some days. MEL, MOTHER OF TWO

Did I miss something? How did I end up here? Making the turn into Struggle Street was never part of any mother's plan. Yet that's where we find ourselves. Lost, lonely, unsure and scared. There are heaps of other mothers stuck in the same location too, but finding them isn't easy. They're hiding. Behind makeup, a smile, the latest baby gadget or their own fancy clothes. But look closer and you'll find you know them, because Struggle Street is a well-trodden pathway of even the most amazing "got it all together" mothers.

And nope, "Tim Tam" power won't get you out. Chocolate's not your answer here, it's more the inbuilt "Tom Tom" you need. Yes the internal GPS device we do all have that's designed to help us out and sort us out. It was short-circuited by the amniotic fluid, but now it's returning to action and ready to get you back to sane street. One block (strategy) at a time.

Great! So where are these strategies? As much as we'd all love it to be the case, feeling better isn't something that just "happens" because we want it to. Without effort, our feel-good factor doesn't multiply as quickly or as miraculously as the cell-division process that created our babies. But just like our babies, we're all unique – which means you need to know which techniques work for you. No point trying to get all zen-like in a yoga class if your feel-good fantasy is a military-style boot camp.

The feel-good factor may seem elusive, but it's not that hard to find. It's waiting for us, ready for action, in these three different dimensions:
  a. my physical health
  b. my psychological and emotional health
  c. my social circle health[1]

In this chapter, the physical and the psychological/emotional factors get their chance to shine, and hopefully help light up your dark moments too.

The "social" factor covers our major relationships (such as those tricky mothers-in-law, our own mothers, our girlfriends and our relationship with our partner). These are addressed elsewhere in this book because they're all potentially problematic enough to deserve their own chapter! So flick over to the chapters most relevant for you, keeping in mind that caring for yourself physically and mentally gives you the best chance of handling social relationships too.

As any mother – myself included – will tell you, our children's health is the most important thing in our lives. And we know that a strong and empowered mother is the best champion a child will ever have (to achieve it). JASMINE WHITBREAD, CEO, SAVE THE CHILDREN INTERNATIONAL, QUOTED IN *SURVIVING THE FIRST DAY: STATE OF THE WORLD'S MOTHERS IN 2013.*

Pushing a teething, screaming baby for hours is so much fun. Said no mother ever.

Number 1. What PHYSICAL TECHNIQUES work best?

Get moving

Walking was my saviour on my toughest of days. I would just walk and walk. Even in the rain sometimes with both me and my stroller with our "raincoats" on. It gave me something to do. It got me out of the house. I got to see adults. It reminded me there was still a world out there that didn't revolve around changing nappies, breastfeeding and my baby's crying. I needed that.
SUE, MOTHER OF TWO

"Life. Be in it" TV ads have been telling us to get off the couch for years (thanks Norm); probably your partner has nagged you to do the same. And yep, I'm going to join the line to gently tear that packet of chips out of your hands and politely shove you off the couch too. At the end of another weary day as a mother, you simply can't hide behind this fact: exercise has been shown time and time again to be one of THE most effective tools for improving our mood[2].

Here are some tips to make working up a sweat a sweeter proposition:

1. **First principle – do no harm!** Realistically, what's your body ready for? Depending on your delivery – whether you had a caesarean, a small perineal tear or an episiotomy – allow yourself time for healing. Four to six weeks is usually a good time, but listen to your body and your GP about when to start.

2. **Aim for 30 minutes.** Preferably you'll go as many days as you can, but if five minutes a couple of times a week is all you can muster, then that's great too. Remember, a little activity is better than none, and more is better than a little.

3. **Pacing counts.** Walking the corridors to soothe your little tiger contributes to the fitness factor. So tie on a pedometer and you'll be amazed how far you've travelled. If you get above 10,000 in a single "soothing session" you know you've both: (a) earned the title of "keeping calm in a crisis": and (b) clocked up your exercise for the day!

4. **Get tech-savvy.** There are some great mobile phone apps to log your workouts and keep you motivated. Many of them will send you reminders and give you inspiration for those days when resting your feet up on the couch has trumped their close connection with the pedals on an exercise bike.

5. **Find a friend.** Line up a girlfriend to exercise together: it's harder to say "no" to someone else than it is to make an excuse to yourself. Research also shows that while talking with our mummy pals is good for our emotional health, we'll get a whole load better bang for our positive-thinking buck if we team our talk with a walk .

6. **Let your fingers do the walking.** Use Google to find out whether there are some strollersize classes or mother and baby yoga classes in your local area. That way you can combine exercise with meeting new similarly-minded people all with a good excuse to have a cappuccino afterwards!

7. **Don't let your crying baby stop you.** Remember when you're walking, the people you walk past are only going to hear your baby for five seconds, even less if you walk faster, so use it as motivation to pick up your speed!

You are what you eat

Some mothers are convinced their baby's crying episodes are linked with their (the mother's) diet. Carry on with this motivation if it's helped you palm off a few pounds, but it's actually not supported by much evidence, unless that is, your baby has some type of lactose intolerance. Anyway, unless you've made the diet-to-crying association, you're probably about as interested in your own diet as in the state of international politics. Which means it's taken a sharp turn down an uninterested and unhealthy hill.

I'm not sure how I didn't see that a diet of cheesecake and cappuccinos wasn't going to be helpful – either physically or emotionally – but I just didn't. When I decided to take more notice of "feel-good" foods, everything started to change for the better.
JULIE, MOTHER OF ONE

The best way to eat for maximum physical and psychological health post-baby is outlined in the table below (a culmination of suggestions from the organisation beyondblue and a review of the current research). You'll soon see that what's good for us is also (surprise!) good for our babies. And as I'm assuming you weren't going to wean your baby onto high sugar, high salt, highly processed baby puree or caffeine-fuelled and alcohol-soaked baby rusks, it makes sense that we consider knocking back the grown-up versions of the same.

Photocopy the following sheet and put it on your fridge so you can take charge of your inner health and your mood all at the same time. Chances are, the same eating plan will also have a positive effect on your outer health (think baby belly) too.

I'd like to cook you any gourmet meal that takes less than 2 minutes and feeds us for a month.

FOOD TYPES	HELPFUL HINTS
Eat plenty of vegetables, legumes and fruit.	Please make the commitment to love your vegies! A huge UK study has just proved what we (should) already know: happiness and mental health are highest among people who eat a good amount of fruit and vegetables a day, with wellbeing hitting a high point at seven portions a day[3].
Eat plenty of cereals, preferably wholegrain.	Wholegrain cereals and many fruits, vegetables and legumes have a low "glycaemic index". So? Well, it means the sugar in these foods is absorbed slowly into the blood stream, which helps stabilise blood sugars and optimise both mental and physical performance. This means it might help banish the mushy-brain effects of new-mum syndrome. (If you want to check the glycaemic index of a food, visit www.glycemicindex.com).
Include high protein foods such as lean meat, fish, poultry and/or alternatives.	Three good reasons to have protein-rich foods in your diet: 1. They're made up of amino acids – essential nutrients for repairing or building new cells (think anti-aging). One essential amino acid is called tryptophan which is used to produce serotonin (the very component most anti-depressant medication tries to increase). 2. These foods prevent iron deficiency, a factor which can lead to anaemia, fatigue and low moods. 3.Oily fish, such as tuna and salmon are good sources of long chain omega-3 fatty acids. Consuming about 500mg a day of long chain omega-3 fatty acids is a good preventative measure for mental health (with some evidence it reduces symptoms of depression), as well as physical health.
Drink plenty of water.	Drinking plenty of water helps prevent dehydration. Even mild dehydration can affect mood, causing irritability and restlessness.

78

FOOD TYPES	HELPFUL HINTS
Eat dairy products, including milks, yoghurts, cheeses and/or alternatives.	In the absence of breastmilk for grownups (kind of a weird thought really), dairy products are a pretty good ready-to-eat, nutrient-dense food substitute. Low-fat varieties are useful too when trying to lose or maintain weight. Milk is also a good source of the feel-good tryptophan factor (see above). Add to this the fact that a warm milk drink before bed can also help induce sleepiness and surely it's big cheers (with milk-filled glasses of course) to that!
Limit processed food in-take.	In case you were wondering whether a "chicken burger" made of only 50% chicken (soy, additives, wheat, emulsifiers, etc making up the rest) was kind to your body, research has made it loud and clear: a diet rich in processed food leads to higher rates of depressive illness[4]. So keep your sanity by keeping *real* food in your diet.
Limit saturated fat and ensure some "good fat" intake.	We actually need *some* saturated fat, but not at the four-serves-a-week-of-pork-crackling quantity. You'll get enough in your lean meats and dairy food. Conversely, the "good fats" (clever name being "monounsaturated fats") are typically associated with health benefits such as better mental health and cognitive function. So chow down on seeds, nuts, fish, and avocados.
Limit your alcohol intake if you drink.	Alcohol is a depressant, meaning heavy drinking can actually contribute to depression or make it worse. Switch to another feel-good drink. A Mojito mocktail is a great alternative.
Consume only moderate amounts of sugar and foods containing added sugar.	Many high sugar foods are not only a poor source of essential nutrients (ie "hollow calories"), they're also often high in saturated fat, which increases blood cholesterol and encourages weight gain. They also rate high on the glycaemic index scale. This may give you a momentary boost as sugar (glucose) surges into your bloodstream but the effect soon wears off leaving us feeling tired and low.
Limit caffeine intake.	For people who experience anxiety, it's wise to avoid caffeine. Caffeine, especially for those who are particularly sensitive to it, increases anxiety and can prevent us getting to sleep when we need it most. Opt for "decaffeinated" or "half-caff" drinks.

Prioritise sleep

My husband kept complaining that I'd lost my libido. I told him he'd find it in the same place as I "lost" all those hours of sleep and my sanity too! REBECCA, MOTHER OF THREE

It doesn't take a research professor to tell you that getting a good night's sleep makes you feel better. You all know that. I remember the envy I felt toward the first mother at mothers group who chirpily announced that her baby had "slept through" the night. Actually, I think I wanted to throw a wet nappy at her.

But did you know that not getting a good night's sleep over a few weeks or months can actually produce symptoms very similar to postnatal depression, including the likelihood of your mood taking a major nose dive. That's because sleep deprivation is stressful and its effect on the brain is really the same as the stress response – the logical, rational, decision-making area (ie the prefrontal cortex) starts to shut down and in its place you've got the subcortical "flight or fight" regions. Which is why in our sleep-deprived state we're much more likely to pick a fight or just want to run away from it all.

As one of the mothers I interviewed said:
When my baby was four weeks old, a well-meaning clinic nurse suggested I might have depression. The truth is I was acutely sleep deprived and her comment did nothing to lift my mood. Sometimes a full night's sleep is all that's required. PIP, MOTHER OF TWO

To make sure your little sleep issues don't evolve into major psychological issues, here are some tips[5]:
1. **It's not all about length!** Good quality sleep isn't necessarily a long sleep – it's having what doctors call "deep sleep" and

"dream sleep". Most deep sleep occurs during the first five hours after falling asleep. Even if you sleep for only four or five hours, you can still get about the same amount of deep sleep as someone who sleeps for eight to ten hours .

2. **Get your pram out and dust off your Nikes.** Regular exercise can improve your sleep, but just in case you *could* actually find any "me time" after 6pm, avoid vigorous exercise late in the evening (unless it's in the form of the ol' "baby soothing backstep" done over and over and over and over...).

3. **Only use your bed for sleeping.** If you do a lot of reading or other activities in bed, your brain probably is confused about what the purpose of bed is. Try to do your reading or other activities in a quiet, relaxing place other than bed and then only use bed to lie down in.

4. **Get up!** Seems a bit weird to say this about getting down to sleep, but the general advice from sleep experts is – don't stay in bed if you can't sleep. For the same reasons as point (3) above, your brain is getting confused by spending time in bed *not* sleeping. Get up, do a relaxing activity (crossword, shower, knitting, etc) and wait for the wave of tiredness to come. Once it does, return to bed and try to sleep again.

5. **OHHHMMM away.** Use the meditation and mindfulness techniques in this chapter to help slow down your thoughts and focus on the present moment. Sleeping is near impossible if we're critiquing every minute of our day or excessively worrying about tomorrow – our brain thinks there's too many life stressors and assumes we need to stay awake to deal with it all. Switch off your brain buzzing or expect a night of major unrest.

6. **OHHHMMM some more.** Take heart that once you achieve a pretty sound meditation "zone", research suggests your

81

brain may benefit just as much from being in that "zone" to actual sleep. So there's no need for that critical self-talk such as "I have to sleep or I won't function tomorrow" or "I must sleep". Switch it to "I may not be able to sleep but meditation's a pretty sound substitute".

7. **Chill out**. If you want to sleep, your brain needs to get the message that it's safe to do so. If you're breathing quickly and your muscles are tense, your brain thinks danger is lurking about. Use the breathing and relaxation techniques in this chapter to calm down your stressed-out system.

8. **Know thyself!** Work out what sends *you* zinging and commit to sending it sideways. If caffeine, chocolate or sugary foods seem to wind you up, avoid them from about noon onwards. If you're the kinda gal who gets annoyed by the news or fazed by your Facebook followers, limit your access to these sensationalist-prone media sources an hour or so before bed.

Once I stopped stressing about how much sleep I got and taught myself slow breathing, I could face night-time again. Until then, I'd dreaded the hours between 10pm and 7am. I'd been like a zombie. HELEN, MOTHER OF ONE

De-stress your system

We're programmed to be more tense and breathe more quickly under stress (it gets us ready for the "flight or fight" response). Problem is that sometimes we keep up our fast breathing and high muscle tension long after the initial stress has passed. This fast breathing almost becomes a habit which means our system constantly gets the message there IS something stressful we're facing, even when there isn't. What's all this got to do with babies? Well, if fast breathing's become a habit of yours, you can end up heading in to soothe a crying baby at the same breath rate of an armed female freedom fighter. It's fast-paced, high intensity and our muscle tension (un)thankfully joins in the tension party. Little wonder our babies don't find us calming. Ever got a hug from someone who was panting like a dog and as tense as a drum? Didn't make you feel calm did it? But in case you're thinking I'm under some delusion that the stress of a crying baby should equal the pressure of pondering on a poolside cocktail (those were the days…), don't worry: I do get it. Crying babies are hard work. It's just that if you get your breathing more regulated and your muscle tension sorted (combined with some of the self-talk tips below), at least you know you'll go to your crying baby in your sanest state possible.

BREATHING TECHNIQUE

Step one: COUNT THE RATE OF YOUR BREATH

1. Sit quietly in a chair for about five minutes (longer if you've been racing around).
2. Count your breath rate (how many breaths you take) over a period of a minute.

Step two: RESULTS CHECK

1. If you counted more than 17 breaths per minute (BPM), it's a sure sign your breath rate needs to be reduced in order for you to deal with situations calmly.
2. If it's above 14 there's still room for improvement.
3. Check your BPM again on a stressful day to see how your breath rate changes and whether there's a cause for concern that you didn't pick up the first time.
4. Proceed with the rest of this exercise to get your breath rate within a safe range.
5. If you want to calm the calamity motherhood mayhem, target the 10-12 BPM rate.

Step three: CONTROLLED BREATHING EXERCISE

1. Breathe in through your nose and out slowly through your mouth. Try to get about a six-second cycle happening (.e breathe in for three, breathe out for three).
2. As you breathe out, calmly say to yourself the word "relax" (or other words, like "calm", "chill out" or "it's OK").
3. Focus on the out-breath rather than the in-breath. The out-breath sends messages to the brain that we're OK. Sharp in-breaths are associated with a panic response.
4. This pace will lead to a breathing rate of 10 breaths per minute.
5. Stay breathing in this six-second cycle for at least five minutes to feel the effects of what slowed breathing can do in invoking a calmer system.

Step four: PRACTISE

Practise this exercise each day whenever you get the chance. I often suggest mothers put some type of reminder around the house (such as post-it notes), especially on their baby's door, to prompt them to practise.

MUSCLE RELAXATION EXERCISE

To get the most out of this exercise, firstly try it out in a quiet place (maybe just as you're going to bed at night). After you've got the technique down-pat, you can then use it when you need to – in any time, place or situation that requires that you remain calm(ish), like babies crying or mothers-in-law coming for dinner.

1. Sit in a comfortable chair, or lie down, in a quiet room.
2. If seated, put your feet flat on the floor and rest your hands in your lap.
3. Close your eyes.
4. Start by using the controlled breathing exercise (above).
5. After three minutes of controlled breathing, start the muscle relaxation exercise below.
6. Tense each of your muscle groups for 10 seconds (for the best results, tense to the point just under your pain threshold), then relax for 10 seconds, in the following order:
   - upper body: clench your hands into fists and lift your shoulders as if you're trying to get them to touch your ears, then relax
   - face and jaw: clench your teeth, then relax
   - lower body: put your feet out straight ahead of you, curl your toes toward you and tighten your buttocks, then relax
7. Continue controlled breathing for at least five more minutes (longer if by some miracle you have the time) and enjoy the feeling of relaxation.
8. If you need to, go over the more tense parts of your body again. Many mums I work with do their upper body at least twice.

*I hadn't realised how tense I was when I was dealing with my
baby. When I relaxed and told myself I could deal with her, it was
like she trusted me to know what I was doing and became more
relaxed too. There were still hard days, but nothing like before I
knew how to calm myself.* NATALIE, MOTHER OF TWO

Pills and potions

Improving our mood through medication, herbal remedies,
vitamins and minerals, or Chinese concoctions is a subject
of much debate. There are so many opinions and conflicting
"research" that we're left wondering how we choose to spend our
hard-earned cash (and let's face it, many of these tiny pills are
large in price).

So let's cut through all the debate and make this distinction.

a. **For more severe mood issues.** If you have a constant low
   mood and other signs of postnatal depression (see chapter
   four for a full list of symptoms), avoid suggestions your
   solution lies in non-traditional medicines. While you may
   prefer to part from prescription-based pills, don't use this
   stance to justify un-substantiated solutions either. Head to
   your GP for the best advice about whether an anti-depressant
   prescribed medication is best for you (and suitable for
   breastfeeding if that's what you're doing).

b. **For less severe mood issues.** If you have lower mood on some
   days and better mood on others, non-traditional medicines
   are increasingly showing signs of success. You might like to
   start with some herbal medication that works in a biologically
   similar way to antidepressants (eg St John's wort). In a recent
   report from the reliable Cochrane database, this herbal
   medication was found to work as well as antidepressant
   drugs for people with mild to moderate depression[6]. But just

because it's "herbal" doesn't mean it's not potent (remember that opium is more than a pretty poppy!) and you should talk over-dosages and appropriateness with a GP who is open to the idea of non-pharmaceutical interventions. This is crucial if you are breastfeeding.

No medication or supplements substitute for making other lifestyle changes such as exercise, breath rate and diet. It also won't stop you getting beaten-up by your own self-talk if that's a well-established toxic pattern.

Medications should always be considered part of an overall "package deal" of wellness.

If you're keen to resort to alternative therapies, do your research before parting with your hard-earned cash. Reliable websites like www.bluepages.anu.edu.au and the Cochrane databases (see www.cochrane.org) provide sound advice regarding which medications, supplements and therapies have been found to give the best results.

I didn't want to take anti-depressants, but when I couldn't stop crying for days on end, my GP finally convinced me to at least try them. I wish I hadn't waited so long. I can only suggest other mothers think about starting earlier. Now I manage my mood through diet, exercise and sensible self-talk, but I don't think I'd have gotten there without using anti-depressants first. KRISTY, MOTHER OF THREE

Number 2. What PSYCHOLOGICAL strategies work best?

The phrase "our perception is our reality" brings good news for those mums blessed with rose-tinted glasses that allow their perception to be – well – rosy. For the rest of us, whose perception is more the totally wonky from hormones/fatigue/over-load kind, we can feel all sorts of things that make no sense to others and lead us to acting like a complete lunatic. Well, maybe not complete...but kinda borderline.

The mums I work with tell me that different techniques are helpful depending on their level of distress, their background, their previous attempts to find sanity and the age of their baby. Some may work for you now, but then you'll reread this chapter in a month's time and find another technique works better.

Meditation

The Buddhist communities have been meditating for centuries, and local ashrams spruiking the benefits of it are popping up faster than an adolescent's acne. My hairdresser swears by it and even my sister seems to have been bitten by the "OHHHHMMM" bug. Yep, unless you're meditating at the moment, you're out of the loop!

But is meditation really helpful? It's hard to ignore the research papers confirming the effectiveness for a range of psychological symptoms including anxiety, addiction, aggression, suicidality, depression, chronic pain, insomnia, and hypertension[7]. Add to this the growing recognition about its benefit for general health[8] and it's hard *not* to think the practice is worth taking a closer look.

But before you close the book in disgust, thinking I'm another do-gooder therapist who has no idea that fitting in a five-hour session stuck in the lotus position is not on your "must do" list today, take heart. Modern meditation is a whole lot more achievable for today's parents. Here's what to do:

MEDITATION EXERCISE

1. **Sit in a comfortable chair** - but only if you want to. You can lie down and even walk around – yep, walking meditation is currently trendier than a hot pink stroller cover.

2. **Have thoughts!** The old idea that your mind had to be "blank" simply isn't achievable for many of us. Instead the idea is that you:
   - train your thoughts to sloooow down a little and to focus on either neutral or positive thoughts (ie not the toxic nasty "I'm a crap mother" ones).
   - stay in the present, the "right now", not the past, nor the future.
   - choose what suits you: you can count your breaths, you can repeat a helpful phrase or calming sound, you can imagine air moving in and out of your body.

3. **Gently maintain focus.** If your mind wanders (eg to how crap you were at parenting this morning), remind yourself you have just a few minutes to stay in the present. Gently bring back your thoughts to what your focus is and try again.

4. **Breathe slowly.** Aim for around 10 breaths per minute. If you want to know more about breathing slowly, take a look at that section (above) in this chapter.

5. **Start with as little as one minute**. Remember, you can also do this while you walk or shower. I know one of my clients finds the best time is while she hangs out washing. The methodical nature of hanging clothes just seemed to help her stay in the present.

6. **Find out more**. If you are still not quite getting into the meditation vibe, or if you want some variety, there are *heaps* of both free and purchasable mp3 files on the internet, including ones for walking (see for example www.buddhanet.net.). And check out Oprah's website for this too, as her recordings are generally of good quality (see www.oprah.com/oprahsbookclub/Download-the-A-New-Earth-Web-Classes)

Get assertive (not aggressive)

Many of the women I work with have no idea how to be assertive. They think it's something only aggressive, self-centred mothers do. So they stay passive, sometimes passive-aggressive. Problem is, when they've had enough and do need to stand up for something, they do switch to being aggressive! Sometimes scarily aggressive. Then the blame game starts – either to someone else (*yeh, well, I wouldn't be that way if you just helped out more*) or themselves (*How could I be so mean to my partner? I'm an idiot*). Sound like a recipe for disaster to you? You can bet your baby's soggy nappy it is!

Being assertive is not being aggressive. It's not about being self-centred either. So what is it? The description below is lengthy but hopefully it's helpful. It's important to have some well-oiled assertiveness tools in your social skills armour to manage this motherhood mayhem.

1. First, imagine everything you believe in and everything you do is contained within a square.

2. Ask yourself whether you have the right to stand up for how you think and behave. Hopefully you answered yes… If you're not sure what's actually *in* your square though then you can do the house and garden exercise in chapter eleven

3. Now imagine there are boxes surrounding you for everyone you know. Each of these contains what these people do and believe in. Like this:

4. Now ask yourself whether everyone else has the right to stand up for their own behaviours and beliefs too. I hope you answered "yes" to that one too.

5. The way to live assertively and respectfully – for yourself and those around you – is to watch your borders and the borders of others. This means protecting what's in *your* square and allowing others to protect their own. In this way:

- **Know your boundary:**

a. If someone makes a strong negative comment about *your* behaviours and beliefs, or tries to change your beliefs and ideas, *they* are being aggressive.

b. If you allow someone to make a strong negative comment about your beliefs and ideas (and don't do anything about it), then *you* are being passive.

- **Respect other people's boundaries:**

a. If you make a strong negative comment about *someone else's* behaviours or beliefs, or you try to change their behaviours and beliefs, then *you* are being aggressive.

b. If someone allows you to make a strong negative comment about their behaviours and beliefs, or allows you to change their behaviours or beliefs (and doesn't do anything about it), then *they* are being passive.

6. Passive-aggressive behaviour is more complex. It means letting someone else comment about or change something in your square and *looking* as though you're not going to do anything about it, then at a later date somehow sabotaging what's in their square. For example, when another mother says, "I think your routine is too baby-centred, you should be more relaxed about it all," you say nothing, but then neglect to invite her to any further morning teas or meet-ups with your mothers group.

7. So how do you be assertive and stand up for your borders?
   - **step one**: say that you understand someone else can have a different opinion (everyone has a different squares) – *"I appreciate we see it differently"*.
   - **step two**: stand up for your own beliefs or behaviours (you have a right to your own square) – *"But I actually feel this is the best way for me"*.
   - **step two**: say nothing negative about what their square contains (they have a right to their own square) – *"I'm sure your way is best for you too"*.

8. Here are some examples to show the difference:
   Situation: Your mother comes over for dinner and comments that the house is a mess. Possible responses:
   - Aggressive: *"How dare you? The only reason you're saying that is because you wash and scrub your house so often you may as well live in a bottle of bleach."*
   - Passive: *"I know. I'm a useless housekeeper."*
   - Passive-aggressive: *"I know. I'm a useless housekeeper,"* then

never invite your mother over to see the baby again.
- Assertive: "*I guess we keep our houses in different ways. This way feels right for me with all I have going on with a new baby. I'm sure the way you keep your home feels right for you too.*"

Situation: A child health nurse tells you the way you're settling your baby will create ongoing problems, but you feel it works well.
- Aggressive: "*How would you know? I bet you haven't even really settled a baby in years, you just preach to everyone else and leave them feeling crap.*"
- Passive: "*OK. I'll do whatever you say.*"
- Passive-aggressive: "*OK. I'll do whatever you say,*" then put in a complaint to her manager.
- Assertive: "*I guess we have different ideas about settling babies. This way feels right for me and my partner. I'm sure your way is right for some mothers, just not me.*"

9. Be aware of "fence line" issues. Just like any old neighbourhood, sometimes the way one neighbour behaves impacts on another – think big oak tree dropping branches into your garden. In the same way, the behaviour of people we're close to can impact on us too. For example, it's all well and good that your partner wants to train for another triathlon, but when it means he's training all weekend and you're left on babysitting duties alone, *it's going to impact you. Big time!* On these issues, we need to politely remind our "neighbours" how their behaviour is "coming over the fence" and impacting on us.

The solution is to consider how you'd deal with a neighbour with the big oak tree, or the wisteria that's growing into your drainpipes.

- Point out that you respect what's in their garden (*I know you love Oak Trees*).
- Point out how it's having a negative impact on you (*but the branches on my side of the fence keep dropping and now that I have a baby I worry she'll get hurt*).
- Offer some possible solutions to the problem (*I was thinking of getting a tree specialist to tastefully remove the branches on my side, perhaps we could halve the costs*).
- But if they choose not to change, you'll have to suggest consequences (*well I'll need to take the matter to the local council to sort out, or I'll just cut it down on my side in the best way that suits me*).
- If it becomes clear that consequences don't change the situation or sparks neighbourly warfare, then it's possibly time to move house.

Now to apply it to the triathlon training.
- Point out that you respect what's in his garden (*I know you love triathlons*).
- Point out how it's having a negative impact on you (*but when you train this much I'm alone with the baby all weekend. I miss you and it's tiring and I feel like I don't get a break. Then when you come home, you're exhausted too and don't want to help out much*).
- Offer some possible solutions to the problem (*I was thinking that maybe you could take just a 12-month break while our baby is so little and return when things settle down; OR: Maybe you could be less competitive and have it as a bit of a hobby for 12 months, that way you could train for a few hours each day but still make time for me and our baby*).

94

- But if they choose not to change, you'll have to suggest consequences (*well, I'll need to pay for babysitters at least one day each weekend so that I can do things for myself too; OR: I'm going to train with you so this whole situation evens up a bit. Let's get all the training equipment so we run, swim and cycle with baby on board!*).
- If it becomes clear that the consequences don't change the situation or they spark relationship warfare, then it's possibly time to move. Unfortunately in some relationships this will mean you need to "move on" – literally. But sometimes it's necessary. We can't live our lives in relationships where there is no regard for damage occurring to who we are and what we believe in.

I'd never understood how to be assertive. My mum was so passive I don't think she ever stood up for anything she believed in, so I didn't know how to either. When I could see being assertive in this "squares" way, it changed everything. I could be respectful of myself and still respectful of others. It was fantastic.
NINA, MOTHER OF FIVE

Acceptance and commitment therapy

I think it was after I'd had another pretty stressful day that I realised my daughter would one day figure out that I wasn't perfect. I was determined that this news was better to come from me than someone else. CATHY, MOTHER OF THREE

One of the "coolest" types of therapy out there at the moment is called "acceptance and commitment therapy", or ACT for short. Basically it stands for: (1) accepting what is out of your personal control; and (2) committing to action that improves and enriches your life.

If that sounds a bit "airy fairy" then here's the more practical version for us mums: (1) accept that there are many struggles in parenting and the only thing remotely close to "mummy perfection" lies in the rushed –but somehow perfect anyway – cappuccino with a sterling set of girlfriends; and (2) make a pact with yourself that you'll take the best possible care of not only your family but *yourself* through even the crappiest (no nappy pun intended) days of parenting.

So then, what do we do?

1. We have to know our *values* so we know who we really are and how we want to take care of ourselves. It's then about committing to actions that ensure we actually do these things. This work on values is a big deal and is deservingly covered in a whole load more detail in chapter eleven

2. We need to be able to identify the "shoulds" and "rules" our thoughts have created that make us miserable and replace them with more realistic self-talk. See below under "the little voice in your head" for more details on how you can shift your thinking this way.

3. We need to learn the skill of mindfulness so that we can be *aware* of our thoughts but not confuse them for facts or become overwhelmed by their content.

Below are two exercises that illustrate how mindfulness can help us when we're getting stuck on a self-destructive negative "beat up" (adapted from exercises at www.actmindfully.com.au).

MINDFULNESS EXERCISES

Exercise 1

- Find a negative self-judgment phrase you often say to yourself (eg "I'm a crap mother" or "I'm no good at this mother thing").
- Really focus on this thought for 10 seconds – get caught up in it, give it your full attention and believe it as much as you possibly can.
- Now silently replay it for another 10 seconds with this phrase in front of it: "I'm having the thought that..." For example, "I'm having the thought that I'm a crap mother".
- Now replay it one more time (10 seconds again), but this time add this phrase: "I notice I'm having the thought that..." For example, "I notice I'm having the thought that I'm a crap mother".
- What happened? Did you notice a sense of separation or distance from the thought?

Recognising that our thoughts *are* just thoughts (and not a reality) stops them being so toxic on our wellbeing.

Exercise 2

- Take the same negative word you used (crap, loser, stupid) and really focus on it (for this to work you have to stick to one word).
- Close your eyes and start your slowed breathing.
- Keep your slowed breathing going as you say it over and over to yourself for at least 45 seconds (*note*: don't stop after a few seconds or you'll feel worse,.You need to keep going for at least the full 45 seconds if you want to feel the effects).
- What happened? Did you notice the word gradually became less meaningful or harder to focus on?

Most people find that the word eventually becomes a series of meaningless sounds or vocalisations. Others find they lose interest in the word and start thinking about other things. In doing so, it loses its power and its destructiveness over us.

There's a whole lot more about ACT, so if you feel the principles seem right for you, take a look at Russ Harris's book, *The Happiness Trap* or alternatively *The Joy of Parenting: An Acceptance and Commitment Therapy Guide to Effective Parenting in the Early Years* by Lisa Coyne and Amy R. Murrell. The website www. actmindfully.com.au is also packed full of great resources and more ideas on using ACT principles to improve your mood.

At some point I realised if I was going to get through this whole baby thing that I had to finish each day and be done with it. I had to believe I had done what I could with what limited resources I had. I had to forgive my stuff-ups, accept myself for what I was and stop demanding things of myself I couldn't possibly do.
CORINNA, MOTHER OF ONE

That little voice inside your head

Before I looked at my self-talk, I had no idea how bad it was. I was literally talking to myself in a way that could only be described as verbally abusive! I needed to change or risk forever feeling anxious and depressed. It took time, but I got there. Now I talk to myself in the same way as I do to my children. Never perfect, but as my therapist says: "good enough" is my goal! LYNDA, MOTHER OF TWO

Until we mothers actually take a moment to look at how we talk to ourselves (our "self-talk"), we don't realise we have set up our thinking to be more like the war-wounded than a spritely sister when it comes to our parenting.

Hopefully the ACT exercises started your journey in reducing the power of toxic self-talk. In addition to these ACT techniques, I give the following task to the mums I work with:

In your moments of being the best mum you can be, how would you imagine talking to your baby about how they are behaving or feeling?

I bet you're being patient, respectful, kind, thoughtful and wise.

Now...Compare this to how you talk to yourself. Still patient, respectful, kind, thoughtful and wise?

If you answered "yes" chances are your self-talk is OK.

If you answered "no", I bet you're more used to being mean to yourself, degrading yourself, or giving up on yourself. In other words, your self-talk is *destructive* – to *you!*

Just as our baby will either grow up with a sense of being nurtured, loved and confident from the way we talk to them

If you found that your self-talk was a little self-abusive, then it will help to start speaking to yourself as if you were respectfully speaking to your child. Here's how:

1. **Are you predicting a disaster or catastrophe?** For example, telling yourself, "It's going to be a morning of hell." Ask yourself, in later years, will you send your child off to preschool carrying this prediction in their little mind (ie, "Goodbye honey, enjoy your morning of preschool hell")? Could you then really hope their headspace is up to meeting the demands of their snotty-nosed and toy-snatching classmates? Talking like this to yourself will result in your brain preparing for a completely horrible experience sufficient to invoke the flight/fight/freeze response. It really limits your capacity to see the situation for what it is and you'll tend to turn potentially *difficult* situations into *definite* disasters. Try something more realistic, eg, "This will be probably be a tough few hours but

I'll deal with it the best I can" or "My baby isn't wanting me to feel bad when she cries, she's just working something through her system that I can't understand".

2. **Are you predicting you can't manage the experience?** For example, telling yourself, "I can't cope with this baby" or "I won't be able to deal with mothers group". Imagine your baby's self-talk including "Learning to walk is too hard, I can't cope, I can't do this!" They'd give up pretty quickly and remain shuffling on their knees forever! That's because this way of talking to yourself leaves your brain assuming *you're simply not up to the enormous challenge in front of you.* And it wants to give up. *No solutions, no creativity, no trying. Nothing.* If you want to set the stage to cope with the day-to-day parenting dilemma, try adapting your thoughts just slightly to be more realistic, eg, "Crying is really hard to manage, but it won't last forever. My baby needs me to stay calm and to wait. It will pass."

3. **Are you labelling yourself into one of life's "losers"?** For example, telling yourself, "I'm a crap mother." Would you want your child to label themselves as "a crap baby" if for some reason they couldn't latch on to breastfeed that day. Imagine how they'd feel if they did. Sad? Useless? Overwhelmed? Sound familiar? That's because just as a child finds it hard to beat off a bad reputation, so too is it hard for us to get away from a label we've always called ourselves. One day of getting things wrong doesn't describe who we are, it just relates to what we *did*. If we label ourselves, we can expect our kids to do the same and they'll soon be calling themselves an "idiot" if they get just one maths question wrong. Try to get some perspective by saying something more like, "I may not have done everything how I wanted today, but that's OK. It

doesn't make me a loser, it means I'm not perfect and that's OK."

4. **Are you focusing on just the bad stuff?** For example, turning a tricky feeding session into a verbal bashing of the "I can't do this whole mother thing" type. If your baby had trouble learning to crawl would you suggest she's hopeless at all things related to being a baby? As a way to turn around this negative focus, see all that you do as a TV screen or screen at the movies. Put up on there all the things you *can* do and *have* done. Note the times you've cuddled and kissed baby, the times you've rocked her to sleep, when you've taken her for a walk. All of these times are essential for baby's wellbeing too. Getting a few feeds out of whack, having a few unsettled nights and a few hard times in-between doesn't *take away* all the good stuff. Kids are happier and healthier with authentic amateurs rather than "perfect parent posers". We have to model that we can *accept ourselves warts and all* if we're going to teach our kids to do the same.

5. **Are you basing your life around "rules" with no realistic basis?** Perhaps you're still using "rules" that stopped being applicable to you years ago (but you forgot to let them go), eg, "I have to be on time" or "My baby should never cry". When mothers tell me these rules, I usually ask them "Who said?" and then "How do you plan punishing yourself for breaking this rule?" How well would your baby cope if they developed rules like "I have to poo once a day" and then couldn't? Or "I must not make a mess when I eat my pumpkin mash". You know the answer, it's simply that we forgot that these self-statements were meant to *guide* our behaviour not *rule* our behaviour. It's OK to be late if you couldn't help it. Life is complicated. People understand, and if they don't it's

because they have an unrealistic "rule" governing them too. To shift your thinking along if you're prone to over-policing your own behaviour, write down all your "rules" (they're all the ones starting with "I must", "I should" and "I ought to") and see whether you can ease up on yourself by replacing them: try starting your new sentences with "I prefer to", "I like", "Things flow more easily when".

6. **Are you mistaking a feeling for a fact?** Often we can get feelings for a whole range of reasons, some of which we have no control over and often aren't accurate. Just because I feel worried, doesn't mean there is necessarily something for me to worry about. Remember, if our baby is scared of butterflies, grass, new people, etc, we need to acknowledge her fear but then help her know they'll be OK. So too do we need to remind ourselves that the most powerful way to change our feelings is not to always agree with them, but to use our thoughts and behaviours to change it when it's off target, eg, "Although I feel lazy, I know I'll feel better if I walk, so I will" or "I know I'm feeling sad, so the best thing for me to do is call a friend, even though I don't feel like it".

7. **Are you forgetting that feelings aren't permanent?** Like the weather, feelings change. Just as you'd be considered a tad silly for ignoring that it's hailing (think possible head injury or hail-damaged car) it would also be unwise not to acknowledge that either you or your baby is upset. But you'd also be silly to think the hail would last forever and that the sun won't ever appear again. Same goes for your feelings – it would be unhelpful for you and your baby if you assumed that just because you're sad right now, that in a few moments or hours you won't feel different. If your baby was upset in the bath, would you say "Oh dear, it's likely your distress is

now permanent"? No? In the same way, we need to catch ourselves out when we say things to ourselves like "I'll never be happy again, it's all too much, life is miserable". Fast-forward your thoughts even a few hours, talking to a friend, a cup of tea (or wine) in your hand. Fast-forward them again to the weekend – partner home, a walk in the park. Your own mind, and your baby, will benefit using a long-term view of your emotional weather pattern, not just your current storm.

8. **Are you basing all of your thinking around what others might think or do or comparing yourself with them?** For example, telling yourself, "I bet they all think I'm a crap mother" or "I bet all the other mothers aren't having this much trouble settling their baby". Would you want your toddler entering the local playground whilst saying to herself, "I bet all the other babies will laugh at how many times I fall over" or "I bet they all think my speech development is crap"? No other person has any idea what you and your baby really need. You are the person who knows best about that. And every baby is different. Try thoughts such as "No matter what people think, I know I'm giving everything I can to do this job" or "Just because her baby settles more quickly doesn't mean she doesn't have other problems. We're just all different".

There are many more suggestions for identifying and changing thoughts, some of which are online such as: www.moodgym. anu.edu.au, www.ecouch.anu.edu.au and www.fiveareas.com. Sara Edelman's book *Change Your Thinking* is also a great book with heaps of ideas that are practical and easy to read on this topic.

Everyone thought I was doing great. I'd put on my makeup, muster a fake smile and act as if being a new mum was the best thing that ever happened to me. But inside I was a mess. Looking back, I wish I'd done something about it earlier. GENEVIEVE, MOTHER OF TWO

Blah blah blah – "positive thinking" doesn't work

I may be one of the only psychologists in the world who says this but I'd have to agree – positive thinking does have its limits. Why? Because just as a negative self-talk comment like "It's going to be a morning of hell" is a **lie** (you can't predict the future any better than I can), so too would be a positive self-talk comment like "It's going to be a morning of absolute bliss". Again – how do you know? Positive thinking without a grasp on reality doesn't prepare you to deal with what's really happening in your life – a crying baby, a whole load of household chores and perhaps a little loneliness thrown in for good measure.

> **This is why the only option for us mums is to adopt what I call realistic thinking. As one of my favourite quotes says: "*The pessimist complains about the wind; the optimist expects it to change; the realist adjusts the sails.*" WILLIAM ARTHUR WARD**

In the examples I detailed in the above section, you might have noticed each one of them prepares you to best get your head into a space to deal with what is *actually* ahead of you. Not for candy land. But not for World War II either. You'll know when you've used realistic thinking because it will be *true*. You won't be able to debate it. If it's a really helpful realistic thought, it will also be *empowering* such as "I don't know what this morning will be like (the *truth*) but I'll do my best to handle it with all the calm breathing and helpful self-talk that I can (*empowering*)".

What a relief not to be told to just think positively! It was good not

to pretend I was in some type of nirvana, when I felt like I was
drowning in motherhood. Learning to use realistic thinking was
the most helpful skill I needed to get through the hard times.
SHONA, MOTHER OF ONE

I'm me. You're you.

There is a definite theme to the popular language of love. Words
such as "I can't live without you", and "two become one" are
lines used within many love songs. The problem is that they
suggest:

a. our survival is dependent on (ie we'll die without it) another
   human being;
b. that love means "morphing" into another person – with
   the same thoughts, feelings, behaviours, ideas, emotions,
   fantasies and perceptions as each other.

Weird? Kind of. Destructive? Definitely. In healthy adult
relationships with people who are "differentiated" (ie you are
you, I am me) there are two well-functioning different people.
They have two different sets of ideas, emotions and values. But
love each other and respect each other just the same. Oh, and if
one partner leaves, the other person continues on living – often
in pain and very distressed – but alive nonetheless.

In the early days post-birth, there is probably the least amount
of differentiation between a mother and baby than there is in
any other healthy relationship. Realistically, a baby *is* dependent
on us to stay alive. But even at this early stage, we need to be
careful that we don't become so intertwined with our baby that
we don't know what's her experience and what's ours.

This is most obvious when a baby cries. Our baby's cry
naturally triggers us to feel upset, but this is so we know *they're*

distressed, it doesn't mean we are. If we don't acknowledge *which person* has the distress then *we end up both feeling the same way.* And as we know, meeting our baby's distress with our own distress is probably the least helpful response in the situation.

Sometimes I give the quicksand analogy to explain this concept. Imagine a scene where for some bizarre reason you happen to be in the Amazon jungle and your baby falls into quicksand. Is the most helpful response to:

a. jump into the quicksand and slowly perish with them? OR
b. stay on safe ground and remain as calm as possible, quickly devising as many strategies as possible to get them out – vines, sticks, clothing lassoes etc?

You know the answer. Just as it's not helpful to dive into the quicksand, our babies aren't helped with their strong negative feelings if we feel the same way as them. What's important is that we're aware of how they're feeling and help them through it accordingly.

When I understood how much I was allowing my baby to determine my mood, I realised I had to change. It was my job as the adult to help him, not get all caught up in his distress. I was soon able to learn strategies that helped me be with his distress without taking it on myself. I wished I'd know about them earlier.
JENNY, MOTHER OF TWO

There has been much coverage of this "I'm me, you're you" phenomenon in scientific literature, and fancy terms have been applied accordingly:

• "*Cognitive empathy*" is the term used to describe our ability to understand the feelings of others and to appreciate the distinction between their feelings and our own.

- *"Emotional contagion"* refers to our tendency to "catch" (feel the same) joy and happiness, love, fear and anxiety, anger, sadness and depression, etc in general from the people around us.

As mothers (ie adults…most of the time), when our baby cries, the goal is to achieve "cognitive empathy" rather than "emotional contagion". But our baby's brains haven't yet developed enough to do the same. As a baby, they don't yet know that they're a "them" yet, nor that you're a "you". So in these early months, they *will* pick up on your strong emotions and find it difficult not to feel similarly to the way you feel. This is usually why they smile at you when you smile at them. They feel joy when you do.

But they will also pick up on your distress, your tension and your sadness…And no, this fact wasn't included so as to make you feel even more pressure to "act happy" or to think that your low-level negative feelings are harmful to your baby.

It was included so we can be aware and responsible for the hows and whys and whats of our strong feeling states and their impact on our babies.

Over time our babies will grow into children and later into adults. Their capacity for cognitive empathy will develop so long as they have a connection with us that says, "I can love you for who you are and you can love me for me. The love we share is not dependent on us having to think, feel and behave the same way."

Meanwhile, next time your baby's convinced an all-night scream-a-thon is on the agenda, keep in mind the quicksand analogy and follow the guidelines below. You'll stay firmly on stable ground (perhaps with some Tim Tams or supportive partner for extra stability) and you'll both come out in the morning in a better headspace. Cheers (with a decaf cappuccino) to that.

When my baby is distressed, I ask myself:

- What feeling do I think my *baby* is having?
- What feeling was I having before this? Is my own mood influencing how I'm interpreting my baby's mood?
- What feeling would be most helpful for *me* to have in this situation (remember the quicksand analogy)?
- Am I sure I'm not "catching" my baby's emotion and forgetting I'm capable of feeling differently?
- Am I reminding myself that I can't always change how my baby feels? She might be working through something I don't understand. But wherever possible I can hold my baby and help her get through it.

Ghosts in the nursery

Ever watched a re-run of "The Brady Bunch"? Does their just-so-fabulous family often seem bizarre? Was it a far cry from your own not-anywhere-close-to-fabulous family warfare? Forget wanting a cutesy Mum (Carol), Dad (Mike), or housekeeper (Alice); some of us would have given anything for a home that was just safe (emotionally or physically).

Many of us grew up in homes where we weren't made to feel special or even wanted. Some of us have suffered significant trauma in our lives including sexual assault or living with alcoholic parents or in physically abusive homes. Some of us had mothers who were so anxious about danger that we rarely left the house.

As much as we hoped it wouldn't impact on us, our past experiences have a huge influence not only on our relationships, but also in what we accept in ourselves and what behaviours from our babies trigger uncomfortable thoughts and feelings inside us.

Where there are difficult experiences in our own childhood, we are more susceptible to being overwhelmed by certain tasks of mothering. Mums with this history often report feelings like:

- complete panic when their baby cries and can't be consoled,
- an inability to ever leave their baby alone *ever* (even when baby is perfectly content to lie on the mat while you *could* quickly run to the bathroom),
- worrying their baby doesn't like them or is somehow thinking they're not doing a good-enough parenting job,
- being petrified about doing anything for fear of harming their baby,
- worrying every other mother in the entire world is doing a better job than them,
- wanting to get away from their baby because it's just too much.

If this sounds like you, then I'm sorry mothering has so far been so tough. The good news is there is now a growing pile of research studies showing that perfect childhoods aren't a prerequisite to becoming an awesome parent. In fact it's quite clear that parents who had a much-less-than-fabulous childhood *can* (with determination and help) raise babies and children who are just as well-behaved and just as emotionally secure as any other parent.

But I'd suggest you make contact with a very supportive therapist with specialised knowledge to help you on this journey. It takes time to work out how to manage unhelpful childhood legacies. You will require patience, reassurance and understanding. Seek out fantastic training programmes such as Circle of Security (see www.circleofsecurity.net for more details). Most therapists who have a sound understanding of attachment theory will also understand the type of therapy you require.

But if nothing else, always remember it's never too late to start. Our children will always be grateful that we took our histories into our hands to forge a secure future for them. No matter how old they are.

I couldn't ever imagine being anything like my mother. But during my hard days, I reckon I became as crazy as she had been when I was a child. I needed to use all the skills I'd learned in therapy to keep me on track and stay the mother I wanted to be and not become like my mum. Each time I stayed calm and remained gentle with myself and my baby my confidence grew. I'm now proud to say that I am a good-enough mother and that's good enough for me! SHELLY, MOTHER OF ONE

The most important lesson of all: forgiveness

To forgive is to set a prisoner free and discover that the prisoner was you. LEWIS B. SMEDES (AUTHOR)

Many women I work with have been punishing themselves daily for years. Not of the Opus Dei kind (although some women do physically self-harm), it's more of a mental cage-fighter variety that they've been honing their skills in for years. Then they become mothers. And instead of getting better, the cage fight becomes more vicious. Every perceived "mummy error" becomes part of a day and night side-kick, left-hook, slap-in-the-face rumination routine. Anything that's not done "perfectly" cannot be forgiven. They are sure that they must punish themselves forever.

And then I pose the same type of question to them as I posed earlier in this chapter. "How would you want your child to think about themselves if they had made the same 'error'? Would you want your child to hate themselves and berate themselves for the rest of eternity? Picture your child in the same mental cage-fight and ask yourself if you want them to be there?"

All mothers answer the same way: "No."

And then I ask: "Would you want them to learn that they can forgive themselves? That they can make up for their errors in some way? That they can like themselves even though they made a wrong decision at some point?"

All the mothers answer the same way: "Yes."

In presenting this last section on the power of forgiveness there is one story of an amazing mother that particularly stands out to me. I'll call her Stephanie. Stephanie had experienced quite an exciting youth and the drugs, alcohol and general partying lifestyle had continued well into her early-married years.

On one such exciting occasion, it resulted in a one-night stand with a good-looking family acquaintance. He was never to be seen again.

But when Stephanie looked into the eyes of the baby born some nine months later, she knew for the rest of her life she would always see a female form of this sexual acquaintance. Her husband might have pondered the birth of a brown-eyed baby in a blue-eyed, blond couple, but she would not give up her secret. Wracked with guilt, she declared she could never forgive herself for what she had done. She deserved to be eternally miserable and she deserved to feel pain. And it was making motherhood miserable.

So I asked her:

- to help me know the level of love she felt for her baby girl – it was mountains.

- to think about whether her baby needed particular care because of what had happened and how her future might unfold – she agreed her baby's future might be more difficult and would require a strong and healthy mother to help her withstand the potential paternity-test storm.

- Tto ponder whether a mother who was constantly punishing herself could be the mother this baby would need – she agreed this was unlikely to be possible.

- lastly, how she would want her baby girl to feel about herself if by any chance she grew up and did the same thing – she was quick to say she would want her to forgive herself and be strong.

Stephanie and I took many sessions on the answers to these questions. We spent many hours pondering on the potential to forgive the self.

The two most powerful images for this client were:

a. to imagine herself again as a little girl. At an age less than 10. She imagined herself with all the dreams and hopes she had had at that age. She imagined the words she'd always hoped to hear from her mother – but hadn't (her mother had been and continued to be emotionally abusive). Then she imagined saying all of these kind words to herself.

b. to imagine talking to her own daughter about how to forgive herself if the same thing had happened to *her*. To use all the kind words she could muster to help her daughter deal with the reality of a very difficult situation.

Over the course of our sessions she came to learn that when she didn't use these kind words in her own self-talk – to her internal "little girl"– she became abused all over again. What she needed to use were words of compassion to make her feel loved and nurtured. She remembered to tell herself every day that although she wasn't proud of what she'd done, she had not done it with malice or viciousness, but rather in her ongoing search to feel acceptance and affection from another. The more she could do this, the more she was able to be the mother she wanted to be.

Stephanie is now a very different woman. She holds her head high. She laughs. She has a beautiful relationship with her daughter. She likes who she is, even when she may not like what she has done.

Perhaps I can share with you something she said at our last session:

Now I know what it is like to have a good relationship. With myself. It is not perfect but it is tender. It is kind. It pulls me up when I'm in the wrong, it gives me a chance to learn to be different, but it loves me all the way on this new journey. Now I can give this gift to my daughter.

One last comment:

So after reading this chapter, a chapter I hope has been a mixture of both some frivolous fun-finding factors mixed with serious soul-searching sentiments, I'm hoping you might tap into your internal "Tom Tom" again. Where's your current position?

Is Struggle Street still your location, or has it headed toward Smooth(ish)-Sailing Avenue?

If it's still Struggle Street and it has been for some time, I'm going to get momentarily serious again. Mainly because the bitumen on that road can get pretty sticky and the longer we're there, the harder it is get you and your stroller out.

If the strategies in this chapter aren't enough to alter how you feel, turn to the next chapter which gives ideas on handling the really dark moments or days of motherhood. Seeking professional help is also always advised. Get a referral from your local GP to a psychologist or counselor specialising in postnatal care.

Asking for help doesn't mean you are a failure or that you should have been stronger. It means you *are* taking responsibility for working through your own issues so they don't become issues for your baby. My experience is that the mothers who *do* ask for help are much further on the journey to Mummy Utopia than those who *don't*. And because your baby will only poo, wee and cry in response to your brave leap in asking for help, I'll thank you on their behalf for changing both their lives and yours for the better.

To finish, I want to share with you what one mother said to me at her last session:

Thank you for showing me I could be different, that I could be the Mum I wanted to be. I can now love my daughter, rather than being scared by her. I can enjoy her without fearing the next moment going "wrong". I can sleep at night knowing I'm doing the best job possible with what I've got. MANDY, MOTHER OF TWO

Chapter 4:

This job isn't just HARD, I'm totally STRUGGLING.

Managing those really dark days of mothering.

Me! Depressed?
That's so hysterical
I could almost cry...
For days...

One night when my baby was four weeks old I had one of the worst nights of my life. I had tried all the techniques under the sun to get him to settle! It was 3am. We'd been awake since midnight. Nothing worked. Feeding wasn't the answer. As soon as he stopped sucking he was screaming at me. So I put him in his pram in the lounge room and started rocking him back and forth. I picked him up when he was really distressed and then put him down and rocked him until he started crying again. Then I'd do it again. And again and again. It felt like a lifetime.

The pram helped me, because at some stage I knew I really was getting worked up and I was struggling to settle my own emotions let alone my baby's. And yes, sometimes I let him cry a little longer before I picked him up than maybe even I would have liked. But at times my crying was just as savage as his was and my heart ached so much at my own uselessness that I couldn't pick him up. I felt it was safer for him to be in the pram at times than in my arms. I hate to admit it, but it's true. I'll never forget that night.
ERICA, MOTHER OF TWO BOYS

Reality bites. Hard. For most of us, by about week four of the "mummy rollercoaster", reality has hit us like an elephant-sized wet nappy. It's knocked us over and man, is it hard to get up. Ironic that a little miracle so small could wreak so much havoc.

And you learn the glossy magazines lied. About everything. Our bellies don't magically turn back into a rippling six-pack (if they ever were…), our clothes still resemble those of the maternity variety (that's if we get out of our pyjamas) and forget the jewellery, our main "accessory" looks remarkably like a stain from a leaking breast pad.

So this chapter is dedicated to the two hardest parts of parenting:
- how to cope with my baby on my hardest days
- what to do with myself on my hardest days

Part 1: what to do when your BABY is too hard to handle

Remember that you cannot force a baby to stop crying.
You can only be *with* them and soothe them while they're using their high-pitched screams to work through whatever it is they're working through.
The only person you can control in this environment is you.

Just like there are helplines for helping us deal with our own struggles, we've also got some really useful helplines (detailed in the box below) that can help us through the toughest moments with our babies. I know dozens of friends, family members and clients who credit the wisdom and calmness of the person on the other end of the phone with saving both their relationship with their baby and their sanity.

But let's make one thing clear: While a crying baby is *usually* best cared for in its mother's arms, the one time the baby is not safe is when we lose control of our own emotions. At these times, our behaviour can also get out of control and the consequences may be life-threatening for our baby.

To reduce the risk of child abuse, the guidelines for all professionals working with mothers is to direct them as follows: **should you feel at risk of harming a crying baby, place your baby in a safe place and walk away**[1].

So, if your frustration is climbing to the same frenzied fever pitch as your baby's bellowing, here's the two-phase guide to managing this heartbreaking situation more safely.

PHASE ONE: IF YOU CAN MANAGE YOUR OWN FEELINGS WELL ENOUGH TO SAFELY CARE FOR YOUR CRYING BABY

Before you enter the room, use the following technique, and write it on your hand if it helps (a spelling variation of burps – BIRPS – is used for ease of remembering):

(B) Breathing – slow it down and focus on the out breath, saying "calm" to yourself as you breath out.

(I) Imagining yourself handling the situation in the way you want to – including being calm and patient. It also includes imagining yourself putting your baby down if your own distress gets too high.

(R) Relaxing your body – tense it up and then let it loosen again, dropping your shoulders and gently rolling your head backward and forward.

(P) Permission to put baby down and take time out to resettle yourself if you get too worked up.

(S) Soothing self-statements such as "we can get through this" or "this crying will end, I don't know when, but it will. It always does".

Now enter the room:
Pick up your baby, keeping your breathing, muscle tension and self-talk in check.

If you remain in control, stay for as long as possible using settling techniques for your baby contained in chapter two

If you find yourself becoming overwhelmed and no longer in control, move to Phase 2.

PHASE TWO: IF YOU FEEL LIKE YOU ARE OVERWHELMED AND STRUGGLING TO STAY IN CONTROL

1. **Reassure yourself that your baby is okay**. Go through your mental list of things to check when your baby cries such as temperature, nappy, clothing, etc (and run through it twice again). If these are all OK, move to step 2.
2. **Put your baby in a safe place**. A crucial part of staying calm is the ability to take a break. Put your baby in a safe spot such as his cot.
3. **Find a place for you**. The next key step is to find a place that offers you a brief distraction from your baby's cries. A bedroom or bathroom will do.
4. **Now you can take a break**. This can be gradual if needed:
- If it's just too hard to go to your safe place straight away, start more slowly. Stay close enough to see him but more than an arm's length away. Close your eyes and take long, deep breaths. After one minute, pick the baby back up.
- Each time you take a break you can increase the distance. Take the baby monitor with you if can no longer see the baby (but keep the volume on low so you aren't as traumatised as when you were in the room with him).
- Remind yourself that you're not *deserting* him, just taking a break to get yourself in the best space to *look* after him.
5. **While on your break, use your calming techniques**.
- Start your slowed breathing, muscle relaxation and self-talk strategies to calm you down (ie your BIRPS techniques above).
- Do some exercises on the spot if it helps.
- Call a friend, or your partner.
- Listen to some music.
- You need to stop any destructive self-talk and get your body back to a calm-enough state in whatever way works for you. Otherwise it's safer to stay away from your baby.

6. **Give yourself time**. Don't expect your chosen technique to work immediately. If you're really worked up, it could take up to five minutes of calming techniques before you start to wind down. Remember, while we don't *want* to leave our babies this long, if you're too stressed out to handle them, it's NOT SAFE to pick them up.

7. **Once calm, return to Phase One**.

BUT...If you can't calm down and you're severely distressed, and you feel like you still can't attend to your baby, YOU NEED HELP.
CALL
Parentline: 1300 30 1300; Karitane: (02) 9794 2300;
Tresillian ((02) 9787 0855 or 1800 637 357 (freecall outside Sydney and within NSW).
In the UK: Cry-sis: 08451 228699; Parentline Plus: 0808 800 2222

AND...If you have any concerns that you may harm yourself or your baby: call 000 (Australia) or 112 (UK) immediately.

Part 2: what to do when it's YOU who's seriously not coping

For some of us, our mothering situation doesn't just momentarily shift onto Struggle Street, we find that it's turned into a full-on daily meltdown territory of Mt Everest-sized proportions. Tears flow more freely than Niagara Falls, our energy levels resemble those of a wet nappy, daily decisions seem harder than any theory of Einstein's, and we rate our parenting confidence as somewhere below negative infinity.

Yep, in case you hadn't predicted it, with all of the stresses, strains, stretchmarks and sleeplessness due to baby's arrival, we're at greater risk of developing a mental illness following childbirth than at any other time in our lives.

But at least we're not alone in our emotional pain. The research consistently shows that as many as one in seven (or around 15%) of mums could be potentially diagnosed with clinical depression during the postnatal period. And for those who are more Anxious Annie than Depressed Diana, postnatal anxiety (PNA) may have received far less attention than its PND cousin, but preliminary studies suggest it could actually be more prevalent – possibly affecting one in six new mothers[2].

And while our mummy-mushed brain can't perform logarithms or quantum physics (if it ever could) it's actually pretty easy to see that there's many a new mother struggling with a diagnosable mental health condition. Look around your mothers group: if there are 10 mums in it, chances are two of them will meet the criteria for either PND or PNA over the first few years as a new mother.

One day I just summoned up the courage to tell another mother in my group how sad I was feeling. To my surprise she told me she felt the same way. It was a powerful turning point for both of us and we supported each other the whole way. I'm glad every day that I took the step to speak up. MICHELLE, MOTHER OF TWO

In understanding your symptoms and emotional state, it's important not to confuse them with the "baby blues". The "blues" is a much more short-term experience, affecting around 80% of us after our baby is born and then reducing over the first few weeks (see chapter three for more details). In comparison,

PND symptoms are both more severe and don't just go away.

If you think you might be one of the mums whose mood has shifted from being sad or worried to more melancholically miserable or permanently petrified, take yourself seriously. Because if *you* believe it's a major problem, it probably is. So be wary of opinions offered by well-meaning aunts, friends and colleagues preaching their wisdom on the "whys, wherefores and what-ifs" of your symptom development. It's highly unlikely they know more about your mental state than you do.

So does that mean you're just a non-coping, weaker-than-most, mothering menace?

The recipe for depression is to create an unrealistic myth about motherhood, offer unfeeling medical care, and then set the new mother down in a social system that offers her little support for her new child and new role. Childbirth is so oversold as women's greatest achievement that women believe something is wrong with them if they have ambivalent feelings after giving birth.
ANN OAKLEY, "POSTBIRTH BLUES," *TIME MAGAZINE* 1980, P 58

Any woman who is led to believe she is somehow to "blame" for her symptoms has been led up a garden path (of motherhood-myth variety). Despite the best attempts of some pretty amazing researchers, we are actually yet to devise one single theory that adequately describes the complex causes and nature of postnatal illnesses. It seems that the best predictive power we've got merely points us to consider the interaction of many factors, including a past history of depression, social support, hormone levels, baby temperament and many more. Only *you* know yourself well enough to know how all these factors impact on you.

And unfortunately there are still significantly outmoded and misguided understandings of postnatal illnesses in our apparently "modern" world. Some still associate it with turning into a "crazed woman", while, in reality, mums with PND suffer in sad silence or an anxiety-induced nightmare. For many mothers, their ability to function on a daily basis while crying for hours in the privacy of their homes or checking for germs hundreds of times won't be understood as resembling a postnatal illness. They're looking out for something more like a hysterical Tassie devil.

Is it serious enough to be a diagnosable postnatal psychological issue?

If you do believe you're at risk of a postnatal mental health issue, take a look at the symptoms below and tick off the symptoms you experience. You could also complete the internationally recognised and respected Edinburgh Postnatal Depression Scale (EPDS), designed to allow screening of postnatal depression in the primary care setting.

But don't go popping open your laptops to fill in the numerous on-line versions in the hope that this one's the definitive on-line definitive "test" for PND or PNA. And don't let any well-meaning nurse, therapist or do-gooder tell you that since your score was "above 13 on the EPDS you're definitely in the PND dumps". Any assessment must be used in combination with a formal check-up by a GP, psychiatrist or clinical psychologist.

SIGNS OF POSTNATAL DEPRESSION OR ANXIETY

The Symptoms	Words Mothers Use
☐ Feeling sad on most days for most of the time	*It's like there's just this darkness all around my thoughts and feelings all the time*
☐ Feeling worthless about yourself or your role as a mother	*I just can't get anything right anymore. Everything I do seems wrong*
☐ Excessive worrying about your own health or your baby's health	*I'm forever thinking what might go wrong or how we might get sick or how to avoid my baby catching anything*
☐ Either feeling slowed down in movements or feeling hyperactive and fidgety most of the time	*I just can't seem to get moving. Everything is an effort*
☐ Feeling irritated or annoyed	*It feels like I'm constantly on edge, like at any minute I might snap*
☐ Difficulty making decisions about daily tasks	*I can't even decide on what to eat, or to what to buy at the supermarket. It seems too hard*
☐ Having trouble sleeping, even when the baby is sleeping soundly	*I'm so tired but I can't drift off to sleep. It takes hours and by then the baby is awake again*
☐ Thinking about death or suicide	*I can't do this anymore. It's all too hard. I don't want to be here*
☐ Feeling like you can't stop crying	*I just cry and cry and cry. All day. About anything*
☐ Feeling anxious on most days and possibly experiencing panic attacks	*I'm constantly anxious, thinking about everything that could go wrong. I never relax*
☐ Lacking in energy and feeling exhausted	*I constantly need sleep. Even when I have a good night's sleep I'm still exhausted*

☐	Losing interest in activities that you used to enjoy	*I don't enjoy doing anything I used to. Nothing interests me anymore*
☐	Changes to your appetite such as eating too little or too much	*I eat to give myself something that's a little bit nice for me. But I can't stop. I want to keep eating everything that's not good for me*
☐	Difficulty concentrating	*My mind just drifts off, even when I'm talking to people. I can't remember things I've said or what I was supposed to be doing*
☐	Feeling overwhelmed and confused with your thoughts	*My mind feels like it's on overload, and then all of my thoughts seem to get jumbled up and things don't make sense*

NOTE: Puerperal (postpartum) psychosis is a very rare but severe mental health condition that is experienced by one or two in 1000 postnatal women. There is no known cause but symptoms include:
- feeling abnormally strong, powerful or totally unbeatable
- having strange beliefs (eg people are plotting to harm my baby)
- hearing voices or seeing things that aren't there (hallucinations)
- believing things that are not based on reality (delusions)

If you are experiencing these symptoms yourself, or notice them amongst any new mothers, SEEK HELP IMMEDIATELY. See below for details of emergency care options.

Firstly, for those who ticked "yes" to many of the depressed and/ or anxious symptoms but *aren't* having thoughts of harming yourself or your baby:

- **Try some new techniques**. Take some time to read through the techniques in this book, especially those in chapter three. They are all designed to assist us mums with just the types of thoughts and/or behaviours you are experiencing.
- **Talk about it**. Wherever possible, tell someone you trust about how you're feeling. A partner, a friend or your mother. Research shows that for women who have experienced distressed feelings, almost 75% agreed that talking to someone about their feelings was by far the most effective strategy[3].
- **Get professional help**. If the techniques aren't enough to shift a constant low mood, and talking to a trusted support person hasn't helped, it's likely you need individualised help to specifically look at what might work for you. Make an appointment to see your GP for a referral to a therapist specialising in postnatal care. Take the list with you to share with them how you're feeling.

Secondly, for those of us whose thoughts have turned to harming ourselves or our baby or that resemble postnatal psychosis, **seek help IMMEDIATELY**. Use whichever of the following best suits your current location:

1. If you feel safe enough, drive to the local accident and emergency section of your local hospital. Explain you don't feel safe to be on your own or with your baby. Ask for whatever help is available.
2. Call OOO (Australia) or 112 (UK) and explain how you feel; they'll guide you through what you need to do.

3. If it's between the hours of 9am and 5pm, call your GP and explain to the secretaries the urgency of your situation. They may be able to see you straight away. If not, use one of the other options.

4. Call a 24-hour crisis hotline (in Australia: **Lifeline 13 11 14;** in the UK: **NHS Direct on 0845 4647**) where trained phone counsellors can help you through the situation and advise you on what services to access next.

Don't let a motherhood myth stop you getting help

There are many mothers who stay mute when it comes to speaking up about sad (or anxious) symptoms. Their reasons for doing so aren't exactly logical – depression and anxiety strip us of that capacity – but they're certainly powerful. Before you sidestep a sound intervention, just make sure you've worked through these motherhood myths about seeking help:

1. **"Someone will take away my baby."** This is probably every mother's biggest fear and is usually based around outdated notions of how child support services work (along with some unhelpful Hollywood hype thrown in for good measure). Know this: having PND or PNA is not a reason to remove your baby from your care. Having worked with child support services for over 15 years, I can confidently say that services know a baby's welfare is best met in the care of its mother. This is of course unless you have any homicidal thoughts. Services will work with you to do everything possible to address your symptoms and increase your connection with your baby.

2. **"Why bother – nothing will help."** I'm always curious as to how so many women with depression and anxiety come to this assumption. I want to ask "based on what

127

information" but a woman with PND isn't usually up for a debate. Researchers suggest that when mothers receive a combination of both cognitive and behavioural therapeutic intervention, up to 80% will have a positive response. Appropriate medication gets good results too, however unless there is also psychological support, the mother is more prone to relapse once medication is ceased[4]. So, no more excuses then – suggesting interventions won't help is simply, well, unhelpful.

3. **"I don't want to take drugs."** There are many misconceptions about antidepressants and medications for mothers. Many believe they are "extremely harmful" to either themselves or their babies. Actually, truth is antidepressants *aren't* addictive and some can be safely taken while breastfeeding. But it is always important to get good quality information about side effects and safety before making any decision, so include your GP in any medication debate. Keep in mind that medication is still only one option and not the only option. As outlined above, psychological therapies are effective too, although it is best-practice to utilise a combination of both in more severe forms of depression or anxiety.

4. **"Isn't this what all mothers feel – isn't this "normal?"** No mucking around, this myth deserves a big boot to the backstage. While it is certainly common to have a few down days, being continuously sad or worried isn't normal. You and your baby deserve better.

5. **"I'm just being a mummy moaner and should just 'get over it'."** Mental health issues aren't a choice and they're certainly not something we can just "snap out of". Ever heard anyone suggest that to someone with heart disease? Or "hey, you there with the diabetes – get over it"? Sure, lifestyle

measures do help. And there are other things that boost our mood or dampen the panic, but just like any illness, they need to be considered seriously and treated accordingly.

How do you find a "good therapist"?

When you've decided to take the important step of talking to your GP about a referral to a therapist or counsellor, it's important to know your options. Many GP's will have psychologists, counsellors and other mental health professionals to recommend to you, but it's worth doing a little bit of investigating yourself. After all, it's *you* who's going to have to feel comfortable in the place you attend for therapy and the therapist you see.

Step one: get some information.

Once you have a recommendation to see someone, contact the person directly (or speak with their secretary who may be able to help). You could ask questions such as:

a. *What experience does the therapist have with PND and other emotional issues for women with young babies?* You really do need someone who has experience in the area you need help with. If they're more familiar working with elite athletes or male sexual problems, I'd keep searching for one more suitable.

b. *What are the therapist's qualifications and professional registrations?* Ideally you will see a therapist with university training in psychology, social work or counselling. If they are registered with a professional organisation then you also know they are meeting all of their ongoing training requirements to stay up to date with current research. No point seeing someone whose last training on PND was when the world was thought to be flat...

My first therapist was this old guy who seemed bemused by my distress. He virtually told me I should just go home and enjoy being with my baby. I felt more alone than ever. Fortunately a friend persuaded me to see a therapist she had used. This time my experience was what I hoped for. My therapist really understood me and I made progress really quickly. COLLEEN, MOTHER OF THREE

c. *How long will you have to wait for your first appointment?* If you're really struggling to cope, it's probably a good idea to see someone as quickly as possible. But if you have advice from a friend or GP that a certain professional is "really fantastic" (word of mouth is often the best way to find the right person for you) then it may be worth the wait.

d. *Can you bring your baby with you to sessions?* Sometimes therapists will prefer you to be on your own to make the most of the session. While this is true, you need to attend a service that can also allow for those times and situations when this isn't possible. If you can't bring your baby, the therapist may not be a practical choice for you.

e. *How accessible is the service for prams?* You need to bring your baby and all the things that make it easier for you to care for baby while you're in session. Find a service where it's possible to wheel your pram into the therapy room and definitely one that has access to a change table and a large toilet (so you can wheel the pram in when you need to use it). Many of my clients are convinced their baby saves up their poo explosion just for me, and given the number of babies who do poo on arrival, I'm not convinced there isn't some kind of weird association going on here.

Step two: reflect on your first session.
During your first appointment and when you think about the appointment later, ask yourself the following:

a. *Did you feel that the therapist "got" you?* Do you feel she understood where you were coming from? Did she seem understanding and empathic? Did she seem to judge your decisions? Having a good connection with your therapist is incredibly important if you are to get the most out of therapy.

b. *What did you learn about yourself and your diagnosis?* It's nice to "click" with someone, but we're not talking about finding a new BFF here. This professional also needs to be skilled at assessing your emotional state and letting you know whether you actually have a diagnosis or not. You want to leave knowing whether they think your symptoms relate to childhood issues, a biologically-based depression, a "tricky" baby, difficulties with your partner or family, or a combination of factors.

c. *What's the plan?* Even when you have a diagnosis, or other explanation of your symptoms, it's still essential to know what to do about it. Did she suggest a programme (such as Cognitive Behavioural Therapy or Interpersonal Therapy)? How many sessions did she recommend? What's the plan if your symptoms don't improve? How much will the programme cost?

d. *How will she communicate with other professionals?* One of the key factors to your treatment will be making sure your therapist and your GP are on the same wavelength regarding your treatment needs. Make sure you give your consent to their communication about you, and make it clear to both of them that you want to know what they're telling each other.

Step three: give it time.

Well, a little bit anyway. I usually suggest people try to come for three sessions before they decide it "doesn't work" (it's a bit like going to one aerobics class and then quitting because it didn't make you fit). Changing thoughts and feelings takes time. Sometimes connecting with people takes time too. When you're depressed and anxious, this can be even harder than it normally is.

But, if you feel like your therapist doesn't "get" you, or you feel like she's doing a lot of talking without much actual focus on changing your symptoms, it's time to take action. Go back to your GP and express your concerns. Ask for a referral to another therapist.

Step four: don't give up.

Just like it might have taken a few trial runs to find the perfect partner (well, a rough-around-the-edges perfect partner) and you've probably had a few BFFs in your time, finding that connection with a therapist can take time too. You *will* find someone you connect with if you keep trying. So ask around. There's bound to be some mothers at preschool or in your mothers group who "know someone" who has needed a therapist for one reason or another.

Step five: end therapy when *you're* ready.

It's not about having six sessions, 10 sessions or even 20. Therapy ends when you feel *you* are ready to manage motherhood without having a therapist's support. Toward the end of treatment I tend to space appointments out a bit – perhaps monthly or two-monthly apart. There are some mothers I book in every six months for a check-up during the first few years with baby.

Check also that therapy hasn't just treated your own postnatal illness and neglected any baby bonding difficulties. Any lingering concerns about your connection with your baby need to be addressed before you boot (gently I hope) your therapist out of your life.

Are these postnatal illnesses just a woman's thing? How do the men manage?

There is a widespread (mistaken) belief that postnatal psychological illnesses are exclusively encounters of the female kind. Quite the opposite, in fact:

- Men can get majorly miserable (or achingly anxious) too, with around one in 14 having symptoms of sufficient severity in the postnatal period to warrant formal diagnosis.
- Worse still, of around half the men diagnosed, their partner will *also* have a postnatal psychological illness.

So it's often a double whammy of parenting pain endured by countless couples. Just don't expect it to get its rightful respect in the popular press. The parents who suffer and the stories they share are curiously absent from the glossy mummy magazines.

Even more problematic is the fact that new fathers don't access services that new mothers do. They don't tend to take their baby to their doctor, maternal and child health nurse or midwife where *our* symptoms are often picked up. Men often feel that they can't talk to their partners about their problems either, for fear of making their partner worse. Many dads also avoid seeking support due to the public stigmatisation of men's postnatal illness. And the specialists often aren't helpful either. I've recently spoken to two "dinosaur doctors" (I think they trained in the Jurassic period) who insisted male PND didn't exist. And they had the nerve to insinuate I was the stupid one...

Anyway, there are now many websites that can help dads whose partners have PND and for dads who feel they have PND themselves, including:

1. **Fathers Reaching Out (www.fathersreachingout.com)** – started in 2011 by a man whose partner had PND, he shares tips, ideas and links for other dads in similar circumstances.

2. **PostpartumMen (www.postpartummen.com)** – started by psychotherapist Dr Will Courtenay, this website is a place for men with concerns about depression, anxiety or other problems with their mood after the birth of a child. It promotes self-help, provides important information for fathers, hosts an online forum for dads to talk to each other, offers resources and gathers new information about men's experiences postpartum.

3. **How is Dad Going? (www.howisdadgoing.org.au)** – created as a part of the Post and Antenatal Depression Association (PANDA) with significant contributions from dads. It was designed to complement the existing PANDA website but focus specifically on men as new dads who either experience antenatal and postnatal depression themselves or whose partners have a postnatal illness.

Dads might also be interested in reading *The Postpartum Husband: Practical Solutions for Living with Postpartum Depression*, by Karen Kleiman, which is particularly good for those partners who have depression too.

These websites and resources will provide sound advice, but here's a summary of how I suggest a partner can support a mother with postnatal distress.

SUPPORTING A NEW MOTHER WITH POSTNATAL DISTRESS – A PARTNER'S GUIDE

1. **Remind her that it's not personal.** Postnatal depression and anxiety are neither a personal choice nor a consequence of being a "bad mum". The causes are so complex that in reality, any one of us could potentially develop the same or similar symptoms.

2. **Remind yourself that it's not personal too.** She hasn't developed this because you're not supportive enough or a bad husband (but do see point 4!). Nor when she cries and screams "it's all too much" does she blame you either. Take a deep breath and don't run away. She needs you more than ever.

3. **Encourage any support she seeks.** Cheer on any steps she takes to address her low mood (even if it's not the exact choice you would have made). Often women take the route to psychological care through the advice of another professional, such as seeing a personal trainer or nutritionist first.

4. **Reflect on your own behaviour.** Are you pulling your weight around the home or expecting her to dote on you because you work 9am to 5pm? Remember, watch a mother long enough and you'll soon realise she never "clocks off" from her work. Pitch in when you've finished your *paid* tasks and join her in finishing off the *unpaid* ones. And if you work long hours, you'll be aware that it's even tougher on you both. Loneliness is a recipe for disaster so encourage her to spend nights over with family or encourage positive supportive friends to report for bath and bedtime duty. Maybe you could start earlier and get home earlier some days to prevent long nights of loneliness.

5. **Sort out your sleep (and hers)**. Sleep is a big driver in the sanity stakes. Get enough and you've got a firm platform to parent. Miss out on your regular zzz's and sanity can slip by in an instant. Call on any help you can or tag team so one gets sleep one night (or goes to bed early) and the other the next.

6. **Make sure she's nurturing herself**. Encourage her to take time-out from the baby such as a walk on the beach or a night with her friends. For those women who aren't yet ready to leave the house, she'll still appreciate you running her a bath or putting the baby to sleep while she flicks through a magazine.

7. **Nurture yourself too**. Having a partner with a postnatal illness is not only frightening at times, it can be hugely draining too. Make sure you're making time to grab some exercise or hang out with your mates.

8. **Nurture your relationship**. The quality of your relationship together is a powerfully protective factor against postnatal issues. Get a babysitter if you need to, but make sure you take time to just be with each other.

9. **Dish out the duties**. If Aunty Rita cooks a knock-out casserole, set her up for a regular Tuesday delivery. Seek out a house-cleaner to carve up the constant clutter. Liaise with the laundromat to wash and iron your laundry (drop if off before work and pick it up at the end of the day). Remember, burning mother martyrs will leave scars on you both.

10. **Seek professional support**. You and your wife both deserve any help available when it comes to postnatal issues. But don't let her unwillingness to see a therapist or counsellor prevent you taking action. Try to get her to attend a session together, but go alone if she doesn't agree.

Learning more about PND

Despite the fact you may feel alone in your feelings, get ready to find out a whole new world of services, support and connections out there in cyberspace. The internet is a powerhouse for finding sites to help you learn more about your symptoms, but I'd suggest sticking to those that have a strong research background or are endorsed by credible sources. Here's a few I'd recommend:

Gidget Foundation: www.gidgetfoundation.com.au
A not-for-profit organisation named after an Australian woman who died after suffering postnatal depression. It focuses on promoting awareness of perinatal anxiety and depression to parents and professionals with great links to groups and projects. A help-line is available Monday to Friday, 9am-7pm: 1300 726 306 (in Australia). The foundation has also recently announced the opening of Gidget House (North Sydney, Australia) – a specialised treatment centre for women, children and partners affected by postnatal illness.

Post and Antenatal Depression Association Inc (PANDA): www.panda.org.au
A partially government funded not-for-profit Australian organisation providing advice, lists of professionals and numerous tip sheets. A help-line is also available between 9am-7pm (EST): 1300 726 306.

Beyond Blue: www.beyondblue.org.au
An independent, not-for-profit Australian organisation aiming to increase awareness of depression and anxiety as well as provide resources to community members impacted by such illnesses. Numerous tip sheets, links and resources are listed, including

educational booklets on perinatal mental health issues in 20 different languages.

Association for Post Natal Illness (APNI): www.apni.org
Established in 1979, this registered charity is one of the UK's leading organisations for postnatal issues. The Association provides telephone support (between 10:00am-2:00pm) on 020 7386 0868, as well as information leaflets for sufferers and healthcare professionals, and a network of volunteers who experienced postnatal illness and now offer support to others.

St John of God Health Care (SJOGHC) – Perinatal Unit: www.beatbabyblues.com.au
In NSW, SJOGHC is the largest not-for-profit provider of mental health care, and the only NSW provider of a mother and baby unit for mothers requiring inpatient treatment. Their website has links to numerous resources as well as sound suggestions for PND and related mental health issues in the postbirth period.

The Black Dog Institute: www.blackdoginstitute.org.au
An educational, research, clinical and community-oriented facility offering specialist expertise in mood disorders. It is attached to the Prince of Wales Hospital and affiliated with the University of New South Wales. It has a wealth of information and suggestions for people with depression.

Postpartum Support International (PSI): www.postpartum. net
PSI is a non-profit organisation aiming to promote awareness, prevention and treatment of mental health issues related to childbearing in every country worldwide. It has members in 36

countries. It provides a huge range of resources and information about PND and related disorders.

The Marcé Society: www.marcesociety.com

An international organisation since 1980, the Marcé society prides itself on combining the knowledge of numerous disciplines including psychiatrists, psychologists, paediatricians, obstetricians, midwives and early childhood nurses as well as women who experience postnatal issues. The principal aim of the Society is to promote, facilitate and communicate about research into all aspects of the mental health of women, their infants and partners around the time of childbirth. They conduct meetings worldwide and provide a range of resources for both professionals and mothers.

Even celebrities are speaking up about their sadness

Perhaps one of the most important contributors to many mothers' journeys out of postnatal illness is the wisdom and support they receive from others. Sometimes these others are the fantastic-friends variety allowing a mother to dump all her sorrows and unload all her anxieties. Sometimes these others provide inspiration merely from sharing their own stories of overcoming the sadness, anger, desperation and fear that overwhelmed them in their PND or PNA.

For many it's been helpful to know that there are celebrity mums out there struggling with depression and anxiety – the ones who "should" be happy with all their cars, clothing, caterers and carats (the pink diamond kind). Learn their stories and hopefully you'll soon agree that postnatal psychological issues are something that can affect any of us – regardless of financial status, culture, age or our previous sane(ish) state.

Here's what some celebrity mums say about their experiences:

1. **Brooke Shields**. This former child-star and successful actress talks frankly about her extreme, sometimes suicidal, feelings in her own book *Down Came the Rain: My Journey Through Postpartum Depression* (Hyperion, 2005). With the assistance of appropriate medication and therapy Brooke's depression was treated and she went on to develop a strong relationship with her daughter. But her down-to-earth account of her experience provides helpful insights into the thoughts of many depressed mothers.

   When her baby girl, Rowan, was only a few days old she wrote:

   Instead of the nervous anxiety that often accompanies panic, a feeling of devastation overcame me. I hardly moved...this was sadness of a shockingly different magnitude. It felt as if it would never go away.

   She goes on to say:

   Why was I crying more than my baby? Here I was, finally the mother of a beautiful baby girl I had worked so hard to have, and I felt like my life was over. Where was the bliss? Where was the happiness that I had expected to feel by becoming a mother? She was my baby; the baby I had wanted for so long. Why didn't I feel remotely comforted by having or holding her?

2. **Gwyneth Paltrow**. This multi-award winning actress shares many of her ups and downs of motherhood in numerous interviews and TV appearances. She also has her own publication, goop, which helps highlight the prevalence and treatment options for postnatal illness. In one interview after giving birth to her son, she told Vogue UK "At my lowest, I was a robot. I just didn't feel anything. I had no maternal instincts for him – it was awful. I couldn't connect, and still,

when I look at pictures of him at three months old, I don't remember that time."

She wrote for goop:

When my son, Moses, came into the world in 2006, I expected to have another period of euphoria following his birth, much the same way I had when my daughter was born two years earlier. Instead I was confronted with one of the darkest and most painfully debilitating chapters of my life. For about five months I had what I can see in hindsight was postnatal depression.

(July 21st, 2010 www.goop.com/journal)

3. **Bryce Dallas Howard**. This young actress who starred in *The Twilight Saga: Eclipse*, talked about her postpartum depression in goop's e-newsletter. She spoke out about her daily crying marathons, her loss of ability to eat and how she lashed out at her loved ones. "(My husband) would ask what he could do to help, but knowing there was nothing he could do, I screamed expletives at him," she wrote.

Of her emotional state she shared:

It is strange for me to recall what I was like at that time. I seemed to be suffering emotional amnesia. I couldn't genuinely cry, or laugh, or be moved by anything. For the sake of those around me, including my son, I pretended, but when I began showering again in the second week, I let loose in the privacy of the bathroom, water flowing over me as I heaved uncontrollable sobs. (July 21st, 2010 www.goop.com/journal)

6. **Elle McPherson**. This international supermodel completed a six-week intensive treatment programme at a private psychiatric clinic in the US for PND after the birth of her second son. She told *Vogue* UK: "I took the steps I needed to take in order to recover...The truth was, I just did what I needed to do and addressed a lot of issues that needed

addressing and had a well-earned break, which I really needed as well."

7. **Melinda Messenger**. An ex-glamour model, Page 3 girl, and current television presenter, Melinda suffered from mild depression after the birth of her first son Morgan, but was to suffer a more severe form after the birth of her second son, Flynn. Of her second experience she says it was like "a dark black pit". In an interview with the *Daily Mail* she goes on to say, "I felt suicidal. I couldn't stop crying – at playgroup, in the car, at home. I remember thinking 'Wouldn't it be great if the car crashed and I died?' I could never have done that to my children, but I just wanted the pain to end."

Melinda has continued to experience episodes of mood difficulties and remains an advocate for regular and ongoing treatment for psychological disorders in women.

8. **Jessica Rowe**. This renowned journalist and news presenter experienced postnatal depression after the birth of her first daughter, Allegra. In her book *Love. Wisdom. Motherhood* she describes her experience of psychological distress in relation to her connection to her mothers group: "I was like the odd one out in this group. I vowed never to go back to that meeting again. I'm sure on the surface I looked like I was coping and, in hindsight, there would have been some other mums in that group who, like me were drowning – floating adrift, desperate to be thrown a lifeline."

She goes on to describe her experience in great detail on the beyondblue website: "Although I knew where to get help, had family support and the financial means to pay for specialists I still felt ashamed. I thought, what right do I have to be depressed? I have everything I could wish for...a beautiful baby, a wonderful husband. I felt like such a failure." Jessica has since become a beyondblue ambassador and patron for the *beyondblue* Perinatal Mental Health Program.

Further Reading

Hunt down some more celebrity stories of on the internet, there's also a heap of information about PND and PNA there too. But if you want a few recommendations for sound reading on your glum days, here they are:

- Catherine Knox, Benison O'Reilly and Seana Smith *–Beyond the Baby Blues: The Complete Perinatal Depression and Anxiety Handbook.*
- Lisa Fettling *– Postnatal Depression: A Practical Guide for Australian Families.*
- Lisa Fettling and Belinda Tune *– Women's Experience of Postnatal Depression: Kitchen table conversations.*
- Susan Maushart *– The Mask of Motherhood: How Motherhood Changes Everything and Why We Pretend it Doesn't.*
- Shoshana Bennett and Mary Jo Codey *– Postpartum Depression For Dummies.*
- Kevin Gyoerkoe, Pamela Wiegartz and Laura Miller *– The Pregnancy and Postpartum Anxiety Workbook: Practical Skills to Help You Overcome Anxiety, Worry, Panic Attacks, Obsessions and Compulsions.*
- Sandra Poulin *– The Mother-to-Mother Postpartum Depression Support Book.*
- Karen Kleiman and Valerie Raskin *– This Isn't What I Expected: Overcoming Postpartum Depression (2nd edition).*
- Karen Kleiman *– The Postpartum Husband: Practical Solutions for living with Postpartum Depression.*

One last comment:

If you've got to this stage of this chapter, I'm guessing two factors are involved here. Firstly, that you've had some pretty tough times as a mum. Secondly, that you're either in an okay mental place right now or are able to maintain incredible reading skills in a crisis!

I feel as though I speak for all the mums out there who have been through dark days fierce enough to rival the most ferocious of storms when I say, "Hold on. This time will pass, and with it your distress. Use whatever it takes – family, friends, neighbours, nurses, doctors, therapists, helplines or hospitals. Just hold on, if not for you, then your baby. Because no child is *ever* better off without the love of their mother. And no mum is ever better off not knowing the love of her child."

May the words in this book give you courage. May the love for your baby give you hope. And may the power of all the mothers of the world give you determination to keep going. Even on the hardest of days. One day at a time.

There were probably about three months of Lucy's first year that I don't remember. I was on automatic pilot. I couldn't feel happy about anything. But then I told my husband how I was feeling and together we got help. Between the therapy and the medication to treat my depression, my world started to change. Where there was just grey now there was colour. Where there was just sadness there was joy. Where I'd felt nothing for Lucy, now I wanted to snuggle her at every moment. My advice to other mothers is – don't wait. Get help. Motherhood can be great for you too, just take that first step as soon as you can. NATALIE, MOTHER OF FOUR

Chapter 5:

As snug as two bugs? Or poles apart? Tips for baby bonding.

Our connection grows stronger with each high- pitched scream, projectile vomit and poo explosion.

Note: This is a chapter for all mothers and all babies. It does not matter how your baby came to be in your care. If you hold a baby in your arms – whether through birth, through fostering, through adoption or through other circumstances – this chapter is for you.

Hanna was born with a problem with her little heart. She required surgery straight after she was born. It was a rollercoaster ride for those first few weeks. So often we thought we'd lose her. I couldn't feed her (except with my expressed milk through a syringe), and I hardly had any skin-to-skin contact time because of her health risks.

When she started to get better and we were able to take her home, I couldn't let anyone else touch her. I felt like I needed to reconnect with her, without anyone else's interference. I hadn't allowed myself to love her completely before then as a way of protecting myself in case she didn't make it. So I had to work hard to love her. I don't think it was until she was about four months old that I felt truly connected to her. GEMMA, MOTHER OF TWO

Love at first sight? A more lengthy elopement? The variation in how us mums connect with our babies is, well, like a box of chocolates, really – from the soft, gooey and "oh so sweet" variety to the hard jawbreaker (confused, bewildered and heart broken) type.

But what if I'm the second type? Unless you fall into the first category (ie the "love at first sight" type), you can be left feeling like you've got something wrong or that you've somehow failed. And I bet you feel you can't tell anyone. It's hard to admit to our gushy, mushy friends and baby-besotted family that our own baby connection is more detached than it is delighted.

So are you all alone in your bonding blues?

The reality is that around 60% of us new mums will bond with our babies either at birth or within the first few days of baby's arrival. It doesn't take a statistical genius to figure out that that leaves a substantial 40% of us who won't.

So, if cupid's bow hasn't quite struck just yet, cast aside any "I'm not normal" thoughts and look around you. Chances are, if you're struggling with bonding, then so too are a whole load of your mummy pals. In fact, as many as 10% of mothers are still finding it difficult to bond with baby even after three months.

If you're wondering how you're doing on the connection

stakes, The Postpartum Bonding Questionnaire (PBQ)[1] (available at http://www.mothersmatter.co.nz/PBQ.htm) will ask you serious questions such as "I regret having this baby", "I feel trapped as a mother" and "I am afraid of my baby". Research has shown the PBQ to provide a reliable indication of the early emotional tie between a woman and her newborn infant[2]. But, in reality, we don't really need a questionnaire to put a statistic to our "level of bonding". We're usually either blissfully or painfully aware of how connected we are to our babies.

After a few health scares throughout my pregnancy, at the 36-week mark we unexpectedly bid an early welcome to our daughter into this world. But, to my complete and indescribable amazement, I found it hard to bond with her, because for so long I had been in complete anguish wondering if it would all be OK. And then she was OK. But then she would not feed from me.
Once again, like birth, I thought this was supposed to be the most natural thing in the world. How wrong can it get? I did not want to be left alone with her; not because I thought I would harm her, I think it was just a case of "what has gone wrong, what have I done, why do you not want me?". This was all so new and soooo not what I had prepared for. We think the world prepares us for this wonderful gift, but in hindsight they don't really prepare us at all. It's not easy. NAME WITHHELD AT THE MOTHER'S REQUEST, MOTHER OF THREE

So why has the love train missed your station?

The answer to difficulties in the bonding process is complex. However, in multiple studies of women all over the world, researchers have highlighted these consistent factors in many disrupted bonding experiences. Perhaps some of these explain your situation:

- **A difficult pregnancy**. Let me suggest a few pregnancy "highlights" – nausea, gestational diabetes, crippling back pain, cracked pelvis, varicose veins and haemorrhoids. If you've had your fair share of these special sensations, it can be hard to associate your baby with being Fun-Time-Freddy. Nope, it's more like Piercing-Pain-Penelope. In making this negative association, our brain will try to protect us – a sort of *cast aside what harms you* message. It's up to us to take charge of our brain and remind it that our babies didn't *mean* to hurt us. In fact, our baby was just doing their growing thing.

- **A difficult birth**. Now for the highlights of birth – episiotomy, third-degree tears, haemorrhages, emergency caesarean. If you've experienced some type of birth trauma this can interfere with your ability to feel anything (other than fear or numbness) for quite some time after birth. Remember our brains just work this way – after severely scary times, our mind isn't focused on how to *love another human being*, it's just focused on *how on earth can I protect this woman from that happening again*. See chapter one for more details on birth trauma, but most of all, be kind to yourself as your mind slowly adjusts to the enormous events you've been through.

- **Premature birth**. Ummm…I thought my baby was meant to look kind of "pretty". Even in the scrunched-up, gooey form that an on-date baby emerges, they look kinda cute. But this isn't always the case for those babies who arrive prematurely. They can often look less "baby-like" than we expected and it can scare us. We can also still be in a state of shock – perhaps we hadn't even bought a car seat or cot yet! Worse still, for many of our premature babies, they need additional medical care which prevents us holding them and this lack of touch can lead us to believe they're not really ours. We might also fear that if we bond with them and then they die, it will be all too much for us to cope with. In a strange way, this is our brain's way of trying to protect us from becoming too attached to something we fear we won't keep.

- **Adult relationships woes**. Did your pregnancy result in the baby's daddy hitting the high road? Was he angry that you didn't terminate the pregnancy? Perhaps it's more that your social circle has slowly vanished? When these things happen we can "blame" our babies for all the hard times in our lives. Our brains are just trying to help us here too – if we can blame something for what has gone wrong in our lives, then we can avoid that same thing next time. But again – it is up to us to remind ourselves that these changes in adult relationships weren't the *baby's* fault. If other people can't manage the idea that a baby is now in our lives, then as adults we need to man or woman up and cast these doomsdayers aside and rally only those who support our motherhood situation.

- **Feeling inadequate**. Feeding, sterilising, soothing, calming, sleep deprivation, health issues…the list of taxing topics for a newbie mum is endless. It can leave us feeling we're nowhere near good enough for the job. When this happens we can avoid creating a baby connection. We start to believe our babies would be better off without us and our brain gets caught in an unhealthy cycle of distancing ourselves. "The baby is better off without you" becomes our dysfunctional self-talk. If this explains your feeling, then remember this – there is not one child on this planet who doesn't want to be connected with their mother. Not one. And there is not one mum on this planet who can't feel and behave differently with the right help. So see your GP and get a referral to an appropriate specialist. The way your life and your relationship is now does not need to reflect how it could be next week or next month.

- **Feeling depressed or psychologically distressed**. Some of us find our own moods can prevent us connecting with our babies. We can feel too sad, too overwhelmed, too anxious or just too "all over the place" to bond. In some way, it's as if our brain is saying to us, "*you're the one who needs to be looked after right now*", which doesn't leave room to care for someone else. If this is you then help is needed. Fast. Turn to chapter four for more information on postnatal psychological issues and turn this situation around for both you and your baby.

Where before there was just a "demanding baby" in my life, after getting help from a therapist, I could see my baby as a beautiful little "person". It was incredible how differently I felt toward him. I urge all mothers to seek help if they're not connecting with their baby – it doesn't have to be that way. NELLIE, MOTHER OF FOUR

If you haven't bonded immediately will your baby suffer?

Before I answer that question, a little bit of background information first.

a. **Attachment is care *seeking***. Our baby's brain is wired to seek out an attachment to someone. It is their instinct. They will do whatever is in their little powers (as small as these might be) to seek out closeness and connection to another human for comfort, protection and to help them organise their feelings about this crazy post-womb world. Their goo's and ga's and their nestling into us when they feed aren't meant to be cute for no reason. And their little (or big!) cries weren't designed to be ignored. They're all part of baby's master plan to seek out a connection with us.

b. **Bonding is care *giving*.** This is where we (as parents or caregivers) come into it. Usually it's instinctive at some level for us too. We want to be close to our babies, to provide them comfort and protection and to help them work out what's wrong with them and find solutions. So we tend to pick up crying babies, we tend to echo a baby's goo's and ga's and we tend to want our babies to be close to us.

c. **Perfectionism not required.** Notice that the words "perfect" and "flawless" simply weren't mentioned in either the bonding or attachment explanations. It's for a good reason – they're simply not important or even required in the baby connection stakes. Our babies don't require us to be perfect, but rather just to be "good enough". And what's "good enough" in the very early days with our babies is for us to follow this rather basic process (picture adapted from www.upsidedowntherapy.blogspot.com.au):

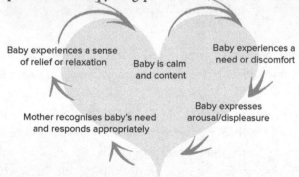

Baby experiences a sense of relief or relaxation

Baby is calm and content

Baby experiences a need or discomfort

Mother recognises baby's need and responds appropriately

Baby expresses arousal/displeasure

What you'll notice about this all important cycle is that babies are healthily attached when we:

a. repeatedly respond to their attempts to alert us to their needs;
b. meet those needs by providing cuddles, shelter, warmth or food.

It *does not* require that:

a. we are *in love with, in awe of and in wonder* with every moment of life with our babies;
b. our mind is free of any anxious thoughts, depressed thoughts, angry thoughts or overwhelmed thoughts about being a mother. The only exception is when we have thoughts about harming our baby, then we need to seek help. See chapter four for more details.

It is very important, however, that we don't:

a. ignore our baby for long periods of time;
b. scare our baby, eg with mean facial expressions or loud noises or by pretending to drop them;
c. harm our babies in any intentional way.

Hold on...don't you have to get bonding absolutely "right"? All the time?

Some media reports have claimed that for mothers who haven't bonded absolutely perfectly, their child will go on to have a lower intelligence or IQ. Others suggest the less bonded child will go on to have anything from severe behavioural problems, to severe emotional disturbance to being more likely to end up in gaol.

Nothing better than a bit of media fear to turn a perfectly well-adjusted mother into a neurotic guilt-ridden shadow of her former self!

Here's the realistic version. Bonding is important. You know yourself that *you* feel better, perform better and are just generally more content in relationships that are thoughtful, kind, caring and aware of your needs. The same goes for our babies. In fact, research has shown time and time again that in a secure attachment relationship, children really do thrive more than children who aren't in securely attached relationships.

But don't believe any media hype that suggests your baby bonding is a "now-or-never phenomenon"[3]. Studies have clearly identified that:

a. **We've got time**. It usually takes infants until they're about two or three months old before they show a strong preference for a particular caregiver. It's like nature just knows that sometimes mothers need time to work through the baby blues, the trauma of birth, the baby's illness or whatever, and gives us a window of opportunity to do this. It means other people can step in and help us to meet our baby's daily security needs while we gradually do as much as we can to increase our connection with our baby.

b. **Our babies will help us**. Our brain is working overtime to help us connect with baby, even when we're struggling emotionally. Scientists at the Baylor College of Medicine have found that seeing our own child smile actually gives us a "natural high" by activating the pleasure receptors in the reward processing areas of the brain. Scientifically speaking, this is called the "dopaminergic area" typically associated with food, sex – and drug addiction. It's possibly not a coincidence then that many mothers say their bonding was assisted by seeing their baby smile for the first time.

153

So know this: Even on your worst days, take comfort that despite how you are feeling about your baby (ie the "bonding" element), your baby is still determined to pursue their end of the bargain (the "attaching" element).

And even if you feel a bit removed, robotic, or exhausted in those first few days, consistently using behaviours that respond to your baby's needs is something virtually all mothers CAN give – even if your emotional connection is yet to develop.

I have a friend who was swept away the instant her baby arrived. For me, I was extremely pleased when my baby arrived, but that overwhelming feeling of deep attachment didn't develop until she was a few months older and we were interacting with each other.
JESSIE, MOTHER OF ONE

Do you have to be 100% available 100% of the time to stay "bonded"?

Some "experts" declare that "attachment parenting" methods, eg constantly wearing a baby in a sling, co-sleeping, never allowing a baby to cry, etc, is the only way for the bonding to occur. I disagree. And so do a good number of researchers too. Yep – they make it clear that the quality of our bond with our baby is not met by a formula of simply 24/7 togetherness[4].

But even without the science, let's consider the obvious. Some babies are born as twins, triplets or more. Some are born as the second or third child, sometimes as far down the birth order as child number 10! It's absurd to think that all of these children have their psychological state permanently destroyed due to their parent's obvious inability to either: (a) meet their needs immediately every time; or (b) because they weren't all worn in a sling all the time – picture the mother of quadruplets doing that! Look around too at any playground or preschool – there are many perfectly secure children who have not been raised by adamant "attachment parents".

What all psychologically healthy parents know is that connection with children can be maintained without immediate touch every time. Known as "distal interaction" methods, it means, for example, looking across the room and smiling and talking or singing while you shower/bath/go to the toilet. For those with more than one child, these techniques help us to connect with one baby while holding and feeding another. Of course, wherever possible, we want to meet our baby's needs and be close. But babies are hard-wired to deal with both our imperfections and that sometimes we just can't get to them first time, every time.

When I had my second baby I realised how different his life experiences were going to be compared to my first child, Evie. With Evie, I could go to her each time she was distressed, but by the time I had two of them, I realised it wasn't possible. I was often dealing with Evie's toddler tantrums, toilet training and running away – which meant sometimes my baby had to wait for me to soothe his cries. But he was OK. He settled when I picked him up. And he seemed to cope just fine. And if anything, I think he's the child who copes better with the ups and downs of life too. BELINDA, MOTHER OF TWO

So what can you do to increase your bond with your baby?

There are some mothers who know right from the start how to connect with babies. They're all good with the goo then ga, then smile, tickle, watch, then snuggle. And then repeat this all over again – and again – and again.

Sound a bit mind-numbing? Don't rush to dismiss how much you might enjoy this interaction. Once you've read through the suggestions below, you'll be surprised at how easy it is to find *some* bonding activities that you enjoy too.

The ways to create or maintain a strong bonding connection can generally be categorised under the five senses[5]:

Smell

Ever notice how many people talk about the smell of a baby? Smelling our baby and being close enough for our baby to smell us is an important part of connecting with our baby. So:

- Take the time to know your baby's aroma and notice how it changes – and it's not just when they have a dirty nappy (!). They will also smell different when they have a cold, when their ears are infected and when they have infected urine.
- Try to avoid heavily scented aromas so that your baby gets to know your real smell. This helps them to find comfort in snuggling up to toys or snuggle blankets, etc that carry mummy's smell when they're a bit older. It also helps our baby to know we're nearby at times when they're trying to settle themselves to sleep…They can sense that we've not left them alone.

Sound

Babies have conversations. Well, not the adult kind, but research has confirmed that babies do converse with others! I don't mean word-based conversations, I mean conversations based on a range of sounds, gestures, mouth or tongue movements and facial expressions. If we do our part by returning the interactions, they'll learn turn-taking too. This helps both bonding and longer-term language development.

And while it may seem strange in the early stages, try the following ideas to develop your baby's inner chatterbox:

- Put your baby in a position where you can see each other face-to-face.
- Say something, anything, just keep it generally positive and brief.
- Allow your baby time to reply.
- Follow the baby's lead for a "topic" of conversation. If for example she is indicating interest in a toy, talk about the toy.
- If you're stuck for something to talk about, have pictures or toys ready and ask the baby which ones they like, or talk about the toy.
- Copy and exaggerate the sounds made by your baby as well as using your own "real" talk.
- Everything you do with your baby (feeding, nappy changes, bath-time, etc) provides great opportunities for a conversation.
- Continue only for as long as your baby seems interested, and then revert to silence or singing or whatever. We all need breaks from conversations (although I do have some friends who would vehemently oppose this suggestion) and so do our babies.

Touch

Since the 1950s and the famous Harry Harlow and his rhesus monkey experiments, we've known the importance of soft touch to our babies. In these experiments, the baby monkeys repeatedly showed a preference to be with a soft and cuddly pretend mother rather than a "hard" (made of wire only) pretend mother even though the "hard" mother provided food. Why? This is what the research tells us:

- Our skin is our largest and most sensitive organ. Which means that even if our "goo's" aren't heard, our facial expressions aren't seen and our baby doesn't smell our smell, they will know of our connection and our presence through our touch.

- Of all the senses, it is thought that the sense of touch is likely to be the most developed at the time of birth[6].

- Touch alters the level of the hormone oxytocin, which means a baby who is caringly touched is therefore likely to be more relaxed. Yes indeed, touch is baby's early "rescue remedy" or "anti-depressant" to counterbalance the stress hormones that can occur in the frenzied, overwhelming first few weeks of life for our babies[7] (oh, and regarding us – a regular massage has similar benefits for mothers too!).

But it's not just baby who's getting something out of this. For those mothers who are concerned about their level of bonding, the research shows that touching baby is your fastest ticket to a love connection .

So try out these "touch" techniques to increase the connection with baby:

- **Wear me**. Yes, one of the latest trends, particularly for those strong advocates of attachment parenting is to literally strap your baby to you and wear them like a slinky Hermès scarf – around your belly or back though, not your neck. Some prefer the traditional methods of using copious amounts of material to strap on their baby, while others go for the back-saving support versions such as BabyBjörn.

- **Cuddle me.** Ever had one of those times when your baby has just dozed off on top of you while you're soothing their cries or feeding them? Use the opportunity to let them snuggle there for a little while. Even if you're not a big fan of your baby sleeping anywhere other than their cot, little exceptions to the rule are important. Of course, opportunities for cuddles when your child is awake are endless, so take every chance you get.

- **Let's go topless!** Whether you're breast or bottle feeding, getting skin to skin during a feed is a great way to stay connected. Usually this is best done in the privacy of your own home, but feel free to explore fellow patron's reactions to your decision to bare your bosom in your restaurant of choice.

- **Kiss me. Kiss me.** Nothing signals a close relationship like a series of kisses. Friends may get one quick one from you on the cheek, but anybody who gets your repeated lip smackers counts in your top few important people. So blow raspberries on their bellies or their bottoms, kiss their little heads while you feed them, reach for their hands and kiss each finger (babies *love* putting their hands in your mouth!). A series of kisses before bedtime is a great addition to any bedtime routine.

- **The day spa experience.** Massages are loved by almost everyone, including our babies[8]. Some are more sensitive than others, some will only like their legs massaged, some

159

only like it during certain times of the day, some will only allow you to massage during a bath or a feed. Be flexible on how and where it's done and don't let any devout yogi or incense-wearing guru tell you what's right for your baby. The most sensitive approach to all things about baby massage can be found at the International Association of Infant Massage: see www.iaim.org.au (Australia) or www.babymassage-uk.com (UK). But here are some ideas if you want to get started straight away.

BABY MASSAGE BASICS

- Make sure the room is a nice temperature for your naked baby.
- Make sure you have a comfortable place for baby to lie down – a small mattress or baby change mat covered in a towel is ideal.
- Make sure you have limited distractions around the room and dim the lights slightly if possible.
- Make sure baby is well-fed and seems content. (If she is really worked up, soothe and cuddle her first, then start again).
- Have an appropriate massage oil for baby – refined sunflower oil is currently the oil most recommended (order from infant massage websites or savvy health stores).
- Warm your hands and then warm the oil between your hands before you start, allowing baby to see and hear what you're doing – this will begin to become a cue that a massage is coming up.
- Ask permission – this can seem a little weird – how would your baby know, right? Wrong. As your baby becomes more attuned to their environment, they will give you cues for whether they want something or not, including a massage. So

start with something like, "Shall we do some massage now?" and see how baby responds. Eye contact and a relaxed body suggest it's a good time to start, but permission signs vary between babies.

- Lay your hands on baby's belly – or a large body part such as shoulders if her belly is tender. Allow it to rest there as you warm to your baby's body temperature. Keep eye contact and explain what you're doing, eg "I'm just resting my hands here before we start our massage."

- Make gentle stroking movements over her body, massaging the parts that baby seems to enjoy – all babies will like some body parts more than others. Their preferences will also vary each time you massage so be flexible and aware of what your baby enjoys each time.

- Talk quietly about what you're doing as you proceed. Explain what you think your baby might be experiencing, eg "You really like your legs being stroked, don't you?"

- Stop and soothe your baby if she becomes distressed, then start again.

- Always let your baby know when you'll be finishing the massage, eg. "That's our massage finished for today", and end it with another ritual – such as resting your hands gently around her head and giving her a kiss – or whatever seems right for you.

Tip from an experienced masseuse: *Babies seem to somehow save their bodily fluid emissions for all massage parties. So always have a few extra wipes and towels ready for the clean up or an intended relaxing moment might just end up one big smelly mess.* Tiffany, mother of three

Sight

As our babies get older, our eye contact becomes another important "love drug". They'll make noises, wave their arms about and move their little bodies with all their might in an attempt to get our gaze right back on them. Why? Because while we're looking at them, their little brain tells them we're *connected* to their needs (emotionally and physically).

As Professor Nugent (Brazelton Institute at Boston Children's Hospital, USA) said in describing the eye contact with a baby, "We believe babies are born to seek out the people and things that are going to be important in their lives so they are drawn to human faces more than anything else. So when a baby and mother look at each other the baby has this sense of 'I'm OK and the world is going to be OK because these people look at me with love.' It's the beginning of trust."[9]

Some mothers can find eye contact confronting, boring or both. If you're unsure about gazing at your baby, try thinking about it like watching a movie – you don't have to do anything when you watch a movie, but your facial expressions will change as you watch, depending on what you see. You can also describe out loud what you're seeing. So if baby yawns you can say, "It's good to yawn". If they grimace, you could say, "Ohh, that face tells me you might have a bit of wind".

Remember though that constantly staring at someone is uncomfortable – for both baby and for us. So, when baby takes a break and turns to the side, allow her time to take a break from your gaze. Your baby will return to looking at you when ready.

I would gaze at my son for hours. I wanted him to be as close to my skin as possible. I wanted to smell him and kiss him and hold him and never put him down. I wanted time to stop and let us stay together forever, in some type of cocoon. I had never loved anything or anyone like I loved this boy. This was the most amazing and beautiful thing I had ever experienced. ERICA, MOTHER OF TWO

More games to play

Most mums I know want more information on what "to do" with their baby when they're together.

Before you start any play session, it's important to gauge whether baby is actually in the mood for playing (just because *you* want to doesn't mean *they* do!). So watch out for these signs to know baby is feeling ready:

- watching you or other people with interest
- reaching out for you
- smiling
- making noises in an attempt to attract your attention.

It's also important to recognise when your baby isn't in the mood for games, or needs a break. Watch out for these signs:

- crying
- spitting up baby vomit/excessive saliva
- looking away
- fussing or being irritable.

So when baby's ready, here are some fun games for you both:
Peek-a-boo. Hide your face behind your hands and then move your hands away while you say, "Peek-a-boo!" Until babies are around nine months old, they don't realise that you're still there when your face is covered, so baby will be enthralled by your disappearing and reappearing act. It also helps baby realise you'll

163

come back even when you "go away".

Throw a dance party. Try dancing around at a tempo and style to suit baby's mood. If baby seems playful, do something more quickly or silly to keep baby laughing. A slower dance with more rhythmic movements helps a baby who is more unsettled to calm down.

Start a band. Babies love learning connections between objects and sounds. Use anything that makes a noise – the click of a pen, a rattle, a little bell, etc. Make the noise for them, and talk about what the sound is. Hide it from their view and see if they can follow the direction of the noise. As they get older, baby will want to make the sound themselves and will reach for the item you're holding.

Know baby's musical tastes. While baby is on the floor or in a bouncer, play a range of musical types. Watch how their body responds and whether they try to "sing" along. You'll probably be able to determine a preferred music type, or maybe different songs for different moods or time of day.

Body parts. To help baby's growing sense of self, ask where each body part is, eg "Where's your mouth?" (try using all sorts of fun voices). Then gently touch your baby's mouth as you say "There's your mouth!" with great delight. Do the same with your body parts too.

Let's play ball! Babies love holding and throwing things. It's so much fun for them to watch us pick something up – over and over and over again. Find ball-like objects (pom-poms are just as good) of all different textures and colours to keep their interest. Start with giving the ball to your baby and see what happens – it might be sucked, thrown, ignored or held, depending on the interest level. See which ball is baby's favourite for the day.

Mirror mirror on the wall. Hold baby in your arms in front of the mirror and talk about and point to her body parts – eyes, nose, mouth, arms, etc. Try stepping away from the mirror and asking, "Where did baby go?" Move back in front of the mirror and say, "There's the baby!" Do the same as you move in an out of the mirror's reflection. You can do the same for toys too: "Where's the teddy?" then "There's the teddy".

Bring in the farm. Babies love all sorts of sounds and pairing animal noises with animal names is a fun and educational activity. Show them a range of different toy animals – pig, duck, goat, etc – name each one then make the corresponding sound. They'll probably have a favourite one!

Read a book. It's *never* too early to start a child's love of reading. Choose books with bright colours and less complex pictures to start with. Ask at your local library for books suitable for babies if you're not sure. As you read, use your imagination and different voice types to keep the story interesting. But don't forget how much babies love repetition, so it's not boring to them to have the same book over and over again – it also helps them to build confidence in their skills when they know what's coming next.

Family reunion. Babies love seeing human faces, so why not get close-up photos of all the important people in baby's life and make up stories about each person. I particularly love this game for getting baby used to the faces of relatives and friends who live far away. Dangle the photos from a piece of string and use different voices and sounds. See how much baby delights in getting to know important people in your life.

"Play" housework. Sometimes jobs just need to get done, but don't always feel it has to wait until baby's sleeping. As you fold items of clothing swish them along baby's skin, or give baby a cloth to hold so they feel what you're feeling. As you wipe or mop, give baby a wet cloth or sponge to touch and feel too. If you're

165

washing up, give baby a clear bottle filled with water mixed with washing detergent. They love watching the bubbles, particularly as they get older and can shake the bottle for themselves.

Take a chill pill. Don't forget that babies like to chill out just like we do. Sit at a park where baby has trees or kids playing to watch as they relax and soak it all in. Read your own book quietly next to them. If they want to "talk" about what they're seeing, they'll try to get your eye contact through gestures or sounds, but otherwise leave them be.

The number of games you can play with your baby is endless, and once you get started, you'll probably invent many more of your own. If you still want more ideas, take a look at the following websites: www.babycenter.com, www.kidspot.com.au, www.parenting.com, www.entertainingbabies.com.

What if I want to know more about how to "do" this bonding thing?

Perhaps unsurprisingly, given the importance that mothers, the media and research studies have placed on bonding, there are numerous programmes ready and raring to go that can help how a mother understands and connects with her baby. While a full run-down on each of them is a book in itself, I've included those that meet two important criteria: (a) that most parents would consider them useful as well as practical; and (b) that there is sufficient research evidence suggesting these programmes are helpful for mothers.

1. **The Wait, Watch and Wonder™ (WWW)** programme[10]. Developed by Australia's Dr Michael Zilibowitz (a developmental and behavioural paediatrician) , the modified form of this approach was designed to increase all mothers'

sensitivity and responsiveness to their babies. There have been some useful video explanations and examples of the programme's effectiveness (see http://vimeo.com/6016065 for an example). So do some internet surfing and learn more about this highly effective and truly beautiful programme.

2. The "Help–Understanding–Guidance" (HUG) programme[11] was developed to improve parents' understanding of how to interpret and respond to their infant's special ways of communicating. The HUG programme includes an educational website (www.hugyourbaby.org), which features a parent educational blog, and a 20-minute educational DVD with an accompanying handout for parents.

3. **The Newborn Behavioral Observations system (NBO)** is a relationship-building, structured set of observations, designed to help the clinician and mother together. It was designed to be delivered by a professional (eg child health nurse or midwife), but there is a lot to learn by simply reading more about the techniques taught in the programme. There is a book available to explain the process called *Understanding Newborn Behavior and Early Relationships* and you can read more on the website www.brazelton-institute.com.

4. **The Institute of Australian Infant Massage (IAIM) First Touch Program**® is currently used in numerous settings across the world to support parents in responding sensitively to their babies through touch, cue-based baby massage, voice, movement and other interactions. See www.iaim.org.au (Australia) or www.babymassage-uk.com (UK) for more information on how to get in touch with a trained worker in your area. As a parent, you are also eligible to become an accredited trainer in this method yourself.

What if you've used all these techniques and there's still no bond developing?

Sometimes, our inability to bond with our babies has gone well beyond failing to fall in love at first sight. For some, it's a relationship that's seriously unwell. Check to see whether your situation is at the point where it could be considered a bonding disorder:

a. **The mild level of bonding disorders**. In this category, we constantly delay responding to our baby's needs, or feel constantly unsure about whether we can care about our baby or not. As a result, we don't want to respond to their needs. Sometimes mothers in this category can feel as though the baby isn't theirs and they're only babysitting for someone else.

b. **The moderate level of bonding disorders**. In this category we can have thoughts about rejecting our baby or it can go further into actually rejecting our baby, including wanting to give the baby away or run away from her.

c. **The severe bonding disorders**. In this category we can feel intense anger toward our baby or not want to care for it at all. As such, we can have impulses to harm the baby, through yelling, screaming, shaking, jerking, hitting or other unsafe behaviours.

The **mild** symptoms are likely to be assisted with the suggestions in this chapter. The **moderate** to **severe** levels will require help by talking to your GP or child health nurse. Request a referral to a mother and baby specialist. Remember, by asking for help you're not failing as a mother – it means you truly respect that both you and your baby deserve the best chance to be safe and build a positive connection for the rest of your lives.

If you feel you may harm your baby in any way, you need to immediately call:
In Australia - 000
In the UK - 112

One last comment:

If nothing else, I hope your mantra to baby bonding has become: KEEP TRYING! Always remember, our babies are hard-wired to give us time to adjust to the crazy whirlwind we call "new parenthood". They're also blessed with a "good enough gauge" regarding our mothering skills – Mother Nature made sure no "perfect parent checklists" were produced in utero. It's only adults that design those caustic creations!

So reduce the self-imposed pressure and give yourself time and togetherness to build up to a love connection. It will come. You will achieve it. And it will be the type of relationship with all the "special" ups and downs that only another mother ever really understands.

How I bonded with each of my three children was entirely different and I've learned not to judge myself for that. I've accepted that each child brings something new and I respond differently to them all. But although some of my babies have taken longer to connect with than others, each bond has eventually been built. Somehow nature gets in right in the end. LIBBY, MOTHER OF THREE

So what is normal? Debunking the motherhood myths that make us feel incompetent

THE TRUTH ABOUT MOTHERS

Average age: 30

Age range: 15 to 60

One in seven will be over 35

Average weight gain during pregnancy: 14 kilos

Average weight loss immediately after birth: 4.5 kilos

Average weight (after dropping the baby weight): 70 kilos

Half will go into spontaneous labour

One in 20 will use assisted reproductive technology (ART)

50% will have a first or second degree laceration of the perineum following birth

Nearly 70% will have a vaginal birth

30% will have a caesarean delivery

14% will have an episiotomy

96% will give birth in a hospital

50% will use nitrous oxide during birth

Nine out of 10 give birth at between 37-41 weeks' gestation

One in three will describe their birth as traumatic

1.6% will have multiple pregnancies

Gets on average seven hours rest but will spend two hours being awake during the night

One in seven will have postnatal depression;
one in three will have a number of symptoms but not reach full criteri

One in 10 will have postnatal anxiety;
one in four will have symptoms but not reach full criteria

Half will have haemorrhoids during pregnancy or after birth

60% will bond with babies within days of the baby's arrival (40% won't)

10% have yet to bond with babies at three months

80% will have the baby blues

THE TRUTH ABOUT BABIES

14% will be admitted to an SCU or NICU

60% will have jaundice

If female – she is likely to be named Charlotte, Imogen, Ava or Olivia

If male – he is likely to be named Jack, Oliver or Noah

Will weigh 7.5 pounds at birth

Will lose 5-10% of birthweight
in first few days and put it back
on again within 14 days

*Will use on average 3500
nappies in their first year*

Will give their
first smile at
around six weeks

*Will roll over between
four and seven months*

*Will have an average of 56 outfits costing
an average of $500 in the first year*

Will gain one-two pounds in weight a month

Will sleep on average between 13 and 16 hours per day in their first 3 months

Will start walking at around 13 months

Will cry between one and three hours per day in their first month

Chapter 6:

My Friends Have Changed.

Coping with post-baby friendship fluctuations and fall-outs.

Before baby, some of my best times
were spent staying up all night with friends.
After baby? Staying up isn't by choice.

Any adult who wakes me up after 9pm
better have a black belt.

My childless friends just had no idea what effort it had taken for me to turn up 30 minutes late for our first post-baby girls' night out. I looked completely bedraggled, I had nothing interesting to say about their world and then suddenly I had to leave early when Jo (my partner) rang to say he couldn't settle the baby and needed me back at home! They were disappointed in me, I think... Yet they had no sympathy for how disappointed I was and how much I needed their support and understanding. BELINDA, MOTHER OF TWO

Yoo hoo...anyone out there? Anyone? The vanishing girlfriend performance is never more noticeable than when babies come on the scene. Unless of course you've coordinated a double act. For those BFFs who synchronised their menstrual cycles and later their labour pains, post-baby relationships can stay just peachy. But if you're the first of the gal gang to enter "parentville" you may have found that one minute your friends were there, pledging their unwavering support, even offering to be your birthing buddy, and then vamoosh. Exit stage right. Busy. Working. Dating. Gone.

At least you're not alone! Large-scale studies of new mums reveal as many as a quarter of us will stop meeting up with our old friends *at all* after baby is born[1]. Add to that the number of women who turned from "forever friends" to "pleasant acquaintances" and there's a lot of mums feeling confused by the buddy back-flip. But that's only how the PC version reads. Get onto some "mummy blogs" for seriously venomous blow-by-blow blogs of with-baby and without-baby friendship bust-ups.

Add to this the recent figures published by the Australian Institute of Health and Welfare suggesting that one in four women will now remain childless[2], and we can ditch the idea that all will be resolved once our childless friend gets her own baby on board.

Before the birth of my baby, I thought I had loads of "friends for life". Now I only have two who talk to me regularly. I miss them, but I get that I'm not the same person I used to be. I'm a mother now and that has changed me in ways I'd never imagined. I like the new me, but my old friends find my new life weird and boring.
TAMARA, MOTHER OF ONE

Why is this happening? They said they were my friends for life...

Before helpful solutions are explored, let's look at some key factors lurking beneath your best-buddy bust-ups.

You mean there's a world still going on out there that doesn't revolve around *your* baby?

In the first few months post-birth, many of us mums can't see outside our own bubble of bliss (also known as sleep deprivation delirium). Between the highs of seeing baby arrive and settle into the family home and the lows of being completely overwhelmed, there is little time to ponder a childless-friends plan. We don't really *choose* to be so obsessively absorbed in our baby, it's a survival instinct for the human species. The problem is that we forget the rest of our social network isn't quite so mesmerised by our little miracle.

So, rewind the clock for a bit. Before your baby was born, do you ever remember being *that* interested in another baby's sleep cycles/nappy deposits/puking habits? Nope? Well, your friends (even your BFF) aren't going to be *that* interested in your baby's either.

I'll never forget the night I invited my childless best friend over for dinner. I'd timed it so she could be there for Lucy's bath and last feed before bedtime. But there wasn't much room in our tiny bathroom and I guess she didn't think watching a writhing naked and crying little baby in water was that mind-blowing anyway. So she sat in our lounge room while I finished the bath, then I fed Lucy to sleep in her darkened nursery. An hour later I managed to join her. On reflection, what was I thinking! The next time, I invited her AFTER Lucy's bedtime.

Jenny, MOTHER OF THREE

But how can *she* be too busy? You're a MOTHER!

You were up six times last night. Three hours is your longest uninterrupted sleep cycle in four weeks. Your waking hours are jam-packed juggling cleaning, settling and feeding and yet still your washing pile is giving Mt Everest a run for its money…and she phones to tell you *she's* too busy to catch up. What? Between the manicure and the degustation dinner she can't slip in a coffee with her old best buddy?

It's impossible to fathom how much work a little bundle requires until we have one. Only then can we truly know what time-suckers they are. And that's the reality. She *won't* have a clue until it happens to her either. She can't believe that a little tiny baby takes more work than a hundred messy office workers. She just can't.

My childless best friend and her husband loved to invite us over to their house to "relax". Yeah right! There is nothing relaxing about having to pack up all our "baby stuff", mess up the baby's half-baked routine and go to their house so they can play with her for five minutes and hand her back when she cries/poos her nappy/gets boring! How about coming to our house, bringing some kind of dinner and properly minding our baby while we take a nap. That's what I'd call "relaxing"! Melanie, MOTHER OF TWO

What do you mean? Being with you and your baby isn't fun?

Almost instantaneously, our post-baby brains compute the need to accept that only 50% of our sentences can be finished, that walking (and rocking and soothing) while talking is nothing short of a necessity and that due to frenzied crying or explosive poo there will be the occasional need to suddenly abandon ship (or restaurant) and head for home.

We'll also be entertained, amused and enthralled by baby's first smile, first rollover or their first air punch that connected with their dangling mobile ("I think he's going to be a *genius*"). Amaaazing, aren't they? Well…I'd take a wild guess you didn't always think so. In your pre-baby days, that is. The "enthralling" bits are considered by many, including our childless BFFs, to be mind-numbingly *boring* or gross or both. That's the reason you didn't have staccato conversations, rave about "rolling over" or discuss poo problems *before* you had your baby.

I'll never forget my first coffee with a girlfriend I hadn't seen for four months since my baby was born. I wanted desperately to show her I could still "do" coffee even with a baby. It was all going fine, even the breastfeeding part. That was until my baby's suckling mouth "unlatched". It was one of those slow-motion "noooooooooooo" moments. My breastmilk sprayed straight into her cappuccino! I was horrified. She laughed at the time, but funnily enough she never asked me out for coffee again!
PENNY, MOTHER OF FOUR

Too protective? Too precious? NO way!

Before I had my firstborn, I'd told everyone my travelling plans wouldn't be altered by his birth. I'd raised my hand in defiance and declared with extraordinary naivety: "I'll pop him in a baby carrier and climb Kosciuszko, maybe even Ben Nevis". Ha! Our first planned blissful family road trip turned into three hours of the following: screaming baby, traffic jams, poo disaster with not enough wipes packed and breastfeeding on side of road in 35 degree heat. Our next "exotic" travel plan (ie a two hour car trip – which wouldn't have even rated as really "travel" by my pre-baby standards) was shelved until he was nine months old.

At some point, most new mothers are struck into an anxiously immobile state by the "what ifs". Not only does it stop us travelling, it can turn any previously classified "normal" social engagement into something requiring the skills of a fancy event planner. What if my baby gets sick and we aren't near a hospital? What if we're in a non-English speaking country and I can't explain my baby's symptoms? What if I get mastitis and can't get antibiotics? What if I run out of nappies and there's nowhere open to buy more? What if? What if? What if?

My childless friends expected me to attend their wedding in Noumea and be at the whole ceremony…as long as my four-month-old baby wasn't there (in case he cried, I guess). They didn't get that I wasn't comfortable leaving my baby with a local babysitter I'd only met as I stepped off the plane four hours before. It created a lot of friction between us.
JENNY, MOTHER OF TWO.

Once baby is born, no matter what naive plans we had before, it triggers a love and a protective instinct – quite lioness like – we just didn't expect. It overwhelms us. It changes what we have to do, say and plan for and it changes our priorities. We'll do anything – and I do mean *anything* – to keep them safe.

So, unless your buddy has had a baby sister or close cousin or other close connection with a baby, chances are she simple *can't* understand your newfound lioness instinct. It's just not possible.

She's not being careless or thoughtless or anything else. It's just how it is.

So what do you do? Well…It's grading time

As much as I'm an advocate for being positive about most things in life, on the issue of post-baby friendships, a tad bit of ruthlessness is in order. Ask yourself whether the friendship is really *that* important to you? Was it really built on hard-core-forever-friend principles, or was it more of a case of being only "job deep", "shopping-friend deep" or "good-times-only deep"?

Be honest with yourself, because for any true friendship to work at this stage of your life, it requires compromise, dedication, patience and commitment – all of which may be more than you're willing to give right now. You may feel too tired, too resentful or just too overwhelmed to put in what's required to keep a surface-level relationship alive. Be as clear as you can in your "baby brain" state as to which ones really deserve your TLC to get back to BFF or even FFF (that's fabulous friends forever) status.

Sophisticated Friendship Sorter

How to use this device: Decide which category best describes the status of your friendship, then use the following advice relevant to your choice

A: Oh yes! She's worth it!
This friendship is worth saving no matter what it takes!

B: Hmmmm...I wonder?
This friendship isn't working right now, but you'd like to think it could be revamped when life gets a little less crazy!

C: Nope. She's outta here.
That little lady ain't worth your time, energy or even thinking about anymore!

DECISION A
Oh yes! She's worth it!

OK. So she's in. Firstly, give yourself a rap. Your girlfriend must be pretty special (and you must be, too) to dedicate yourself to the friendship during these years of chaos. I'm guessing she's one of these types:

a. She has no idea about babies but loves yours to pieces anyway.

b. She has heaps of experience with babies and is super-comfortable with them.

c. She's just super-cruisy and goes with any old flow (you're still wondering if she's noticed you *even have* a baby now).

d. She's secure enough in herself to adapt and take into her stride the changes in her friend without taking them personally.

Now look in the mirror. A real friendship is about both sides making some compromises and adjustments. It's easy to see what a friend is not doing for you, but not so easy to see what you're not doing for a friend.

Photocopy the following page and give it to your girlfriends. Then be a good friend by photocopying the one on the other page and sticking it on *your* fridge.

Top 10 things
I'd like my **childless friends** to know

1. It's hard to believe, but babies are total time-suckers. I'm truly busy, exhaustingly busy (with many ground-hog day monotony moments), all the time.

2. I can't be sure *where* my time goes. And I often can't tell you or have very little evidence for what I've done. I just know some days I struggle to even use the bathroom or have a shower.

3. This job is heaps harder than I ever realised. I've never felt so responsible. And most days I feel I get heaps of it wrong. If I have a little cry, please just tell me I'll be OK (and make sure my house has Tim Tams in it for when you're not there for reassurance).

4. It feels right to make my baby the centre of my universe. My partner revolves around in there somewhere, and you do too. I love you, but give me time to sort out this new whirlwind. I know it won't always be quite this chaotic.

5. When I don't call for ages, it's not that I don't care. Please see my tiny texts or group emails as a huge effort to stay in touch, because they are.

6. I worry about loads of things I never even knew I could worry about. This takes up heaps of my headspace and sometimes sends me a little loopy. Please forgive me if I forget your birthday, your phone number and even maybe your name – I forget my own now too sometimes...

7. I WANT to make sacrifices for my baby. It's OK. Truly. I'm all good to stay home when you're out partying, but if I join you, can we start early? I need to be in bed before 10pm.

8. If you come over to my house would you mind ignoring all signs that a tornado has just ripped through? Please only comment if you are offering to help me out...

9. If I suddenly have to change plans, run late or can't meet up, please know I'm as upset as you are. If my baby's sick, that's what I'll have to do. If I'm late because of an unexpected 10-minute clean-up after baby's poo explosion then that's what will happen. I'm doing those things because my baby needs me to. It's not that I don't adore you and want to be with you too.

10. Even if you loathe my baby, pretend you don't. Even just for a moment. Smile and pick him up. It makes my heart sing to see my special friend with my special baby.

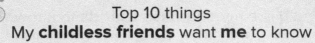

Top 10 things
My **childless friends** want **me** to know

1. I'm busy too. It's not the same kind of busy as with a baby. But it's still busy.

2. I still have a life. I know I'm not raising the next generation of humanity, but the things I do are important too.

3. I have a brain. And I know you used to think it worked pretty well. Please don't assume that without my own baby I don't have any idea about your new parenting world.

4. Your baby is special, but I don't love him as much as you. That means I can't celebrate his poo like you do. And if you talk for 30 minutes straight about his sleep patterns, please don't be offended if I yawn...you would have too in your pre-baby world...

5. Tell me how I can help. I love you, but I'm not a mind reader. It's easy for me to pick up some frozen dinners or a loaf of bread on my way over, or hold baby while you take a shower.

6. Don't ask "Has she got any children?" every time a new name comes up in conversation. I feel like suddenly being a mother is the defining characteristic of a woman. And then I feel I'm inadequate in your eyes.

7. Don't ditch me from all your social events. If it all gets too baby-centred I can leave. I'm a big girl now.

8. Don't laugh when I try to relate to your parenting woes by talking about my interaction with my dog. I *know* it's not the same, but I'm trying to somehow connect our worlds again.

9. I KNOW you're busy. But just one text a week would be cool. When you're too busy for me but have time to post 50 photos on Facebook, I get hurt.

10. I'm patient. I can wait. I am not another pressure. I believe our friendship can handle going off-course for a baby. We can find a new path over time. It'll be different, but our friendship's worth the wait.

Here's a more in-depth guide to keeping you and your BFF or FFF from wandering off-track:

1. **Acknowledge you aren't in Kansas anymore, Dorothy. But she is**. If you want your worlds to collide again and race down that yellow-brick road with matching ruby-red shoes, here's what to do:

Solution a): Work out what things you still have in common.

- Does an old episode of "Sex in the City" still send you both into hysterics? Then perhaps invite her over to watch a show for a "girls' night in".

- Less time than that? Flick her an email with a memory of an event, song or experience that is forever etched in your memory of times spent together in raptures of laughter or tears.

- Do you both still love a massage? Get a mobile massage therapist to come to you (she might have the baby just for the half hour while you get some much needed pampering). Then go crazy – well, the "crazy" that now exists in your new mother scene – and paint your toe nails over a cup of tea.

- Is fashion your mutual "thing"? Just because you might be working off your post-baby "bump" (or "mountain"… all depending on the amount of cheesecake eaten during pregnancy) doesn't mean you can't head to your closest Westfield and watch *her* try on this season's latest arrivals. Sit back in a change room with a comfy couch and feed your baby while she entertains you with her fashion show.

Solution b): Stay interested in her world.

- Watch your waffling! Many childless friends complain that conversations about their own life are contained to a few brief sentences while conversely they're compelled to discuss every moment of the baby's life in minute detail ("she slept for how long? Ten minutes more than yesterday? Oh and then she woke up?" Ho, hum…).

- So stay focused. If you notice eye-rolling, yawning and a third toilet break in half an hour, your friend wants you to *stop talking about your baby*.
- Keep up to date with what she's doing – with her job, her studies, her relationships, her hobbies. Remember, you didn't *not* exist prior to a baby and you never thought your pre-baby life was completely *meaningless*. So find meaning in her world.
- Email or text her when something great happens to her, be it a promotion, a first date or the purchase of a great new handbag.
- Mobile phone apps that instantly share photos help you stay in touch, too – she can send you pics of her "must have" pair of Jimmy Choos and you can trump it with mmmm… another snuggly sleeping shot? Anyway, your baby won't mind if you take the focus off feeding just for a few moments to look at your phone, plug in a few letters or send a few photos to stay in touch with the girlfriend who feeds your soul.

2. **Accept she doesn't have to loooooove Toto (aka baby).** It's wonderful that we live in a world with choice. Choice to have babies. Choice not to. Some women know themselves enough to steer clear of breeding, since it's not the life they really want. She may genuinely prefer a life where she never has to wake up before 9.00am on weekends and jets off on exotic trips at a moment's notice (yeah right, as if you'd want that nonsense…).

So, to keep a friendship *without* a mutual love connection for baby, here are my tips:

- Dig deep…your friend isn't selfish for not being in the mood to hang out with your snotty, crying, but *gorgeous* baby. Respect her for where she's at.
- Remember, *you've* decided to keep her in your life, so it's up to *you* to make arrangements where you catch up *without* baby. This can be while you get your hair or nails spruced up (may as well get something done at the same time since you have *no* time for exotic flings in even more exotic locations) or a planned night out where Dad (or Nanna or Aunty) has some "bonding time". Even if you only get the time between feeds, an hour with a good girlfriend can give you positive energy for an entire week.

3. **Admit sometimes there *are* scary things along the Yellow Brick Road.** And just because they're not of the "lions and tigers and bears" variety, there are things we face in the post-baby world that are jaw-droppingly freaky. Remember your first baby's meconium poo? That *freaked* me out! The solution to not scaring your friend out of your life requires gauging her level of fear:

   - If she's seriously spooked, give her time to see how you do things. Let her gradually learn what babies need, just as you did. Let her join you in bathing the baby or perhaps just pushing the pram. Simply let her hold the baby for a few moments.
   - If she's more eager to learn the mysterious world of babies, let her look after baby for slightly longer periods, perhaps while you take a shower. Then start letting her have the baby for increasing amounts of time, maybe for a couple of hours – just enough time to head to your bedroom for a nap!

4. **Go gently if she's desperate to be in the Land of Oz too.** This is perhaps the most sensitive of issues between friends. When our friends long for their own baby but infertility, miscarriage or not finding "Mr Right" (also known as Mr Darcy) prevents their journey, your new life with your "bundle of joy" can come to represent one huge dose of heartache for her. Here are some suggestions for managing this delicate relationship:

- Choose your words carefully. Avoid complaining about your sleep-deprived state to this friend. She doesn't want to hear it. She'd give her right arm (in fact her entire soul) to be losing hours of sleep to her own baby's presence.

- Be ready for her huge oscillations between delight and avoidance with your post-baby world. Each unsuccessful IVF trial, each time another test result shows the "negative" sign, she'll experience her devastating grief all over again.

- Be flexible and patient. It could be that you can only catch up for short periods of time *without* baby because she struggles so deeply to see you *with* baby. Remember that you've made the decision to keep her in your life, so try to meet her where her head's at on any particular day.

- Don't avoid her. A good friend with these issues needs you more than ever. She doesn't want to lose you and you don't want to lose her. Just try to think how your baby news and baby presence might be received from her end.

- Never forget the power of the words "I'm sorry". If, in your sleep-deprived state, you said a few words you know would have unintentionally hurt her. Apologise. It's the grown-up thing to do.

DECISION B
Hmmmm...I wonder?

I've been working with people who have experienced trauma for over 14 years. Of all the suggestions out there to help get them through this difficult time, one of the most important is this: **hold off making any big decisions during times of significant distress**.

The same applies to us in the post-birth whirlwind. If it's all too hard and you can't see beyond the haze of nappies, feeding and sleep deprivation, hold off a bit. Basically, it's a case of "If in doubt, wait it out".

If your friendship really was at the *soul* level, at some point it will find its way back on track. Perhaps when she has her own children. Perhaps when yours grow up and you can see beyond the baby haze. Many older and wiser women have shared with me that while the baby-bearing years brought a whole range of new people into their lives, their old friends often re-emerged later down the track.

So if one of your *soul* sisters is veering off your intended paired-up pathway, maybe just see her a little less. Maybe just put less energy into trying to arrange a catch up. Instead, put energy into those friendships that are working for you right now. Soul sisters will eventually reconnect with us when the time is right, and when they do, it'll be as if you were never apart.

Two of my best friends didn't have children until they were in their late 30s. So while I was dealing with the whirlwind of two young children, they were out travelling the world and doing all sorts of amazing things. They had no idea how much motherhood changed things until they had their own babies. Then all they could do was apologise for how little support they'd given me and wished they'd been more around to help. That's just the way it goes. How could they have known what having kids was really like until they had their own? Now we catch up a lot more regularly and we're back to being close again.

JENNA, MOTHER OF TWO

DECISION C
Nope. She's outta here.

OK. If your girlfriend fell into this category I'm guessing she either:

a. can't or doesn't want to understand how completely overwhelming and mind-blowingly life-changing having a baby can be for you;

b. can't or doesn't want to cope with all the changes you've made in your life as a result of (a).

So put your hand on your heart. If you really are sure you've done your best, if you've been as patient and kind and thoughtful and as sensitive you can be but she's being downright *mean, nasty and wicked-witch-like*, pull the plug. There is no shame in ending a friendship, if you do it right. Here are some tips:

1. *Hands by your side.* While there are ways to end and ways *not* to end friendships, often in this post-baby period the only behaviour required by you is to simply *do nothing.* This works a treat with those friends who have echoed the very same sentiment since you started your first contraction, ie they did nothing, said nothing, brought nothing. *Became nothing*, in your life, that is. The only way to keep connected with these girls is to extend *your* hand of friendship, so by keeping that hand firmly by your side, the relationship simply ends. No need for tearful farewells or emotion-filled emails. This is a

great solution for those women who *loathe* conflict or where the friendship was really only "chardonnay deep".

2. *Salute to the fallen.* When we've enjoyed years and years with a certain BFF, it often simply wouldn't feel right to just watch the friendships fade into nonexistence. Sometimes it's only respectful to acknowledge that while it's now turned to enemy territory, it was once a gloriously united front. If you can muster the energy, a note reflecting this sentiment can be a respectful end point. It could also potentially leave a door open for future reunification. Words such as, "Our worlds seem to be moving in two different directions and somehow this means we can't connect right now. We had a great friendship and perhaps one day this will lead us to find our way back together again".

3. *Blame the innocent (ie the baby).* In some ways, it really is the baby's fault that all this has happened. Sort of...I mean, they didn't ask to be brought into the world, but couldn't they have done it with less catastrophic impact? Anyway, you don't need to attach harsh words to your baby (eg "Since that nightmare came into our world she's made everything, including our friendship, one massive disaster after another"). Rather, choose a far safer swan song such as: "A new baby is much more of a commitment than I'd ever imagined. I just can't find the time to keep up what's needed to maintain our friendship right now".

BUT what if you exit your old friends, and then you're LONELY?

It's a sad fact that many of us cling onto unhealthy relationships simply because we're not sure a new one is waiting in the wings, let alone likely to sweep us off our feet. Some women get stuck thinking: "better to be in a toxic relationship than none at all". If this has been your approach to life so far, then let me firstly express my sadness that you've probably endured numerous unhealthy relationships. Next, get out your pom poms and strike up the music, because research suggests that this stage in your life can potentially be the best opportunity for changing these old patterns.

Last year, one of the UK's largest papers printed the headline: "Motherhood increases friend count by eight." The *Telegraph* was referring to the poll of 4000 mothers of young children[3] which found that before having children, women reported having only three close friends, while after baby, the old friend fall-out was replaced with a whole new larger circle.

But, before you boil the kettle, dust off the china, pop the scones in the oven and stand in anticipation at your front door, remember these new friends aren't coming to you. Making new friends means *you* must get out of the house! Research tells us that the most likely place we meet new friends is in mothers groups, coffee mornings, playgrounds and preschools. No mention of finding them curled up in front of the TV in your lounge room wearing flannelette PJs.

What if you haven't made new friends since high school?

Many mothers were born with friendship-finding skills equivalent to Einstein's knowledge of quantum physics. For others, this social genius skill missed their production line. So, if you're more Timid Tina than Social Suzie, here are some ideas that might help you increase your social circle:

- **Watch your body language**. Picture the meek mouse cowering in the corner or the hungry wolf glaring at his intended prey. Now picture the bored bank clerk. Compare all three to the gestures and facial expressions of your average Fijian hotel worker. Which one would *you* want to talk to? Yep, it's a big BULA to that! We sometimes forget the power of body language in preparing the stage for friendship. So look as though you're a friendly, relaxed person (well, as relaxed as any new mum can be) who wants to be friends with the people you're with.

- **Talk to people**. You can join any group, church or organisation under the sun but you still won't make friends if you don't actually talk to people. It's like trying to have an email discussion with someone who won't type...doomed. In these early days you don't have to worry about having something in common with other new mothers. You're all obsessed with your babies. So, talk to your heart's content. She may be the only other person who actually *is* interested in the colour of your baby's poo.

- **Know thy name**. If you haven't already done so, make sure by the time your conversation ends, you've at least exchanged first names. It can be as simple as saying "Oh, by the way, my name is...".

- **Make a "date"**. You can chat your heart out but it won't get you a friend if you don't close the deal for round two. You need to make an opportunity for another conversation or meeting, even if it's a case of "Can I talk to you more after mothers group about that?". This is especially important if you meet someone who you aren't otherwise likely to meet again. Seize the day and make sure you exchange contact details too so you can call her if there's a change of plans

191

(new mums are notoriously late for their "dates").

- **Be interested**. Many people think that in order to be seen as "friend material" they have to appear *interesting* when in fact it's more important to be *interested*, in the other person that is. Try to remember important details about them and their baby and refer to these details next time you talk. She'll feel important to you and this creates a good groundwork for friendship.

- **Share your good qualities, not just your struggles**. In the new phase of mothering, most women are pretty puffed out – emotionally and physically. It's unlikely a fellow newbie mum will have enough resources or motivation to pick you up emotionally unless she senses you'll reciprocate down the line. If all you share are struggles, she'll be reaching for the exit button before long.

- **Think like an owl (wisely that is)**. Which part of *The Sound of Music fits* the emotions of your growing relationship – the part where they're singing merrily in unison or the part where they'd running for the hills? If you finish conversations feeling worse rather than better or if you're starting to dread your contact together, then heading for the hills (as gracefully and respectfully as per Frau Maria) is a safer place for your relationship in the long run. And remember, if you made *this* friend, you can make others too.

I'd moved to the UK a few years before my son was born, but I didn't realise how much I'd miss my family until he came along. I was unprepared for how much time I'd spend on my own. Then I made friends with the local mothers group and they became like my family. I'll always be grateful for their friendship. It saved my sanity. TAHLIA, MOTHER OF THREE

What if most of your pre-baby friends were blokes?

One of my most divine-looking girlfriends is unsurprisingly popular with the boys. But it's not just that they like her (wink-wink, nudge-nudge) they *like* her. And it's mutual. Many of her friends always were and probably always will be male. But this was tricky when she was in those first few months of baby bedlam. She understood that these buffed buddies weren't going to rally to her bedside and bathe in baby puke to help her out (it was hard enough to get her husband to report for duty). It was just that, well, making new friends in the post-baby era was limited to making friends with other...women. And she recalls it being a lonely time:

I needed something other than mothers group. It was all I had and I relied on it. But I didn't realise how much I'd miss male company. I'd been on the public speaking circuit and always out to dinners, always talking to loads of different people about loads of different things. Now the only conversation was about babies, babies and more babies – all the female talk just bored me to tears.
MEL, MOTHER OF TWO

And like my gorgeous Amazonian-looking friend, if your main friendship tone was more testosterone than tea-party, those first few post-baby months will be tough. Even more reason to stay connected via text messages, Facebook, emails and phone apps. And a great excuse to make Saturday your family's daddy-Day or nanna-Day, so you can sit down with the paper and immerse yourself in the non-baby-focused world out there that still exists. That'll ensure you have a few topics other than baby poo at your next male catch-up.

And remember, despite your disappointment in the sudden MIA of the males in your life, it's *you* who chose to enter the world of families. Your male buddies didn't. So don't expect them to get clucky over your baby or excited about falling over all your washing piles to make their own cup of tea at your place. Maybe invite them over for a beer once baby is safely tucked up in bed and invite at least two of them so they can entertain each other if feeding demands call you away. Most genuine male friends *don't* want to see your breasts (which is why they made friend status to start with), but some über-amazing ones will take it in their stride. Adjust accordingly. Take them for who they are, not who you want them to be.

And remember, babies don't stay babies forever. My gorgeous friend's children are now aged five and seven and she's surrounded again by *both* male and female friends.

One last comment:

Friendships aren't always easy. No long-term relationship ever is. When we work out who we want in our lives and who we don't, we're one step toward a solution. The next step is physical and emotional investment of effort. Serious effort. But for good friends, this will repay you a hundred times over. Because good friends are like a safety net for those times when our little bundle of joy is more like a trailer of trouble and the only thing remotely "better" about our supposed "better half" are his snoring skills.

Stay patient wherever possible and allow time for motherhood to sink in before you make too many big decisions. And keep a bottle of champagne – of the non-alcoholic variety for the breastfeeders out there – chilling in the fridge ready to celebrate your friendship decisions, be they with the old buddies or the new.

Having my baby made me grow up. I had to take charge. I had to choose friends who were good for me. I had to stop putting up with people who didn't value me or my baby. Once I valued myself, I found I could make friends who valued me too. It's been an awesome time in my life. KELLIE, MOTHER OF ONE

Chapter 7:

Now we're a family of three, what happened to the two of us?

Getting the zing back in your relationship.

Judy couldn't decide whether it was her husband or the Tim Tams that best helped her through baby's first year.

Creating a baby was the best thing we had ever done, yet I was the only one enjoying it – for 12 hours each day alone with our baby. Even though he tried to do as much as he could, I felt strange doing "our thing" but with only me present. It took time for us both to adjust. MARGIE, MOTHER OF TWO

I really resented my partner most of the time. I was jealous of his freedom, annoyed with his lack of understanding and angry at his laziness. The first few years were really tough. ROSE, MOTHER OF TWO

My partner fell into it perfectly. He almost knew more than me. He helped with everything and I'd have been lost without him. He is a really hands-on dad and every mother deserves that! SHARNA, MOTHER OF ONE

196

My partner tried to help out, but I wasn't in the headspace to let him take a more hands-on role. I just kind of did it all, even when I knew I wasn't coping. Looking back we'd have all coped better if I'd just shown him how to help. MARYANNE, MOTHER OF TWO

Supportive Sam? Hands-off Howard? Or more of a Laid-Back Liam? The attitude our partner adopts in his new role as dad makes a difference bigger than an episiotomy needle when it comes to how we cope with our new baby. So much so that the research tells us if our partner is a bit of joke in the support stakes, there isn't a dry eye in the house. But these aren't tears of joy. Our likelihood of developing postnatal distress or depression is heavily impacted by the role our partners choose to take in the postnatal period[1].

So let's just blame the men! Well…Not so fast. The research is also clear that if we're struggling then our other halves are probably struggling too. In fact the rates for male postnatal depression (PND) suggest virtually half of all partners of women with PND also meet the criteria for a diagnosis.

Then this is about both of us? Absolutely. The reality is that for both of you to sanely navigate the first year with baby, you're both going to have to raise the pom poms and choreograph the cheerleading routine, because it's all about embracing the team. *Your team* that is. Because when it all boils down, the summary of all the research is this:

a. If he provides a strong level of support, you're less at risk for psychological craziness (or sadness).
b. When you're more sane because of his support, then he's generally happier too and his own craziness or sadness is less at risk.

c. When you're both sane, everyone's a winner, including baby, because research also tells us that kids fare best in a harmonious home.

But it's all just too hard...

Time to ditch the IKEA attitude here. I know...it's hard. I too once adored the idea of the cheap, expendable, flat-packed furniture regularly being thrown out and replaced as I went through a new "design phase". It's just that the same attitude doesn't bode so well for healthy long-term relationships with your partner...

So abandon the idea that if the relationship's hard it's time for a new model. All relationships need nurturing, with a bit of "buffing and polishing" from time to time. Unless there are issues of abuse, the tough times need to be turned into opportunities for growth. So man- (sorry, "woman-") up! And get on with changing your relationship from flat-packed to fully-formed.

My husband was interested in being a good dad, but just didn't seem to get it. He wasn't totally understanding about how much my life had changed either. It took a few arguments and deep discussions for us to work together and understand each other.
JADE, MOTHER OF THREE

Wasn't a baby meant to bring us closer together?

There are some pretty depressing statistics out there when it comes to the modern family and the relationship between the parents in them. This is our reality:

- **Our parents knew better than us!** Despite the bugaboos, the feeding schedule apps, the baby monitors and the digital thermometers, our yearning for "more" has actually given us "less" on the relationship satisfaction stakes. An analysis of around 90 studies showed that after the first baby's birth, our parents' satisfaction level was 42% higher than it is in our generation[2].

- **Being "without baby" equals "with happiness"**. What? Yep, the research suggests that our friends who have remained childless are more satisfied in their relationships than us. Ouch[3].

- **The women are the more woeful**. It seems it's us women (and not our partners) who are more likely to report a decline in our relationship's "feel good factor". So while we're crying ourselves to sleep, our partners might well be blissfully unaware of the issues – until we throw a feeding pillow in their direction…

- **Even perfect partnerships are at risk**. Yes, even in the healthiest and most amazing pre-baby relationships (you know those ones where the birds seem to swirl into heart formations when they walk together), the general rule is that these couples will also experience some level of decline once the baby comes along[4].

Enough already! Let's switch to the good news…kind of. Well, does it help knowing that:

- **You're at your most dissatisfied right now**. It seems the period of our relationship's greatest discontent is during the years of infancy, then there's an upward trend and we tend to get our relationships off the critically ill list as our babies get older[5]. Yee ha!

- **Statistics have two sides**. Remember that research data doesn't necessarily explain *your* circumstances. As some researchers have found, there are those relationships where the couple gets more in tune, sings from the same hymn sheet, and generally "gets their groove" when baby becomes the third band member[6]. Any hey – who says your relationship can't be the one in this category!

Initially my husband was overwhelmed, but I just expected him to be part of everything and always showed him how to do things if he was unsure. He soon responded and we did it as a team.
JULIE, MOTHER OF TWO

So how do you make sure your relationship heads north not south?

It's possible that you're already there. You know, you've got the whole relationships thing going on, and you don't even know it. Possible, because, well, a lot of amazing things are. Including the bizarre concept that babies can be delivered through a hole one-quarter the size it needed to be.

Anyway, you'll know soon enough, because below is the health test for your relationship. My suggestion is that you and your partner both take the test together and see whether your relationship is fit as a fiddle, or in the chronically ill category. Note: it uses the words "spouse" and "marriage" but just convert these in your own mind to best suit the relationship style and status for you and your partner.

THE MARITAL HAPPINESS SCALE

For each question below, rate whether you are very happy, pretty happy, or not too happy with this aspect of your marriage. If you are very happy, assign a number 3. If you are pretty happy, the number 2, and if not too happy, the number 1.

1. How happy are you with the amount of understanding you receive from your spouse?
2. How happy are you with the amount of love and affection you receive?
3. How happy are you with the extent to which you and your spouse agree about things?
4. How happy are you with your sexual relationship?
5. How happy are you with your spouse as someone who takes care of things around the house?
6. How happy are you with your spouse as someone to do things with?
7. How happy are you with your spouse's faithfulness to you?
8. Taking all things together, how would you describe your marriage?
9. Compared to other marriages you know about, do you think your marriage is better than most (3), about the same as most (2), or not as good as most (1)?
10. Comparing your marriage to three years ago, is your marriage getting better (3), staying the same (2), or getting worse (1)?
11. Would you say the feelings of love you have for your spouse are extremely strong (3), very strong (3), pretty strong (2), not too strong (1), or not strong at all (1)?

Now add up your total score. It can range from 11 to 33. Here is where your score fits with national norms for married people in the USA.

a. The average marital happiness score is 29.
b. If your score was 27 or less, you are less happy with your marriage than 75% of married people.
c. If your score was 32 or higher, you are more happily married than 75% of married people.

What were your scores? If it was lower than you hoped, be more supportive to yourself than your maternity bras on this one. Remember that the first year after baby is the hardest on most of our relationships. But that doesn't mean things can't be better.

From the Marital Instability over the Life Course Study conducted by Alan Booth and Paul Amato. This scale is in the public domain. Published by The Guilford Press in *Take Back Your Marriage* (2nd ed.), by William J. Doherty.

How do you get your relationship back on track?

Suggestion: Get your better/worse/other (whatever word fits best) half to read this section with you. Because you BOTH need to take responsibility for what each of you are bringing into this relationship that turns it toxic or helps it heal.

First the Unhelpful Factors

Before giving you the whole run-down on what factors need to become part of your new healthy relationship, we firstly need to dispose of the toxic parts. So here's the run- down on what *not* to do if you want that relationship feel-good factor back.

1. **DON'T get stuck in a negative rut!** Quickly reflect on your last conversation with each other. Do some quick maths. For every negative comment, how many positive statements did you make?

If your relationship was on the healthier side, chances are there'll be more positives than negatives. And it you want your relationship to enter a wellness wonderland, you'll need to switch over to that style of communicating too.

Try a quick experiment tonight over the dinner table (if by some small miracle you manage to be together at that time) or any other time you're in the same room together and not asleep. Tally up both your positives and negatives as you discuss important issues (eg who'll be getting up to the baby, who gets to sleep in tomorrow) and make sure there are more positives than negatives.

I can pretty much guarantee that if you sort this issue out, you'll be the couple every other parent looks at green with envy.

2. **DON'T dish the dude's daddying!** We women can be our own worst enemies. We somehow think we can shoo the dads away when they can't soothe the baby as well as we can, then suddenly expect them to come back and sort it out for us when we've "had enough" and need a break! It's about training, ladies. The only reason you're good at it is because you had to be. You kept trying. You persevered. Let him do the same!

Remember, he won't parent like you do. Nobody will. But if you want a partner, not a clone of yourself, then you need to accept he'll soothe the baby differently to you. Having different soothing techniques is good for your baby too, because they'll get used to a range of different ways of calming down and going to sleep. This means they'll be OK with having the care of a babysitter or a grandma when you and husband need a romantic night out.

My husband felt left out when our son was born. I breastfed him until he was 19 months old. I think my husband felt useless and as though the baby came between us. He later told me he hated the little baby stage. JENI, MOTHER OF TWO

3. **DON'T underestimate the time-sucking capacity of a baby!** We *know* that babies only have few basic needs, but on some days it seems that meeting them goes waaaaaaay beyond the capacity of even the most awesome female superhero. Dishes pile up in the sink, laundry stays unwashed, general "to do" lists are never done, a shower becomes a luxury experience.

So – for the dads this time – don't ever ask in anything other than a positive tone, "What have you done all day?". Firstly, because we can't answer the question. We don't know how we can do so much and yet on the surface achieve so little. Secondly, because we're hardly jumping for joy at this newly-found "lack of apparent productivity". Some of us used to manage teams of hundreds of people, or financial accounts worth millions of dollars, or made creative decisions that influenced entire companies. So, if you are brave (or stupid) enough to ask the question, be prepared for either a tirade of abuse or a flood of tears. And don't say you weren't warned!

Instead try to see it like this – the messier the house, the more she stinks like vomit and the crazier her hair is – the harder the day has been! This is your opportunity to acknowledge this frustrating truth (for both of you) and say, "How are you, honey? It looks like that little baby of ours was in high demand mode today. How can I help?" Then give her the biggest hug possible. Grateful wife now created. Job done.

4. **DON'T underestimate the parenting complexity factor**. Dads, here's another *major* recommendation for you. Beware of making any comment that indicates "it can't be that hard". Unless, that is, *you* have taken the full responsibility of your baby for three days straight and found it a breeze. Taking care of the baby for a few hours or even one day doesn't count. Firstly because tasks can still be left "for later" (ie for when the mother reassumes responsibility), and secondly because it doesn't account for the life-sapping monotony of doing the same tasks repeatedly throughout the day, every day, and yet never really getting anything finished.

Remember too, that it's not just that mums are physically exhausted – the brain strain of meeting all of baby's developmental needs is a killer. We think about those things *a lot*! As we should. We're not raising a goldfish here. In contrast, most dads *don't* take the time to read the baby development books. They *don't* therefore know the importance of introducing certain activities and tasks at different ages and stages. So when we're helping baby with "tummy time" it's not just for our own enjoyment – it's because we need to factor that into our day for our baby's gross motor development.

So for the dad who still isn't keen on reading the developmental books and sharing the responsibility of meeting baby's developmental needs, avoid saying "it can't be that hard" and try this instead: "Wow. You're amazing. I love the way you take care of our child's cognitive, emotional and physical development." Then step back and watch. Firstly, she'll be gobsmacked you knew those words, but she'll also be one happy mumma knowing that you've noticed how much energy she puts into your baby.

5. **DON'T compare oranges with apples**. Ever heard the words – "temperament", "normal range" or "individual"? Hold onto them like your best friend, because they'll help remind you that what your baby brings to the world (temperament) has to be managed by what you and your partner bring to the world (your temperaments), and that the typical child's and parent's responses can vary significantly (whilst still considered "normal"), and all of this is because you haven't partnered up with a clone nor have you given birth to one (which is why we're called individuals).

So take into account the following:
- **Your baby is unique**. Your baby might sleep for up to six hours a night within days of coming home from hospital. Alternatively, your baby might be up every two hours.
- **You are unique**. You may have been the mother with significant health problems due to the birth and be unable to move about quickly (or even to pick up baby or drive a car if you've had a caesarean).
- **Your social system is unique**. You may or may not have copious amounts of social support to take the baby for a couple of hours to enable a quick house tidy/rest/cup of tea!
- **Your partner is unique**. While Super Simon down the road might have a job that allows him to be super flexible with his work schedule and can get home each day for bath time, yours might be away on international business trips.

Use the knowledge about your individuality to make a pact with each other to accept each other for who you are and what your circumstances are. Unless you do you'll never make decisions that are based on what really is important for *your* family, or be able to solve the problems that *you* have.

6. **DON'T let your mind get stuck in "la la land"**. Most of us suffer the psychological torment of coming to terms with what the reality of parenting looks like. Those Kleenex ads sold us a *completely* different picture…! But, it's actually not us women who mostly feel the pain of the "fantasy versus reality" difference. The research is clear that for the men in our lives, failing to get their heads around what they hoped versus what they're actually faced with is one of the biggest risk factors for their decrease in relationship satisfaction.

Realistically, dads should have known that parenting didn't equal mother and baby staying home all day while they worked/partied/played golf, etc. But there *are* dads who somehow generated this vision. It must come from the information source that suggested we all like to wear super-uncomfortable lacy and racy red underwear even when we're breastfeeding.

Remember dads, it's hard to stop doing all the things that *you* want to do, but your child needs you to harness your inner father instincts and lose the bachelor brain. And yes, this means you won't make every "work drinks" or "Sunday surf" that you used to. Being part of a family means being a *team* player. And if one team member needs you, you step up. Or you can be pretty much guaranteed you're going to get kicked off the team at some point. And then everyone suffers, especially your child.

Same goes for us mums. Holding onto visions where we lunched all day while our baby slept peacefully in the pram need to be squashed super fast. Long days wearing pyjamas, hair claggy with baby vomit, households turned upside down *is* how it will often look.

But – I bet you also didn't imagine how much you'd *love* your little miracle. There are parts of this unexpected new world that blow your socks off! Like when your baby gives you his first smile, or his giggle has you in fits of laughter. Accepting your reality helps you to see what is truly *beautiful* about what you have. And it *is* truly extraordinary watching your baby grow and develop…if you just let yourself see it.

7. **DON'T point score**. If ever there's a relationship grenade, this is it! I so often see (and am occasionally also guilty of it too) couples who start to get competitive about who's had the worst day or who's working the hardest. Some want to set up chalk boards to tally up the number of nappies changed, hours slept, loads of washing done and meals cooked just to prove a point.

There are some big problems involved in taking this competitive approach to your parenting team. Firstly, it destroys the capacity to share moments of joy in your day for fear it will result in your partner declaring that you should therefore do the most work that night! Secondly, it can mean you're so focused on tallying up how many hours you do (or he does) that you fail to *enjoy* your baby and instead turn every parenting task into just one long list of chores.

The solution is to be adult about your workload – if you think it's likely your day was easier, then declare it and take the initiative to do more when your husband gets home. Dads, if you're lucky enough to have had an easyish day at work (or a golf day) then take the mature step of then offering to do a bit more around the house that night. If one of you has a good night's sleep, allow your partner to have a sleep-in if they can.

The parents who work best as a team assume that on most days they have worked *equally* hard. That means, when the husband arrives home, they both have *equal* responsibility for any remaining household or parenting tasks that need to be done. In these highly functioning relationships, there's no room for the mother still carrying on as a solo worker when the father comes home from work, puts his feet up and watches the TV. Dads – I have one phrase that will get you a dozen brownie points every time you say it: "Honey, before I sit down is there anything else that needs to be done?" And then *do* what it is she asks.

Now for the Helpful Factors

1. **Stay physically connected**. OK, hold up. I'm not talking about the S-E-X word here. Affection and sex are not the same thing (and if you think they are, you need a load more help than just this book!). And mark my word, dads, if every time your baby's mother shows you even a slightly affectionate glance, you make some type of bedroom moves on her, then you can pretty much guarantee the affectionate gestures will dry up faster than a cracked nipple. You must remember, *we* want to be affectionate with you too. We *love* a cuddle. But don't interpret every bit of affection as a sexual advance! If you want to know more about sex though, read further down in this chapter.

In addition, please know how much a cuddle means to us. When we've been cuddling and cajoling, rocking and holding, feeding (and then more feeding…) our babies all day, we could use a bit of that in return. Well, not the breastfeeding, but all the rest of it. It feels great when you want to *give* affection to us and not want anything in return for your gestures. It makes us feel like you truly care.

For us mothers: remember that men *looove* physical affection. You'll often get them to agree to participate much more if you're being affectionate while you're talking about it. This doesn't mean you have to make sexual advances, but rather the small stuff – perhaps hugging him when he arrives home from work, or standing close to him when you're together in the kitchen. Use the ordinary moments to make your relationship a special one.

I felt so useless as a partner. I felt like I couldn't connect with Amy anymore. When I ran out of ideas all I wanted to do was hold her in my arms and keep her close. But she didn't even want that from me. I had no way to bridge the growing gap between us. DAVID, FATHER OF TWO

2. **Pile on the praise**. Remember dads, even the most competent woman will have many, many, many doubts as a new mum (often hundreds of times a day!). Regularly letting your wife know that you think she's pretty amazing is crucial to how she feels about herself as a new mum. Don't be fake about it: keep it genuine. Don't wait for big moments and take even the smallest of opportunities to recognise a special moment, eg "I really think it's fantastic how you can keep your cool for so long when the baby's crying" or "I can't believe how patient you are when you're breastfeeding for what looks like hours on end".

Now for us ladies…Sometimes we can be so desperate for reassurance that we forget our other halves need it too. Letting the new dad know that he's getting the hang of parenting helps him feel better than his team winning the grand final (well, maybe not that good) and increases the chances he'll keep trying when the going gets tough. Which means he's more likely to persevere with a screeching baby in the middle of the night without calling in the reinforcements (ie, us). And in baby's first year, isn't that of greater value than the best bargain buy in the Boxing Day sales (and I bet that pre-baby you never thought *that* would be possible!)?

My husband was amazing. He helped so much and supported me immensely. He still does four years on. I know I'm very lucky to have him. KARIANNE, MOTHER OF ONE

3. **Remember that change is stressful**. Remember the old days. Your partner came home from work to a composed woman who eagerly sat down to a civilised conversation and dinner together. Roll on to the same scene in the post-baby era and he walks home to find his partner a crying wreck who shoves a screaming baby into his arms, yells at him for forgetting to pick up the bread and then throws herself onto her bed sobbing about everything being a complete disaster.

When baby's arrival shifts a happy twosome to a tired-out threesome, the changes required to accommodate the transition process challenges some of the greatest revolutions in history. There's a reason big companies pay hundreds of thousands of dollars to decrease the impact of change: it stops their employees "losing it". And it's the same process even when the change is perceived as being positive.

Often we can feel bitter about our husband's lives seemingly staying the same (except for returning home to a raving partner where a sane version once stood). They still go off to work, keep up their friendships, maintain their hobbies, while we seem to have become mere shadows of our former selves.

So both partners need to be aware that even though our little bundles were meant to be a positive change, it's still highly stressful. It's even more stressful if the positive aspects of parenting seemed to skip your household and left you with the colicky and sleep-deprived version. Talk about which changes are the hardest for each other. Talk about any changes that are making you doubt your importance or role with the other.

4. **Choose equality in your relationship**. Most of us women enter a relationship with a male when we're pretty independent kind of gals. We're earning our own money, we have our own cars, and some of us have our own mortgages. So it's a right-hand turn of astronomic proportions when we find ourselves having to "ask" for money from our partners. We can feel embarrassed, controlled and disempowered. In some ways, it's as though in becoming a mother we have become our partner's "employee"!

It's of great importance that a woman feels as confident in spending the family income as her partner. Remember, just because the partner who stays home doesn't *earn* money, it doesn't make her job any less important, or less worthy. The woman is putting aside her own career to raise *the children that both of you created*. Which makes her as entitled to any incoming earnings as her partner. Otherwise, she might just say that she is more entitled to the children, since it was her "work" that fed, cleaned, clothed and nurtured them. And I'm guessing there isn't a partner on this planet who wants to "ask" for permission to hug his children any more than his partner wants to "ask" for money to buy them nappies, clothing and food. You're both equal. Both of your jobs are important. Respect each other for what you both contribute to the family.

The hardest part for me has been my husband's attitude. He thinks he is somehow now more important than me because he earns the money and I don't. It makes me so angry. I'm thinking of going back to work sooner than we'd planned just so I can stop feeling this way. SELINA, MOTHER OF TWO

5. **Remember who you both are (and aren't)**. Heaven help the couple where one member hoped their partner would somehow

magically morph into the ideal parent after the baby was born. In our mad dash to the parenting prize, sometimes we create babies with people we hope will meet our needs (and our baby's needs, too) but who have never shown any signs of being capable of either before! Having a baby means we have to make many, many changes. But rarely does it mean someone can have a personality exchange.

So, if we want our relationship to work, we need to accept our partner is still a person – with all the needs, wants and desires they always had – and work gently to change the parts necessary to be the best parent possible but also to stay in touch with as many parts of themselves as practical.

OK, so there are limits to "being the old you". Dads, even though you can't train for your footy team three nights a week and take all of Sunday for your "match day", you can probably train one night as well as an hour either side of your match on Sunday to get in some "me time". If yoga floats your boat and all weekend retreats are a thing of the past, it's possible you can still get to the 6:30pm class each Tuesday. If you liked sleeping in before – get over it because that's a luxury equivalent to a Chanel-diamond-encrusted disposable nappy.

Sit down once a week (or more regularly if you can) and write down together on the calendar how you will support each other getting "me time". But be realistic – it simply won't look anything like what it looked like before you had a baby. And if you can't cope with the idea that you're going to get less "me time" than in your pre-baby life – then you need to get help from a professional about whether you've made the emotional transition to parenthood. This isn't a criticism, sometimes many of us struggle with the transition, and it's better to get help now than allow your family to suffer.

In addition, if knowing who you are, or staying true to who you are, is an issue, you'd probably both get a great deal out of completing the "house and garden" activity in chapter eleven.

When Brad wouldn't give up his surf life-saving after the baby was born I was so jealous of all the time he was out having fun at the beach while we stayed at home. He said it was his "thing" and also served the community. A year later, when he hadn't changed, I just decided I would become a surf life-saver too. Now we both had our "thing" and our community service to divide equally. It really shocked him and forced us to make our "me time" more fair. I guess if you can't beat 'em, join 'em! KERRI, MOTHER OF THREE

5. **Steal yourself away from screens**. Possibly the only time you get to unwind and get close to each other is when you fall into bed at night. Don't make the mistake of losing this precious time to a meaningless TV series when the person lying next to you is the one who can truly make your life a thousand times better.

I'm often frightened by the women who can tell me more about what a fictional character in a TV show has done in the last week than they can about their partner. Similarly, thanks to Facebook, we can know about the moment-to-moment movements of a distant friend (yes, some people really think we want to know what they ate for breakfast…every day…), but not that our partner is having a tough time at work. Likewise, there'll be men out there who know every fixture for the next 10 weeks of their footy team's games (as well as who is injured/sidelined, etc) but have no idea what their wife's preferred coffee variety is.

Seeing couples out for dinner where they both keep looking at their smart phones instead of each other makes me incredibly sad – and then cranky. Don't be fooled – technology can lure us all in with the illusionary offer of an intimate relationship without any of the hassle. But this illusion has a high price – ultimately, when you need real support most, these illusionary relationships can't hold you and it's only a truly emotionally intimate relationship with your partner that can. They can also never share the real intimacy that comes from holding a baby of your combined creation in your arms.

So, declare whole days "screen free" times. If that's too much, get your fix in before 11am and then put it away for the rest of the day. People can wait to talk to you. Facebook posts will still be there tomorrow. But the relationship with you and your partner will quickly evolve back to "single" status if you don't pay it the attention it deserves. And I'm guessing you won't "like" that post.

6. **Find time to play together (and apart).** There's an old saying that I share with most couples I work with – "the couple who play together stay together". It speaks volumes for how we can really have the relationship that's sizzling hot rather than fizzling out.

Some mums I know have this mistaken belief that being a "good mother" involves sacrificing any joy (unless it's about her baby). In the short term it might help with all the baby turmoil, but ultimately it will make you "boring mum" *and* "boring partner". Remember how much kids engage and learn through play. The better we are at playing – with our kids and our partners – the better off the whole family is. It also teaches our kids how to get a balance between work and fun in their lives too, which is particularly important for those parents whose child seems more intense or anxious.

Go to the "house and garden" activity in chapter eleven and make sure you've included some fun factor in your world.

7. **Talk it up!** You're probably not surprised that communication is a pretty key ingredient in the recipe for a healthy relationship, but during the postnatal period, the significance factor of being able to talk to your partner increases ten-fold. Research has shown that new mothers with babies who cried for long periods had significantly more severe depressed symptoms if they were unable to confide in their partners[7].

But both partners need to step up to the communication plate here. The Bringing Baby Home Program[8] suggests that couples spend at least 20 minutes a day talking with each other. It directs couples to ask their partners questions that go beyond talk of hum-drum household stuff and baby babble.

But keep in mind, we all know what a conversation killer a critical response is. Same goes for minimising any problem our partner shares, or when we only show vague interest in what they're talking about. You know: "Oh... The baby cried for three hours straight... That's nice... Can you pass me the remote control..."

For dads especially – don't feel the need to solve every topic we talk to you about. Most of the time we kinda *know* the answer to our issue – but we just need another adult to share it with and to express it out loud (instead of it whirring around inside our heads). While men do prefer to problem-solve rather than problem-listen, for us women, the listening is often all that we need – so give us your listening ear or your helping hand, not your solutions.

For us mums – remember that we're usually light years ahead of most men in coping with strong emotions. We can sit with girlfriends and bawl our little eyes out, then make a cup of tea and move on. The same flood of tears would send many men into a fear frenzy ("what do I do with this woman??!!") and they'll just want to figure out how to "fix" the problem in their desperate hope it will stop our spooky feelings tirade. You'll usually fare better in communicating with males if you can save the emotional outbursts for a female confidante, then give your husband the toned-down version later on.

BUT...there will be times when the raw emotion of adjusting to new parenting can't be contained and it can't be regulated until the next coffee with a girlfriend. Sometimes too, there are issues that you don't even want to share with your BFF. And other times, our babies have been so tricky we haven't managed to have an adult conversation for days...At these times, dads, you simply need to deal with her strong emotion. Hold her. Listen. Reassure her. It *will* pass. Emotions always do. But try not to intellectualise her issue or "solve the problem" or it might well turn into an emotion the size of Mt Vesuvius. You've been warned.

Divorce. The natural flow-on effect when Eric complained his sleep was disturbed by their crying baby. Gina had been up nine times.

He said it was harsh.
She said he was lucky
to be alive.

217

8. **Halve up the household responsibilities**. Dads, as I said earlier, assuming that taking care of a baby is "easy" is a mistake. Firstly, because it's wrong. Secondly, because saying this to any new mum may well result in undesirable physical consequences – to *you* that is.

Don't let yourselves be sucked in by crazy society stereotypes. Even in our everyday language, we often define paid employment as "work" and mothering responsibilities as "not work". Don't believe me? Think about how many pregnant women are asked when they are "giving up work" and how often mothers of newborns are asked when they are "going back to work". Hilarious. I know of many women who go back to "work" just to get a break!

All of this means that we stand up – loud and proud – and declare that "caring for baby and traditional work roles are kinda equal". Right then. Now that's said, it means that any remaining tasks required to run a household are going to have to be equally divided too. And this includes housework. Research shows time and time again that when a new mother suspects she's holding up significantly more of her fair share in the housework stakes, it's her feelings about the relationship that get a bit dirty (and no dads, that's not of the sexy dirty kind…).

Make sure you get down to the nitty-gritty specifics of the housework division, too. Instead of a vague "You need to clean up more," try "Can you fill the dishwasher while I put a load of washing in the machine?" Many couples also find setting up a regular system for the household tasks is particularly effective. The dad might take on vacuuming, dusting and dishes while the mum can be in charge of cooking, general tidying, cleaning the bathrooms and the washing.

And dads, in all the sleep-frazzled states we often find

ourselves, when you are super-busy and overwhelmed by your work, most mums really only want you to do the grown-up thing of looking after *yourself.* This means simply picking up *your* own clothes, putting *your* own plate in the dishwasher, ironing *your* own shirts and generally putting away anything *you* get out to use. Not rocket science. When you leave stuff around we feel like you're treating us like a housekeeper, not your partner. And remember – housekeepers rarely put their hands up for bedroom action (X-rated movie versions excluded!).

9. **Learn how to fight (or have heated discussions) fairly**. We all know that parenting has brought with it many things, not least of which has been plenty of topics to disagree about – from circumcision to feeding on demand to who's doing (or not doing) their fair share – you could argue all day (if you weren't so exhausted to even speak).

Remember too that stress doesn't do much for our capacity to think calmly. Stress fires up the sympathetic nervous system and the sections of the brain that are linked to the "flight or fight" response. The rational parts of the brain get increasingly disengaged the more stressed out we are – hardly helpful when this is the very part we need in sorting out our relationship issues, but that's how it goes. So, if we're going to give ourselves the best chance of learning how to disagree with our partner, the best solution is to have a plan for how we want the discussion to go *before* the friction starts to rise.

I'd recommend the following as a safe starting point:
- **Pick your timing**. Baby's feeding time, a man's favourite football game and a sleep-deprived woman's first cup of coffee for the day are all times when raising an issue could result in WWIII. Try to schedule a couple of times a week where you

both commit to communicate about any big issues, perhaps after baby goes to bed. If there's no time, think about getting a babysitter even for a couple of hours to give you time to talk. The $40 babysitting fee to keep your relationship on track is worth thousands in the long run (and that's just in solicitors' fees!).

- **Fight nice**. Most problems in conflict arise from someone getting *mean*. You know – belittling, name calling, aggressive behaviour. In using these, your partner is likely to get angry, and then you'll just get a tirade of nasty comments right back at you. Result? Rapid escalation into a hurtful frenzy where the purpose becomes more about hurting your partner rather than searching for solutions. Agree not to swear at each other, belittle each other or get aggressive and you're well on your way to fighting more fairly.

- **Stick to the point**. Most people don't appreciate big generalisations about their behaviour ("you *never* think about what the baby needs") and you'll also lose any reasonable point you were trying to make because it's usually inaccurate. He probably *has* thought about the baby at some point! So keep to the exact issue you want to change ("you need to change his nappy when he wakes up in the morning").

- **Know when to call a "time out"**. If either of you has got to the point where you're so heated up your words are completely irrational or heavily hurtful, take a break. Don't get stuck on "I need to resolve this issue right now!" Because when communication is that heated, a resolution is the last thing you'll come to – other than to break up! Make a pact with each other that you need at least 20 minutes to calm down when a "time out" is called before starting the discussion up again.

- **Know when the disagreement is to do with *your* stuff**.
So, dads, if you're still struggling with intimacy because of
what you saw in the delivery room, she'd rather know the
truth than feel the pain of your excuses every time you avoid
touching her. Ladies, if you're anxious about being apart
from your baby, don't use lame excuses like "he doesn't seem
to settle with anyone else" to keep your baby constantly in
your arms and therefore never cuddling your partner. You
need to talk about your anxieties and work through them.

10. **Preserve the sanctity of sleep**. With a baby's arrival, sleep
suddenly becomes a hot commodity. I've known couples to offer
money or sexual favours just to get an extra couple of hours! And
while I'd steer away from the same barter system, it highlights
what desperate measures we'll resort to, all for a few extra zzz's.

And it makes sense. Ever known anyone who functions
better on repeated nights of sleep-deprivation? That's because
sleep deprivation is stressful and its effect on the brain is really
the same as the stress response – the logical, rational, decision-
making areas (ie the prefrontal cortex) start to shut down and
in its place you've got the subcortical "flight or fight" regions.
Which is why in our sleep-deprived state we're much more likely
to pick a fight or just want to run away from it all.

So, my advice is not to enter into competitions about who's
the most tired. Take it as a given that you're both exhausted and
that you both need help. If you can afford a babysitter, consider
hiring someone on a short-term, regular basis so that you and
your partner can catch up on rest. Or accept assistance from
family or close friends.

And *please* don't ever think that you have to both be there
for every moment with the baby. Don't be the couple where

both partners become exhausted because you both get up every time to your screaming baby in the night. Embrace the tag-team phenomenon and you'll never look back.

There's no shame in making adjustments to your parenting ideals or getting help so that you can both get more sleep. In fact, it's a responsible thing to do. The health of you and your baby require that you sort out the sleep so you don't want to opt out of parenting.

11. **Put the issue of sex on the table**. Woo hoo! Now we're talking – and no I didn't say have sex *on the table* – it's just the issue that needs to go there! (Rats, I hear you men say…) Sexual intimacy is important. But I hope you're not the type to be confused (or immature) enough to think that sex is the only type of intimacy that's important.

You see, in a healthy adult long-term relationship, sexual intimacy is an extension of the emotional intimacy you experience together. It's about working together, listening to each other, communicating about what you like (and don't like), trusting each other and sharing your innermost desires. If you can't do that outside the bedroom, I bet you can't do it *in* the bedroom. Or if you do, it's kind of like a "bonk session" which is actually one person getting their physical needs met, or a mutual masturbation session. And let's face it – we have our hands and plastic toys for that purpose, so revert to them and stop pestering your partner if that's all you're really looking for!

So, dads, if you want meaningful sex to be on the agenda, focus on gaining ground on all the areas that create emotional intimacy, too. Which means taking the following factors into account:

• **We're not *exactly* what we once were**. Our bodies have undergone changes of a magnitude to rival any fancy makeover show. We've been stretched and cut open, torn or pierced by needles, become milk-vending machines, had uterus contractions and those parts of us that were for "love making" have been ravaged by our "baby delivering". We really don't think our bodies are attractive. And when we don't find it attractive it's *really* hard to believe anyone else would. And when you salivate over 20-something models who've never borne children and then tell us we look just as amazing, the only word that comes to mind is "liar". So ditch the leering at other non-mothers and keep up the regular reminders that our post-baby body is still loveable because it truly is hard to believe.

- **When we say it hurts, it hurts**. Which is why the research repeatedly shows those of us mothers who experienced perineal tearing lag behind our intact mummy mates in resuming sexual activity. Same goes for those of us who had anal tearing or otherwise traumatic births – research shows we're still not keen on the whole shimmying up for sexual action even six months post-birth. Good news is though that by 18 months post-baby we're getting jiggy with it on par with our girlfriends again. So please, be patient…we'll get our sexual mojo back in time.

- **Don't go thinking we ought to be getting back in the sack by six weeks**. In fact, only around 50% of western women report they've done the deed at the six-week stage. The good news though is that this figure jumps to around 80% by three months and around 90% by six months (but make sure you keep the above point in mind)[9].

- **In case you hadn't guessed it, we can be quite hormonal in the post-birth period**. This seems to lead to excessive wetness around the tear ducts (our crying can rival Niagara Falls) but unfortunately a drying of the vaginal area. So it's not that you've stopped turning us on, we just might need a bit of lubing up (of the KY jelly kind) for a while.

- **Help us out with our emotional states to increase the bedroom stakes.** When we experience significant depression or anxiety in the post-birth period, we're likely to have lower sexual desire for up to 18 months. So make sure you notice signs when it's the emotional distress preventing the bedroom "undress" and encourage us to get professional support.

- **Help us to speak up.** It's well-known that western women are pretty reticent when it comes to talking about their postnatal sexual problems with health professionals. So, if you're keen to start up the sexual encounters, encourage us to seek help by agreeing to discuss it together with our GP or child health nurse.

HOW WE HONOUR OUR BABY'S FUTURE IN OUR CURRENT RELATIONSHIP

1. **We understand that we are role models.** For you to act with dignity and respect as you grow up, we need to show you how to do the same.
2. **We acknowledge that words can hurt.** We avoid saying things that are harmful. But if we slip up, we say "sorry" because you'll need to use that same word plenty of times in your relationships too.
3. **We agree there is no room for physical violence in our home.** Not now. Not ever. We hope this teaches you to keep the same standard in your own home.

4. **We respect the true meaning of the word "team"**. We will show you to work together to support those you love when they need it. Relationships that are about one person only end up with one person.

5. **We ditch perfectionism**. We neither strive for nor expect perfection from you or from each other. But we will model what genuine effort looks like, because no team survives without relationship energy and enthusiasm.

6. **We pursue praise**. We search for the positives in each other and within ourselves so you can learn to do the same in your relationships, including the one with yourself.

7. **We value the power of touch**. When words can't be found or there is nothing left to be said, we will show you how hugs can heal and how closeness can calm.

8. **We honour individuality**. We will model each day on how respecting our differences strengthens our togetherness. Because you too need to know how to value variations in your future relationships.

9. **We search for solutions not blame**. In showing you the power of focusing on possibilities we assist you in avoiding excuses for staying stuck.

10. **We prioritise**. In our love for each other you will see we give our best not our worst. In this way, we hope that one day you too will find that special someone to say – "there is no one I adore on this earth more than you". Not just when you get married, not just when you're creating a family, but every day of your lives. This is our promise to you.

Further reading

If you're keen to read more about how your relationships can blossom in the post-baby bedlam, take a look at these publications:

- Stacie Cockrell, Cathy O'Neill, Julia Stone and Rosario Camacho-Koppel – *Babyproofing Your Marriage: How to Laugh More and Argue Less As Your Family Grows.*
- John Gottman and Julie Schwartz Gottman – *And Baby Makes Three: The Six-Step Plan for Preserving Marital Intimacy and Rekindling Romance After Baby Arrives.*
- Trisha Ashworth and Amy Nobile – *I'd Trade My Husband for a Housekeeper: Loving Your Marriage after the Baby Carriage.*
- Michele Weiner Davis – *The Sex-Starved Marriage: Boosting Your Marriage Libido: A Couple's Guide.*
- John Gottman and Nan Silver – *The Seven Principles for Making Marriage Work: A Practical Guide from the Country's Foremost Relationship Expert.*

One last comment:

Regardless of the state of your relationship before you read this chapter, if you stick to these suggestions you should soon be all "gooey-gooey" for each other again even when you're exhausted from your baby "gaa-gaaing".

Our kids need us to sort our relationship problems out, not to run away from them, or to spend years living in misery. So, permission to book a dinner for two (in-house if necessary), pop open the champagne (even if you just have a sip), and toast what you're doing to give your little family some well-deserved harmony, now and in the future.

Ben and I decided to have a baby very early in our relationship. Looking back, it was too soon. We really didn't even know each other, so a baby just highlighted all the weaknesses in our relationship. But we both worked really hard to communicate better and respect the other person. There were some hard days, but we got there. And now we're even confident enough to have another baby together. My advice to all other couples is to get help when you need it and don't give up hope. If we can turn our relationship around, anyone can! REBECCA, MOTHER OF ONE

Chapter 8:

The other mothers. Handling your mother and mother-in-law.

My mother-in-law lives just close enough so that we don't clash on day-to-day issues.

She's somewhere deep in the Himalayan Mountains.

My mother-in-law tries so hard but she just doesn't get it. She buys the kids things that are the wrong size or for the wrong gender – I think because they were "on special". She gives me tips and ideas that seem bizarre – like bathing Sophie in vinegar, or mixing my breastmilk with some Weet-Bix so the baby will sleep longer at night. I never quite know what to say and I don't want to offend her, but I just wish she'd read some of the current books on babies and at least then we could kind of be on the same page. JENNY, MOTHER OF TWO

Bustling Beryl? Dominating Deirdre? More like Judgmental Judy? When baby arrives home, it seems these nanna types can simultaneously descend on us like a toxic tornado. And while I know there are some nannas who are more like a gift from heaven, based on the mere fact we *are* mere mortals – and hence slightly imperfect – any relationship, including the ones with our baby's nannas, will have *some* difficult times.

And there's plenty of difficult subjects on offer. Issues can range from baby-routine stand-offs (*the baby doesn't need to be fed just because it's three o'clock*) to silent feuds over baby clothing (*the baby is not always too hot, too cold, too exposed, too covered…*). Yep, there are ample opportunities for conversations as icy as the cold-pack on your episiotomy wound.

So I'll just avoid her then? Well…you would if you could. But chances are you're one of the 40% of new mums who will ask nanna to baby-sit – for an average of 2.5 hours per week – just to get done what needs to get done! Think meetings with bank managers, GP visits for your own war wounds, even just getting your hair done – possible *with* a baby, but typically *far* less stressful without.

So how about I just spend time with the nanna I do like? Yes, when it comes to nannas, they really weren't all created equal – with newbie mums reporting that baby brings them closer to their own mothers, but not their mothers-in-law. Actually, over 60% of us describe our relationship with our mother-in-law as simply "stressful"[1]. Which is probably why around 45% of us will turn to our own mums as the first port of advice and only 5% will tune into our mother-in-law's words of…umm… wisdom (or not)[2].

Well, she should just sort herself out. Maybe. But it's possible your relationship could be cheered up by a bit of your own changing. And don't forget – if you're miserable, she could well be, too. And it looks as though there's many a nanna who has been. As far back as Old Testament times, woman such as Rebekah (wife of Isaac) was complaining that her daughters-in-law were making her so miserable, she'd rather be dead! (Hmmm, hope your situation's not quite so dire...)

I felt awful inviting my mother around all the time while at the same time avoiding my mother-in-law as much as possible. Both of them had the same love for our baby, but it was me who couldn't cope with my mother-in-law. Around her I became a silent emotional wreck and I couldn't stand up for myself. I just avoided her and hoped my baby could eventually have her own relationship with her nanna that was more positive than mine! MICHELLE, MOTHER OF TWO

So what's the health of your nanna connection?

Perhaps one of the easiest tests for the seriousness of your "nanna problems" is how soon you turned to this chapter. If it was in a "Tazzie devil"-like frenzy I'm guessing your relationship isn't too pretty.

Actually, the general rule of thumb is this: how you get along AFTER baby's birth will be pretty similar to how you got along PRIOR to baby's birth (give or take a bit). If she regularly sparked paranoid, delusional and aggressive tendencies in you before, it's likely she still will. If you tolerated your differences and were generally pretty in tune with each other, you'll carry on doing so.

If you're not sure whether your relationship sits in the good, the bad or the ugly category, this quiz might help you decide whether you need to spend your very precious and oh-so-limited time on this chapter (or turn your attention back to figuring out why baby is crying…again…).

	Question	Answer A	Answer B
1	When nanna phones and suggests she drops over to help you with the housework, do you:	Snap back at her that you don't need her help and you're doing just fine (despite the 10 loads of dirty washing piled up and the lack of clean plates in the cupboards).	Delightedly accept her offer. You can put up with her thinking she knows everything for a few hours if it means getting on top of some much-needed housework.
2	When you are showing nanna the new nipple shields you're using for breastfeeding, does she:	Tell you your ideas are ridiculous because those "fancy gadgets" weren't used in her day.	Applaud modern inventions and support your choice to feed your baby in whatever way is most comfortable for you.
3	When nanna invites you over for dinner AGAIN after you've told her hundreds of times that your baby can't sleep in other people's homes, do you:	Tell her she's got the brain of a pea and should stop thinking of what she wants and start taking more notice of what you and the baby need.	Politely remind her AGAIN that you're still not in a position to be out with the baby at night and suggest you catch up for lunch at your place instead.
4	When you ask nanna to mind the baby for an hour while you race to the shops to get milk and bread, does she:	Tell you she can't possibly fit it in because she's already booked in to play tennis and then meet the girls for lunch, which really will tire her out for the rest of the day. Probably tomorrow too…	Tell you she's got a busy morning but would love to see you in the afternoon.

5	When you get home to the "surprise" of a completely clean house because nanna has let herself in with the spare key and "helped you out", do you:	Shout a few choice words at her, change the hiding place for the spare key, and mess up the house so it looks like it's yours again.	Tell her that you sincerely appreciate what she has done, but that you'd feel far more comfortable if she asked your permission in the future before entering your home.
6	When you ask nanna to purchase a few essential items for you at the shops, does she:	Return home with items not on your list because she decided she knew which brands and items were better for you than you did.	Buy precisely what was on the list because she realises that if *you* asked for them they must be what *you* wanted.
7	When nanna comes over to help you out with the baby for a few hours, does she:	Seem to want to take over every task, or adds suggestions on how you can do everything differently or better or more quickly.	Step back and congratulate you on all that you're doing well, but then thoughtfully step in to help you when she can see you're struggling or when you ask for help.

What do your answers mean?

Look at your answers for questions 1, 3 and 5: these are about how well *you* are doing as the daughter or daughter-in-law.

1. For those who answered mainly As: you probably need to look a little harder at yourself and pay a bit more attention to how you react to dear ol' nanna! You are possibly a little oversensitive, probably a bit defensive and need the ideas in this chapter to help soothe a few relationship sore points.

2. For those who answered mainly Bs: you are probably managing nanna quite well (give or take a few moments of crazy rage about her behaviour). Read this chapter to see why you're doing so well and how to keep it that way.

Look at your answers for questions 2, 4, 6 and 7: these answers are about how well nanna is doing in her role.

1. For those who answered mainly As: you are likely to have a tricky nanna on your hands. Hold on for the ride, because for a range of reasons (outlined below) she may well pose quite a problem in your role as a mother. It would be a great idea if you could *both* read this chapter and get some ideas on how to change things around to be more supportive of each other.

2. For those who answered mainly Bs: you sound as though you probably have a well-rounded nanna in your life. Lucky you! Give her an extra big hug next time you see her and perhaps read the chapter to help you keep it this way and identify any smaller issues before they become big ones.

As soon as she walks in the door, I can just feel her judging me. I begin to doubt the things I was feeling confident about doing just moments before she arrived! It's just so hard having her around. I have to admit it, I do avoid her. BELINDA, MOTHER OF ONE

Is it her? Or is it you? Who's really the problem here?

My grandson was born in January so when he was a couple of months old my daughter and son-in-law bought a bottle warmer for the colder months. The first time I used it I took the bottle

out of the warmer and said to myself, "I hope it's the right temperature"'. Overhearing this, my wise son-in-law (first time father of a three-month-old baby) pulled up his sleeve to expose his wrist and said, "Denise, if you put a drop of milk on your wrist you can see if the milk is too hot". With this, I smiled and responded with, "Wow Benny, thanks for the tip. I haven't heard that one before."

I find it quite humorous that my daughter and son-in-law seem to think that even though I'm a first-time grandmother, they have forgotten that I brought up two babies – my daughter being one of them. It seems she has forgotten that I too have been pregnant (with her), given birth (to her), brought her home as a newborn baby and raised her safely and successfully. She has forgotten that she was once my baby. I have even reminded her that I do have some knowledge of parenting by saying, "Please see exhibit A" (pointing to her).

Every stage of my grandson's development comes with "wise words and knowledge" from my daughter and son-in-law informing me of the way things should happen and what I should expect. Two years later (things haven't improved), I now just smile to myself and respond with "Oh really?" DENISE, MOTHER OF TWO, GRANDMOTHER OF TWO

Remember, the difficulties between you both – whether they be on the scale of an international disaster, or just over small stuff – are a product of what the *two* of you bring to the relationship. So look at yourself – *your* level of sensitivity about yourself, your home and your baby will have a huge impact on how you cope with nanna's attitude, comments and behaviour. On the other hand, *her* sensitivity about her role in life, her own success (or not) as a mother and her relationships will have a huge impact on how she behaves towards you.

To determine what you both bring to the relationship, you'll need to:

a. allocate yourself to a "Mother Type" presented in chapter eleven (and don't forget to ask your partner or a girlfriend for their opinion too);

b. allocate nanna to a category below. If you're brave, ask her which one she thinks she is too!

The Nanna Sorting Exercise

The Critical Nanna

Sick of hearing "*I wouldn't do it that way, dear*" or "*Oh no, I don't think the baby likes that*"? Yes, this type of nanna has a single-channelled strategy – to find fault in how you do, umm, everything! Oh, unless it's her way or her idea, of course. But don't expect just an oral onslaught – that's far too obvious. This nanna has been honing her stealth-like systems since your baby bump blossomed. She's plotted to buy different brands, to purchase different products, to dress baby in different outfits, because her ways are just, well, better! She'll even have those little old sarcastic compliments in her artillery, like "It's great you find time to get to the gym even with a really unsettled young baby who clearly needs you soo much." OUCH!

I felt like my Mum watched my every move. It was like she had NO confidence that I could do this whole mother thing myself. Actually, I didn't have much confidence in me either, but I knew I'd just have to find my way, one day at a time. Even when I told her not to be so critical, she denied she was, so nothing really changed. It's easier now that Ellie is older, or maybe it's just that I'm more confident in myself. JACKIE, MOTHER OF ONE

The Comparer Nanna

Do the words "*Benny was doing it by this age*" or "*I'm sure Olivia never cried so much*" sound familiar? Yes, this type of nanna will find any other child – even some distant relation's baby – who walked faster, slept more soundly, breastfed more calmly and had pooey nappies of better consistency than yours. She's probably just trying to identify your baby's developmental stage, but the message that rings loud and clear in your ears is this: in the family pecking order your child is a bit of a dud.

Does she really think I want to hear all about how amazing Jack is and how much my son, Gus, lags behind? What is wrong with that woman? The nasty side of me is desperate to let her know how unfavorably SHE compares to all the other nicer mothers-in-law out there and then see how she feels! JENNY, MOTHER OF TWO

The Delusional Nanna

Ever wondered if nanna's under some delusion that YOUR little bundle is actually HERS? She might pop up at all times of day, whisk the baby out of your arms and say in a soothing tone that sends *your* blood boiling, "*Don't worry, nanna is here*". She'll not only find fault with what you've done and suggest you do it her way (message – your baby would be better under her care), but will also seem to take over what you're doing and make you feel like you're not really needed (additional message – the baby might actually be better off without you entirely).

My mother-in-law didn't have an easy life with her first husband

who was abusive. So when Ben was born, it was like she wanted to relive being a new mother again but with MY son! I understood why she was doing it, and I tried to be patient, but it still annoyed the crap out of me. ANGELA, MOTHER OF TWO

The Super-Nanna.

Is there something bizarrely Mary Poppins-like about your baby's nanna? Does it seem like she is just an unlimited supply of help, support, advice, wisdom and all things just super-dinky and amazing with a cherry on top? Yet does it feel that every time she tidies the room as soon as you walk out that the real message is *"You're just not capable of cleaning the house yourself"*, and when she calms your baby within seconds of arriving (who has screamed all day for you) there's a hint of smugness in that little smile she gives you? Oh yes – you might one day get the hang of being a mother, but you'll never achieve her picture-perfect parenting standards.

My mum is an amazing woman. She's good at everything and she's so confident. She raised four of us as a single mum and here I was not coping with one baby. Sometimes I just needed to sit in my unclean house with my imperfect self and not invite her over. I just couldn't cope with her telling me one more time how easy the whole mothering thing was. OLIVIA, MOTHER OF THREE

The Laid-Back Nanna.

Frustrated by her *"It'll be right"* attitude? A little over the *"let it all come naturally"* approach? Research, science and books containing sound advice aren't for this type of nanna – they're all seriously overrated, don't you know? This type of nanna leaves you wondering how she raised either you or your partner (depending on whose mother she is) without either of you befalling serious harm. She's absolutely, 100% sure that everyone – including you in your worst baby-bedlam state – can be best supported by doing, well...nothing much at all!

My mother-in-law had grown up on a farm and she'd raised my partner on a farm too. So they both approached the care of a baby in what I can only assume is how a cow looks after a calf! It was pretty much a "fend for yourself attitude", which meant any anxiety I had about anything to do with Millie's wellbeing just sent them both into hysterics. I felt unsupported by them both. Thank goodness for my mothers group who made me feel normal.
BRITTANY, MOTHER OF THREE

The Look-After-Me Nanna

Wondering whether nanna has registered that *you're* the one adjusting to newbie mum chaos? Heard the words, "*I'd love to help but I just don't have the energy. Why don't you come over here and help me with my shopping instead?*" Yes, this type of nanna really can't see past her own needs or her own situation. She might deal with this with regular tearful outbursts: "I just don't see you half as much as I used to" (duh – that's because you had a caesarean and still can't drive – she needs to come to you). Or she might get more stroppy: "*I think you're obsessed with that baby*" (what? I'm still in hospital and my baby's in the NICU...!). Either way, unless you place her at the top of your attention and adoration list, she's not going to be a happy chappy.

I remember my mother just couldn't see that I needed to be settled at home at night in order that I could settle my baby. She was always inviting herself for dinner or expecting us to be at her house. When I didn't give in to her constant demands she would cry over the phone and tell me how much she missed the baby. She just couldn't stop making it all about her. I don't think she really cared about me or the baby at all. KAREN, MOTHER OF ONE

The Zero Boundaries Nanna

Your house? Your personal space? Whatever! All fair game as far as these "lovely ladies" are concerned. These nannas presume they can do as they please in your life – whenever and wherever they see fit. What's yours is hers, including your home, your partner and possibly the baby! Don't think a locked door helps – these grandmothers will find a way to let themselves into your home and clean your entire house! Plus your bedsheets. Oh, and they'll rearrange your baby's clothes drawers too. And then expect you to just be so absolutely and entirely *grateful* for all that's been done. Then sulk when you're not.

I'd spent most of my marriage trying to keep my mother-in-law from interfering in our lives, but I just didn't have the strength to do it after my first baby was born. It felt like she took over everything. I lost all my confidence and I thought I was a hopeless mother. When we had our second daughter I had more strength and I put in more boundaries. She didn't like it and it was hard to put up with her "drama queen" reactions, but at least I felt more in control. JULIE-ANN, MOTHER OF TWO

The Absent Nanna

Umm…problems? No chance…she's still not actually even met the baby. These grandmothers can be clear in their need to be absent: "*I've done my time with babies, I don't need to do it again*", or more elusive: "*We might be able to drop over some time this year*

239

but we're pretty busy". Whichever way it's said, the message is the same – you and your baby just aren't, well, important.

My mother-in-law visited the hospital once when I had my first baby and that was probably the only time in the first year when she saw her. She is basically a once-a-year kind of nanna: Christmas and maybe birthdays. I've just come to terms with it because there's no way of changing her. KYLA, MOTHER OF ONE

The Well-Rounded Nanna

Held you in her arms while you wept? Helped you sort out your breastfeeding dramas? Made you feel like you could actually *do* this whole mothering thing? For some lucky mothers, we'll have scored the well-rounded nanna in our lives.

This nanna combines all of the best characteristics of the other nanna types. She is emotionally balanced enough to understand that we are individuals and to want us to achieve our own independence and confidence in parenting. She doesn't think she's perfect, but rather she meets her own deficiencies with a smile and a determination to do better next time. AND she does it all without blaming others. She will do her best to be there for us when we need her and support our decisions – even if she wouldn't choose to do it the same herself. Basically, this type of nanna rocks!

My mother has been my saviour and I could not possibly put into words how much help she has provided. She has been a mountain of support for me, both during the last trimester of the twin pregnancy and after the babies were born. I cannot thank her enough for her support and I don't know what I would do without her. JENNY, MOTHER OF THREE

I couldn't have done it without my mother. Not just what she taught me on a practical level, but what she made me feel on an emotional level. She really wanted me to feel confident and to feel like I knew what I was doing. Looking back, she'd been preparing me to be the best mum I could be from the time I was born.
ERICA, MOTHER OF TWO

So do our styles just clash?

If you are a grandparent – maternal or paternal – who never bites your tongue, never says the opposite of what you really mean, never pretends to approve when you don't, or never in any way tiptoes around your highly sensitive adult children, please contact me at once. I want to learn from you! INTERNET MESSAGE POSTED ON WWW.GRANDPARENTS.COM

No doubt your classification highlighted some "interesting" facts. Additionally, I hope your reaction to your own parenting type also emphasised some factors for reflection. You've probably become aware there are some "needs" in your nannas and in yourself that can make adjusting to baby a little, well, "tricky".

1. **When you're both the type that needs regular reassurance.** If the confidence boat left you or nanna up the creek without a paddle, time can get super tough when a new baby arrives. If you're *both* caught up in a confidence crisis you can predict a full-sized anxiety festival: decisions are impossible to make and nobody's sure what on earth to do. Everyone's either crying about how hard it all is, or desperately dialing the local baby experts for advice.

2. **When you're both the type that "needs to be needed"**. Do you or nanna float your self-importance boat by hoping people can't cope without you? Do you both silently wish people couldn't make a decision without you or perhaps couldn't manage life in any sensible way unless you're at the helm? If so, a baby addition means you're both in for stormy seas. Nanna might take over anything and everything so that your confidence never builds enough to cope without her. But if you *both* "need to be needed", it can be quite a show of the put-down variety – with you both trying to make the other look less, well, competent, so they neeeed you. No, no – you need me. *Hilarious* – unless this is your experience of course.

I don't think mum really wanted me to grow up. She never did any paid work and seemed to get all of her identity from being a mum. She always fussed over us and we really had very few responsibilities as kids. It felt good at the time, but as I grew up I realised I really lacked the skills to be a responsible adult, which was a problem when my baby arrived! I think she liked it that way. Because it meant I was always asking her for help and advice and she could continue to "mother" me. EMMA, MOTHER OF THREE

3. **When you're both the type that needs everything 100% right**. Sort of doing kinda average? Cruising along even though you're unshowered and your house is a mess? Not on your Nelly! You're absolutely convinced that unless you're 100% perfectly performing your chosen area of focus you're a failure! If your nanna's need to feel "right" outweighs the need for you to feel "competent", it can look like a take-over bid on your entire life. When you *both* work this way it can end up in some feisty

fireworks aimed at each other. Unfortunately, at times your need to be right will outweigh the more important need of getting along.

4. When you're both the types that get stuck in happiness traps. Traumatic birth? Look on the bright side! A baby with colic? Things could be worse! Yes, life has only two piles: "just peachy" or "just not discussed". Negative feelings – ooh, they're for weirdos – so snap out of them. OK? It can certainly be hard to share the ups and downs of mothering with a permanently positive nanna. It's better if you're *both* this way inclined, then life can just be one dandy moment after another! Well at least that's what you'll tell each other anyway…Enjoy!

5. When you're both the type that need to be "looked after". You're busy? I'm busier – so help me out. You're tired? I'm exhausted – so come over and let me sleep. Yep, you can always manoeuvre situations to always seem worse off or in need of more attention that anyone else. If your nanna's need to be looked after arises because she believes it's other people's "duty" to do so, it can be achingly annoying. But do refrain from writing "just grow up" on her fence! The most enthralling combination – if you like your dark humour – is when you *both* want the other person to care for you. You should be looking after *me*. No, no – *you* should be looking after *me*. *But I need help. Well I need more help*…Superb watching really, unless you're in the real-life show of course.

6. When you're both the types that prioritise "looks" over "connections". Just gave birth? Yep – but no photos until my hair's done, OK? Babysitting duty? Might be late because I'm

243

getting my nails done. If it's *you* who's obsessed with appearance, it can drive well-rounded nannas up the wall. She'll probably struggle silently, but inside she'll want to ditch your fancy shoes and makeup with the baby's dirty nappies. But if you're *both* this way inclined, it *can* be funny to watch. Your determination to outdo each other can result in masses of makeup, sky-high stilettos and slink satin gowns – all for a…family backyard BBQ?!

How do you better connect two different mother generations?

My "top tips" to you and to nanna separately are contained in the next section. Photocopy them. Pin them on your corkboard or stick them on your fridge.

The interesting one is the "combined tips". If you can *both* agree to these principles as well as your own, you're likely to navigate this first year with a little less hostility and loads more harmony.

But remember, while top tips are great, they're always better if you dedicate yourselves to understanding each other's world. So here's some information to hopefully boost-up the knowledge barometer – about each other.

If there was one thing I wanted from my mother-in-law it was just to be nice to me. I know it sounds simple and maybe pathetic, but that's all I wanted. If I stuffed up, I wanted encouragement not sarcasm. If I was overwhelmed, I wanted support not criticism and when I occasionally got it right, I just wanted some acknowledgement. Is that really too much to ask? MOLLY, MOTHER OF ONE

The shift in financial burdens over time

My mother always treats any work I do as a bit of an unimportant hobby that I "indulge" myself in. Yeah right. Who wants to pack shelves and deal with crappy bosses for 25 hours a week. I do it so we can afford to live in a safe area for our kids and send them to a good school. There's nothing about my work that is either fun or "indulgent". JACKIE, MOTHER OF TWO

The contribution of male and female earnings to the household budget is light years' away from how it looked in previous generations. Recent statistics suggest that double the number of women are now in the workforce compared to the 1950s and 1960s. The main reason for this? Women declare the answer is quite simple really – they can't afford not to[3].

ADVICE TO NANNAS:

- Re-read the last few words of the previous paragraph. Many women aren't deserting their babies so early in their little lives because they desperately want to – it's an economic necessity. Without knowing her household budget, you really don't know what economic factors are driving her life decisions.

- If deep down you still think she should feel guilty about her return to paid work, then don't worry – whether she wants to work or not, guilt is part of any mother's return-to-work package.

- Where possible, spend your energy supporting this stressed-out, guilt-ridden mother and avoid making her life harder. Even if you don't want to (or can't) help out with child-care, most mothers I know would never knock back a frozen lasagna in their fridge, and none would complain about a bunch of flowers acknowledging how hard they're working.

245

The right to education and to work

Sound the horns, put up the streamers, kick up your heels (if your pelvic floor muscles can take it). Believe it or not girls, there IS a shift toward working mothers being more "accepted" in society! While men of the '70s, '80s and '90s thought we were just focusing on "fashion" as we transitioned from bellbottoms to mullet haircuts to minimalism, we were actually gaining massive momentum! On asserting our right to work, to receive payments in our own right and to putting to use the training we received prior to having children.

University statistics show that in 1970, only 9.1% of students who earned a bachelor's degree in business were women, compared to 50% by 2002. The male-female ratio in higher education has been steadily moving in favour of the females ever since 1970 and we have steadily increased our numerical advantage ever since. Who's a clever girl then?

Additionally, women in the 1970s would marry (and have children) within one year of graduating, whereas by the 2000s we'd given ourselves another four years in the boardroom before creating little munchkins in the bedroom[4]. Give any women four years at anything, and she's going to be carving a pretty nifty pathway.

ADVICE TO MOTHERS:

Breathe deeply and stay calm.

- Nanna may not have moved with the times enough to know that you *can* be a great mum *and* have a career. All of her social networks would have reinforced it was either "right" to be at home, or certainly put a career on the back-burner and support the man's career.
- She may also be slightly jealous, perhaps harbouring some

deep-seated frustration at never realising her own dreams of having a role other than as a mother. Or taking a role that didn't reflect the education she received.

- Trust yourself in your decision-making and know that on the whole, our society is getting better (I know we're not there just yet) at supporting women to make the choice that best suits them too. Only you can know which pathway is the right one for you as a mother.

The role of partners

Every time my husband even lifted a finger, my mother-in-law would comment on how amazing he was. It didn't matter that I'd done everything else, I didn't get one bit of praise. He cooked dinner one night for us and the way she went on you'd think he'd solved the problem of world poverty. I didn't handle it very well and sulked all through the meal. It got worse too – every time she praised him from then on, I let her know all the things he hadn't done. It just made me look like a brat. I keep hoping I'll handle her more maturely on her next visit.
CONNIE, MOTHER OF ONE

Unfortunately, for mothers in the 1970s, transitioning to increasing equality in work and education didn't mean parallel shifts on the domestic front. Housework duties stayed strangely outdated, almost as though the increased hours in study or paid work didn't "count" for the female workers.

And while we modern women still do the lion's share of the housework, we do expect (quite rightly) more from our partners than the women of the last generation. But this can leave our mothers or mothers-in-law shaking their heads – perhaps out of envy! In any case, they're not always positive about us encouraging – OK sometimes incessantly nagging – our men to be as familiar with the laundry duties as they are with the internet.

ADVICE TO NANNAS:
- Remember that women and men of today will not have the roles you and your husband did. And isn't that a good thing?
- Please don't heap never-ending praise on the new father who simply does his fair share around the house, unless you sprout equal praise on the women who – as statistics continue to tell us – probably do more.
- And please don't tell any new mother she's soooo lucky that her partner helps her at all. She's not lucky. She deserves it. She works really hard too.

The media

You can bet nanna never worried about her mothering mistakes being broadcast to thousands via a Facebook post. Or that sharing a funny incident – by some innocent tweet – could end up causing a media sensation – headline: *Mother pees her pants at local supermarket.* (Ahhhh! I just sneezed OK! The pelvic floor wasn't up for that yet!) And no other generation has had to experience the same bombardment of information from the media as our generation of mothers. We can't compare ourselves to JUST the other normal mothers in mothers group any more, we have all the celebrities you can name touting their post-baby figures on the news and the magazines.

ADVICE TO MOTHERS:
- Without this media madness, nanna's main avenue for mothering advice would have been her own mother. It's not

too big a leap then to think she'll have spent much of her life looking forward to passing on her wisdom in the same way with her daughter or daughter-in-law. This isn't just sentimentalism.

- If nanna feels her advice is not accepted unquestioningly, she fears you're dismissing her as having no valid place left in the world. So be aware and be sympathetic about what an enormous loss this will be to her.

- Listen when you can. Don't always dismiss her ideas – she probably really does have some helpful words of wisdom to share.

- And always be kind in letting her know if you've chosen to follow someone else's opinion other than hers.

Parenting fashion cycles

Brace yourselves ladies, but here's some information than might blow you away: up until eleven years ago, the Bugaboo pram didn't exist! And get this: the digitally-screened baby monitor wasn't even mainstream until around 2009! Actually, if you can imagine it, there are far more important changes in recent years than that – 15 years ago smacking was still being advocated by some child behaviour "experts" to help parents manage their kids. Parents could only visit their sick children in hospital twice a week until the 1960s. In the 1950s only around 5% of fathers attended their child's birth. Mums were advised to put babies to sleep on their tummies in the 1970s and in the 1950s and 1960s formula feeding had received so much positive press that around 60% of babies were exclusively bottle fed.

When we become parents, we can get caught in believing that whatever we do now must be "right" – automatically labelling any previous generation's parenting approaches as "unsafe", "dangerous" ,"unhealthy" or just plain *wrong*! Remember when grandma mothered the way she did, it was with *the best of intentions.* When we declare their methods as being "ridiculously unsafe" we only leave our mother or mother-in-law in a position where they have to either:

a. admit putting their much-loved child in danger – and who would want to do that!

b. deny that there was any danger in the method and "poo poo" the latest research, describing it all as "nonsense, because you turned out just fine"!

So it's probably best if you avoid pushing her into this thorny corner.

ADVICE TO MOTHERS AND NANNAS:

This is all about acceptance. Acceptance that:

a. You are doing the best you can do at any particular time given the knowledge that you have.

b. You did the best in the past with what you knew then.

c. And remember – the current way we parent will one day be "outdated" too. Let's hope our kids don't criticise us too much for it...

My daughter was quite angry with me when she found out she was bottle-fed as a baby. She didn't want to accept that I had done it on the advice of the medical staff. I did it for her! She wasn't gaining weight and she was my first baby, so of course I listened to the medical specialists. But I think she felt I let her down. I wish she could understand that the information we had was different back then. All she can do is push articles my way that say "slow weight gain in babies is no indication to stop breastfeeding". I want to keep screaming, "Yes – but this information is dated 2014 –nobody showed me this in 1980!" But I hold my tongue. I don't think she'll get it until her kids have their babies! GLENDA, MOTHER OF TWO, GRANDMOTHER OF ONE

TOP 10 TIPS FOR NANNA

1. **Enter with caution**. If you've been trusted enough to be given a set of keys to her home, use this privilege wisely. She really doesn't want you in her home when she's not there – even if you do have the best of intentions for being there.
2. **Give warning**. Don't drop in without calling first and give adequate notice, particularly if your last unannounced drop-in was met with an unenthusiastic response.
3. **It's her baby**. Maybe you *do* know more about a newborn baby then she does. But that's not the point. To be the best mother for her baby she needs to feel connected and confident. Which means you need to step back and allow her to do it her way and tell her she's doing well. Hard to do, but fundamentally important.
4. **Share the love, not the advice**. Time and time again, research shows new mums want and need emotional support from their mothers and mothers-in-law far more than they desire practical advice . And avoid giving "unsolicited advice" (ie advice she hasn't asked for). Mothers across the world are united in viewing this type of advice as unhelpful.
5. **Her house, her rules**. Remember that what is right for you and the rules you live your life by are perfectly acceptable and fabulous, but don't get caught out in thinking that she must live as you do. As TV personality and psychologist Dr Phil concisely suggests, "You are a guest in their marriage and a guest in their home. You have to fold into their rules and their lives if you want to be welcome there."

251

6. **Remember her vulnerability**. Keep in mind that there is **no** topic more sensitive to a new mother than "Am I doing a good job?" Always take this vulnerability into account and choose your battles very carefully. If in doubt, say something you think might make her feel *better* about herself, never *worse*.

7. **Think first**. Be careful you don't turn your own mothering experience into "the glory years" where you seem to have forgotten being overwhelmed, frightened and unsure yourself. Don't be the nanna who declares she soothed all cries within seconds, or whose baby slept through the night from day one. Even if it's true – honestly, what are you going to get from sharing that information other than a newbie mum who feels she's a floundering failure in your eyes.

8. **Support the partnership**. No baby is better off with warring parents. If your grandchild's mother is in a good relationship, help it stay that way. If there are issues, support them to get help. Hold your tongue if you need to. Don't be the wedge that drives them apart.

9. **Find your own tribe**. Grandparents need their tribe as much as a new mother. Keep up your own friends, and make new ones through websites dedicated to linking you up. The better connected you are, the easier moments of frustration will be.

10. **Use technology**. Get savvy with the world that exists online. Try: www.aarp.org; www.grandmagazine.com; www.grandparenting.org; www.grandparents.com.; www. grandparentsapart.co.uk; www.grandparentsasparents.org. Don't forget too: your grandchildren will grow up assuming everyone can communicate by email or text message, so work on your Facebook profile, and figure out how to be a "Granny tweeter". Unless you keep up, you'll end up missing out on a key way to connect with your grandchildren in the future.

TOP 10 TIPS FOR MOTHERS MANAGING THEIR MOTHERS

1. **Remember it comes from love**. OK, so her behaviours annoy you – big time – but deep down she's probably doing them because she loooves your baby. She's just a little preoccupied right now on what she needs and forgotten that it's actually *your* needs that are important if your baby is going to be best cared for.

2. **Set some worries aside**. Despite any of her apparently delusional attempts for the baby to love *her* more it won't happen. The love between a mother and child is not breakable by any of nanna's try-hard tactics.

3. **This could all be a blessing**. Unless nanna is abusive, all behaviours can usually be cast in a positive light if you dig really deep. Sometimes really, *really*, deep. So, if she's the nanna type who chooses to be missing in action, then perhaps it's for best: who needs someone around who doesn't want to be there? If she's a little over-the-top, then who knows when an emergency might require her ability to "just take over" for a little bit? It's easy to see the negatives, but better for everyone if we can try and see the positive, too.

4. **Stand up for yourself**. Nanna's needs are important. But not more important than yours or your family's. You have the right to run your home and care for your baby in the way that best suits your family's values.

5. **Guide her behaviour**. Research has told us this for years – everyone changes faster if they're told what *to do* rather than what *not to do*. So let her know the roles you'd like her to have – helping you with the grocery shopping, making a few extra lasagnas. Popping over so you can pop off for a nap...

253

6. **Rally your partner**. Particularly if your issues are more with his mother than yours, *he* needs to step up and be assertive. If you're the only one asserting the ground rules, her mind starts to believe *he* doesn't agree with you. Stay a team. No nanna can conquer a confident couple!

7. **Get solution focused**. Think "having a conversation" rather than "hoping for an ESP connection". To get solutions, you have to be clear on the concerns. So present them to her – be civil but be definite. Talk them through and come up with clear solutions that sort out your roles.

8. **Don't limit the "love options"**. So nanna drives *you* crazy. Problem is, your baby might end up thinking she's the bee's knees. A child is better prepared for this crazy world with maximum love connections, so only limit your *baby's* contact if you've exhausted all other avenues. Perhaps the baby's dad can spend time with baby and nanna instead of you. You might only see her every...century.

9. **Keep her informed**. Most nannas aren't twits. Most want what's best for baby too. Give her credit for what she *is* likely to know – remember she did have at least one baby herself! But when her knowledge base is a little outdated, give her brief handouts on important facts and research regarding how to care for your baby.

10. **Don't sweat the small stuff**. So she fusses more than you do. She swaddles the baby differently too. Try not to create relationship mayhem over minor matters. Your baby will suffer less from adjusting to minor differences in care techniques than from a family who has declared internal warfare.

MY TOP TIPS FOR YOU AND NANNA

If you judge people, you have no time to love them.
MOTHER THERESA

Here are some quick reminders for you both:

1. **It's NOT a competition**. You can both be amazing mothers, even if you happen to do things differently.

2. **"Being family" doesn't permit "being rude"**. Don't make the mistake of treating strangers with more kindness than your kinship network. Family deserves respect and politeness at the very least.

3. **Accept individuality rather than judging differences**. You're not the same. You never will be. No two people are. You deserve to be you, and so does she. Nobody's better than another. Just different.

4. **Choose to forgive**. Hatred is unhelpful at best and destructive at worst. Adjusting to your new roles brings stress. Stress brings errors – in behaviours and in communications. Give each other some grace and some space when needed. And use the word "sorry" when necessary – grown-ups regularly forget they can use that word too.

5. **Never underestimate the power of a kind word**. In the heat of relationship friction, a kind word is like a cool glass of tonic. Heart rates get lowered, tensions get tapered, and emotional wounds are mended. Use them often.

6. **Sort out your own issues – don't blame someone else**. Being adult is about taking responsibility. If you're anxious, demanding, needy, depressed or otherwise needing some psychological shifting, make an intervention happen. As soon as possible. For everyone's sake.

7. **Choose to learn something new**. Most people know things you don't. Chances are if you take the time to learn about each other's values and behaviours, you'll probably be more tolerant of your differences.

8. **Save your energy**. Anger at each other helps you by making you feel...umm...angry? Not much else. If you're hurt, work it through and then let it go. Let the people and places that inspire you take up your brain space, not issues that just rile you up.

9. **Sometimes relationships need a heroine**. This means one of you has to "woman up" and be the wiser person. One of you has to make the first move, be the first to compromise in order to heal the relationship. Swallow your pride and be that person. Think about what the future holds, particularly for your baby, if you don't sort out your differences.

10. **Nurture yourself**. Sometimes there's just nothing you can do to fix a relationship with someone else. But you can always nurture the relationship with yourself. Use your kind words, take some deep breaths. Love who you are, and seek connections with those who do love you, even when others don't.

How does your own relationship survive this nanna nonsense?

If you weren't already arguing over the big questions of baby-raising, the topic of "the Nannas" provides many couples with copious material for caustic quarrels. As Susan Forward (author of *Toxic In-Laws: Loving Strategies for Protecting Your Marriage*) says, "When you have in-law problems, you have marriage problems."

So to help avoid ongoing partnership problems, here are my suggestions:

1. *Your* **relationship's the winner**. Yep – no need for debate. Quite simply the relationship between an adult couple trumps the one between and mother and her adult child *every time*… It's just that nanna may not think so! But it goes both ways, so:

- **Be sure *you* aren't prioritising your own mother over your partner**. Your mother may have words of wisdom, but leaving your partner out means he could well end up walking out. Seek out his advice wherever possible. And if you and your mum have come up with some awesome ideas, at least run them past him and let him be a part of the decisions for *his* baby.

- **Be sure *he* isn't stepping back from his own mother's meddling madness**. If his mother's behaviour hurts you, then it's up to him to step in and step up on your behalf. He needs to tell her assertively and calmly to modify her behaviour, or risk reducing the contact.

2. **Don't force anyone to be an orphan**. Unless your nanna is super-destructive to you both, don't ask your partner to cut all ties. It's mean and it's harmful. Imagine never seeing your own parents again if you loved them very much. As difficult as nanna can be, it's always better to figure out a solution, even if it means *you* don't see his family anymore. So don't make him choose between the two of you – let your partner keep a relationship even if *you* don't.

3. **Limit her place in your head-space**. So she drives you nuts. You don't even *like* her. You've severely reduced how much contact you have, so why are you still talking about her…five

hours straight for the third day in a row! It's your partner who'll be nuts soon – because *you'll* have driven him there with your fixated dialogues. If she's not on the phone, no need to talk about her. If she's not in your home, no need to think about her. Draw some boundaries around the permitted extent of your granny groans – like ten minutes after each contact. Then let it go.

4. **Show respect**. *You* might wonder if his mother's got a brain the size of a pea, but he thinks she's pretty switched on. Putting her down is therefore going to achieve, well, just another senseless argument: *She's a twit. No she's not*…Ho hum. Let each other have different opinions, but always avoid senseless put-downs of your respective parents.

Further Reading

So I said you had to reduce your attention to a nanna who was driving you nuts. But before you do, you might find there's some wisdom in further reading about the dynamics of adult relationships. Try these for some guidance on your difficult granny issues:

- Terri Apter – *What Do You Want From Me?: Learning to Get Along With In-laws*.
- Terri Apter – *Difficult Mothers: Understanding and Overcoming their Power*.
- Victoria Secunda – *When You and Your Mother Can't Be Friends: Resolving the Most Complicated Relationship of Your Life*.
- Gloria Horsley – *The In-Law Survival Manual: A Guide to Cultivating Healthy In-Law Relationships*.
- Elisabeth Graham – *Mothers-in-Law vs. Daughters-in-Law:*

Let There Be Peace.
- Susan Forward – *Toxic In-Laws: Loving Strategies for Protecting Your Marriage.*
- Susan Forward and Craig Buck – *Toxic Parents: Overcoming Their Hurtful Legacy and Reclaiming Your Life.*

And for Nanna:
- Leanne Braddock, Ileene Huffard and Zanette Uriell, Ty Jones – *Taming the Dragon Within: How to Be the Mother-in-Law You've Always Wanted.*
- Olivia Slaughter and Jean Kubelun – *Life as a Mother-In-Law: Roles, Challenges, Solutions.*
- Susan Lieberman – *The Mother-in-Law's Manual: Proven Strategies for Creating and Maintaining Healthy Relationships with Married Children.*
- Arthur Kornhaber – *Between Parents and Grandparents.*

A few last comments:

If you started this chapter on the verge of calling for 10 rounds in the ring in a prize fight with Nanna, I hope it has ended with the feeling you could probably remove your gloves and call for a cup of tea with her instead. At least for another day.

If you started the chapter feeling you merely wanted to shut the door on her when she arrived, I hope it has ended with the feeling you may be able to invite her in, even if just for a quick cuddle with the baby.

If you started the chapter feeling blessed with the nannas in your life, then I hope it has strengthened your bond. Because we all function best in loving relationships and we all want people to genuinely tell us we're OK through our toughest of times. And a good nanna is worth her weight in gold.

It took a few weeks of uneasiness and the exchanging of a few harsh words before my mum and I finally sat down and talked about what was going on. It turns out that both of us were feeling unsure of what to do and what to say in taking care of Ellie's needs in the first few months. Ellie was a tricky little baby and she cried constantly. In the end, talking about our issues was the best thing we could have done. Now we can both take care of Ellie without fearing the other person's feedback. TRISH, MOTHER OF TWO

Kind words can be short and easy to speak, but their echoes are truly endless. MOTHER THERESA

Chapter 9:

Mothers without mothers.There's a hole in my parenting. It's where my mother should be.

Oh really...Your mother – who gives you unlimited emotional support and minded your baby all day – left the kitchen a mess. How terrible! Why don't you refuse all her help and deal with this entire parenting job without your mother. Like I have to. you self-centred COW!

WARNING: This is the least fun chapter. It delves into the very heart of sadness. A sadness so deep for many women that it seems it will never end. I cannot pretend to know this feeling, for it is not mine to know. So I have drawn on my own professional experience working with mothers-without-mothers and combined it with the wisdom of all the mothers-without-mothers I have ever met. I have no doubt you will be as moved, but also as inspired as I have been, in collating all the memories, stories and messages of hope for this chapter.

For some it's like a constant ache. For others it's like regular waves of intense sadness. Other mothers say it seems more like something is just "missing". When we become mothers yet have lost our own (through death or estrangement) their absence produces a grief response we could never have fully anticipated.

261

Was I like this as a baby? How did you cope? Am I doing a good job? All questions the new mother wants to ask her own mother. Yet for those who cannot ask these of their own mother, who do you ask? Who knows the answers? And who can provide the reassurance?

These are the stories of some of the mothers I have worked with:

Now that I'm a mum, I'm struggling more than ever that my mum's not around. I miss our morning coffees. I have nobody to call when I feel like I might lose it. I wish I could call her just to go for a walk with me so I can get out of the house. I hate going out shopping and seeing mums shopping with their own mums. I never realised how much I would need her. I miss her so much. NATALIE, MOTHER OF ONE

I lost my mum eight weeks before my son was born. My mum never met any of my kids even though it was her calling in life to be a grandma. I can't imagine how she coped with that loss as well. Amazingly stoic in the end. It took me many years to be able to even think about Mum properly as the pain was too much. CATHERINE, MOTHER OF THREE

My mum's a heroin addict. She hasn't really ever been my "mother", more a person who gave birth to me. She's never been interested in me, never wanted to know me. I thought having a baby might make her want to make more of an effort, but she couldn't care less. So I don't miss her as a mother but I miss what other mothers have. When my friends complain about their mothers I feel like saying, "Do you know how lucky you are?", but I don't because how could they know? My mother-in-law tries to help out sometimes, but she never thought I was good enough for

*her son because of my background, so I think she'd like me to fail.
But I'm determined to be a different sort of mother to my children.
And I won't fail. I never want my children growing up feeling like
I did.* NAME WITHHELD, MOTHER OF ONE

*Mum passed away 14 years before my first child was born and yet
her absence seemed even greater in the first few months of my son's
life than it ever had before. I wanted her there to share in my joy
and for her to hold her very own grandchild. I wanted her there
for advice on feeding, swaddling, strange body rashes, and even
weirder strange bowel motions! I wanted to ask her what I was like
as a child. Did I scream for hours in the middle of the night, shake
with fear at the sound of a rubbish truck passing, laugh hysterically
at the ripping of newspaper...but those questions will forever
remain unanswered.* TIFFANY, MOTHER OF THREE

*Mum died when I was 25. My husband's mother had passed away
too. I had my first baby at 32. I had expectations my sister might
be someone I could rely on but I didn't see her for two-and-a-half
months after the baby was born. I was so disappointed and I was
so alone.* MEL, MOTHER OF TWO

Are you as alone as you feel?

It's no secret that we are deciding to have our babies later than
any other generation before us. Our desires to develop careers,
to travel or to establish financial security before bringing a baby
into the world are among many of the reasons for motherhood
being put on the back-burner. For others, infertility has made it
a long, frustrating, unanticipated wait over many years for our
much-desired baby.

New figures from the Office for National Statistics (ONS) in the UK show the number of live births to mothers aged 40 and over has nearly trebled from 9717 in 1990, to 27,731 in 2010, and almost half of all births in England and Wales are now to mothers aged 30 and over. In Australia, data from the Australian Institute of Family Studies shows the number of births to women aged 35-40 has had a five-fold increase from 1989 (2.5% of births) to 2008 (12.2% of births).

This means of course that, if we're older when we're having our babies, the generation before us is likely to be older when our babies are born too. And so, it inevitably increases the chances of our parents' ill-health or terminal health problems or diseases. The net result is many of us are saying goodbye to one generation while we are simultaneously welcoming another. This co-occurrence of intense grief with unsurpassed joy is an emotional combination that knocks many women off their feet and leaves them lying weeping on the floor.

I'd waited so long for my baby to arrive. This was meant to be one of the greatest moments in my life. I'd never anticipated I'd also be farewelling my mum at almost the same time. She was meant to be my birth partner, but if I allowed myself to believe she was "gone" I couldn't have coped, so I gave birth believing she was somehow at my side anyway. I could hear her words and sense her support. I do the same thing on my hardest days. The only way I get through is continuing to believe part of her has never left me. AMY, MOTHER OF TWO

There are also the mothers who have lost the relationship with their mother, or lost the ability to call on their mother to play a "mother role" for reasons other than death. Some of us have grown up with mothers who didn't seem to care, or didn't seem to want us. Perhaps they chose alcohol or illicit substances over being a parent to us. Others have mothers with severe mental illness or other forms of disease which have meant we have spent our lives caring for them rather than with them caring for us.

Whatever your reason for feeling this way, the grief response will be part of your experience. So as I refer to grief, I refer to grief in terms of loss – whether through death, through estrangement or other circumstances. This chapter is not about classifying some mothers-without-mothers as sadder or more alone than another. This is a time for compassion not competition. So if you identify as not having a mother in your life, for whatever reason that is, then this chapter is for you.

How will it change how you are as a mother?

I took a lovely picture of Jesper a month ago sitting on a quilt Mum made and holding a picture of her. My kids may not know her, but they know me, and I am always going to be a piece of her, so in some ways they know her really well. CATHERINE, MOTHER OF THREE

The way grief will impact *your* parenting will be unique to you and unlikely to be the same as anyone else. Since no one has even really walked a day in your shoes, it's unlikely they'll know what it's like to spend a lifetime treading the same path. However, there are some common experiences between the mothers I work with. You may have some of these, or you may not.

What might happen:
a. **An overwhelming sense of responsibility**. It's like we feel we have to be our baby's "everything" to make up for what

265

they have missed from having a grandparent in their lives. So we feel obligated to play more, do more, enjoy more and even buy more to make up for what a grandmother might have done. It can be exhausting and it can be endless and, despite our best efforts, still leave us with a sense that it wasn't enough to make up for the role their grandmother would have played.

I feel in some way, that everything I do is overcompensating for the lack of my mother's presence in my baby's life. I want to show her everything, to give her as many experiences as I can, to spoil her and be ridiculously overgenerous with unnecessarily over-the-top outfits like I know my mum would have bought her. I know birthdays and Christmases will be a HUGE deal for us in the future. I don't want her to feel like she is missing out on anything by not having her grandmother. FELICITY, MOTHER OF ONE

Try to remember that for many reasons *many* children will grow up without grandparents. It does not lead to maladjustment, nor any predisposition to depression or anxiety. But if we overwhelm them with hectic schedules or over-the-top "everything", our overcompensatory efforts to make things better can actually have the opposite impact. Children need a balance between "doing" and just "being" – they need a calm environment to process their world and calm parents to set the tone for the home. Matching plates, cups, spoons and cupcakes for baby's first party might be *nice* but if you've turned into a nervous wreck trying to produce the perfect party, it's your baby who'll ultimately miss out on the security of a sane(ish) mother.

b. **The need to keep our baby close at all times**. With death and absence comes a greater understanding of the meaning of life and of presence. We can cherish moments with greater intensity. We feel the need to stay connected because we know what it's like to feel disconnected. And so we can get caught in a pattern of never allowing our babies to be alone, EVER, sleeping, feeding, and generally just "being" in a permanently "attached" state. We can refuse all other offers to care for our baby, wanting just to cherish them for ourselves. While this behaviour makes sense to someone who has lost a precious person in their life, ultimately our aim with our babies is to gradually allow them to learn how to cope without being permanently attached to us (remember, this starts from the time the umbilical cord is cut!). So if we find ourselves struggling with this concept, professional support is advised. Or else we risk our babies becoming a function of serving our needs, rather than us being there to meet their needs.

My mum never cuddled me. She never told me I was special or important. She never even wanted me and she certainly wasn't interested in any baby I had. I was so determined that my baby would never feel what I felt, but I knew on some days that I'd taken it too far and was becoming obsessed. I couldn't let her cry without wondering if I was becoming neglectful like my mother. If I let my husband care for her, I worried she'd think I abandoned her like my mother did.

Once I got professional help I could make better decisions about what issues were about me, and what issues really related to being a healthy parent. I knew I had to let her form strong relationships with other people, not just me. My therapist really helped. SOPHIE, MOTHER OF ONE

c. **Never being sure we're doing this mothering thing "right"**. Many mothers take great comfort in receiving positive feedback and guidance from their mother. There are few words we cherish more than our own mother saying, "You're a great mum". So when there is no mother to share these words, it can leave us questioning what we're doing and how we're doing it. We can also wonder what our mothers would have done in the same situation and wonder whether we're coping better or worse. It's like we've lost our mothering "barometer" to gauge our mothering skills. This is what one of the mothers I worked with said:

I just seem to question myself all the time. "Am I doing OK? What could I do better?" I go back into my childhood and question all the things she did for me. I want to know what she did and whether I'm doing things the same way. I want her to be OK with the choices I make as a mother – even if it's different to what she did. But the biggest thing I miss out on is the reassurance. Every day I yearn for her to tell me I am doing a good job. SHELLY, MOTHER OF THREE

There are many different ways of managing this lack of reassurance, and although it's not the same (or perhaps even close) women cope with it in different ways:

- Some "adopt" an older female friend who cherishes the idea of supporting a new mother (and believe me – there are many daughterless older women out there who would *love* to be asked to help out).
- Some declare that their mothers group plays the role of the reassuring "other" person.
- Some insist their mother was so disconnected from them anyway, that a sibling or aunty is better suited to the

reassuring role.

- Some build strong networks with a child health-care nurse or worker from a family care cottage (or similar) who can provide regular reassurance.
- Some remind their partner so as to ensure he gets the picture that the regular reassurance needs to come from him!
- Some become the "research scientist mother", taking solace in the knowledge that if her mother can't reassure her, the experts' "wisdom" is being incorporated into most aspects of her mothering.

d. **A sense of loss in knowing ourselves**. It seems that before we become mothers, we have zero zip zilch interest in how we behaved as babies. The day our babies arrive, however, our interest levels shoot up the Richter scale. How were we born, how did we feed, did we sleep well or did we just howl the house down? Did we crawl early or late? Were we an easy baby or did we need constant entertainment? But this information is lost to us forever without our mothers. Even if our father is still present in our lives, fathers of the previous generation really didn't know much about this stuff. While dads are amazing in their own way they're generally quite useless on the baby-biography front!

Mia was such a difficult baby. Nothing seemed to be easy with her. Feeding didn't go well, she didn't seem to like sleeping and there were days when she screamed more than she breathed. I wanted to know whether I was like this. It was like, if I was, then that's OK because obviously Mum was able to cope with it, so I can too! And she could have shown me how to deal with it as well. If I wasn't like Mia, then Mum could reassure me that Mia was a difficult baby and it wasn't that I was a bad mother. I just felt like I would have coped better with it all by just knowing this stuff. JULIE, MOTHER OF TWO

This is a hard one to overcome. Information gets lost with every generation, and when a mother dies before we become a mother ourselves, it can be lost forever. Sometimes, however, there is an aunt who recalls how we behaved, or an old friend that can remember our mother's despair at lack of sleep or gloating about how "easy" we were. So find out information where you can, but do remember, that even for mothers-with-mothers, they'll often have limited memories of our baby year (especially if there were more than two children in the family). Know that every baby is different and comes into the world with their own set of circumstances (caesarean vs water birth), temperament (chilled out vs wired for play) and biology (reflux vs illness vs everything-just-fine). Your job is only to know your baby and their unique characteristics they bring to the world. It's not the same as knowing your history, but after being angry about what you have lost (you have every right to be!) try to refocus on what you do have. One day at a time.

e. **An awkwardness with the mother-in-law (MIL)**. Well, it can also look like full-blown warfare, but if that's the case, refer to chapter eight. But all jokes aside, after having a baby, there is certainly more "pressure" (perceived or assumed) we will work things out with any previously disconnected MILs "for the sake of the baby". Some mothers find this pressure only fuels their sense of loss for their own mothers. Others say if they do try to get along, they somehow feel disloyal to their own mother. Some however, use it as a chance to bond with a MIL who is probably very keen to influence her grandchild's world.

To be honest, I don't think my mother-in-law and I would have ever started a relationship had it not been for the fact I'd married her son. We were just different types of people. And even though I knew she had very different views on how I cared for my new baby, her overwhelming desire was to support me in those early days and she did try to make me feel I was doing OK as a mother. I'll always be grateful to her for that, but we're still not that close. And I still wish it was my mother providing me support and not her.
BELINDA, MOTHER OF ONE

We can also fear that the "in-laws" will exert a greater influence on our baby, rendering their knowledge of their family history a little unbalanced. In her book *Parentless Parents: How the Loss of Our Mothers and Fathers Impacts the Way We Raise Our Children*, Allison Gilbert talks about how she would have pushed her in-laws away in a "misguided" attempt to level the playing field. This same theme was reflected in what a mother shared with me:

My husband is German and so I feel like there is a great pressure from everyone in his family to raise Max in German ways. But I'm not German and Max is only half German, and I know if Mum was here she'd be pretty clear on making sure Max knew the non-German parts! So I tell Max lots of stories about being Australian and buy outfits with the Australian flag on them. It's my little way of exerting my family's influence too. MARGIE, MOTHER OF TWO

f. **No one to brag to.** Beware the mother who tries to divert the "bragging" ordinarily reserved for grandmothers to her own mothers group – it can produce one-upmanship warfare! But then who else can we turn to? Who else other than our mothers wants to hear how amaaaaaazing our baby's smile was? Or moment-by-moment run-downs of tummy time? Mothers-without-mothers often talk about loss of a "bragging buddy".

I remember an older lady bumping into me in the shops as I proudly walked around with my baby in the pram. She thought my baby was so gorgeous and she just gushed over him. For a moment I was so happy – this was what my mum would have been like. Then she wanted to show me pictures of her own grandchildren. I looked at them, but I couldn't wait to get away. I raced back to my own car with tears streaming down my face.
TINA, MOTHER OF THREE

Take some heart in knowing that all your baby needs is just to have you, not a whole swarm of family, believing in how amazing they are. More people makes it easier and it does share the load, but it's not essential. Babies don't gain anything from being the star performer in a "bragging book" or "granny photo stream". But because it's still a sentimental issue, many mothers I know create scrapbook pages, write poems or even write "baby blogs" in the same vein as they feel their own mother might have. Others offer eager aunts or great-aunts to take over the bragging rights of an absent grandmother.

g. **All that was never said**. Many of us mothers weren't always the angelic (!?) creatures we are today. In fact, we were all probably stroppy teenagers or self-obsessed students at some point. At these ages and stages, our mothers were important to us, but so were lots of people (like boyfriends) and lots of things (like the latest fashion). It's not until we have a baby of our own that we realise how much our mother might have loved us and sacrificed for us. Because if she loved us even half as much as we love our babies, then all those times we forgot to call her, or took her for granted, or could have done more to help her must have meant far more to her than they did to us. And now, we have an overwhelming desire to let her know how grateful we are for all those hours she must have spent listening to us cry or the sleepless nights she must have endured for us. Except she's not there to thank. The unsaid words of gratitude can become guilt grenades of painful proportions.

I grew up feeling I deserved to have everything I wanted and rarely thought about others, particularly my parents who always seemed outdated and uncool. My mum never bothered with her hair or her makeup and she was often an embarrassment to me. Now that I've had my daughter, I want to take all that selfishness back. I realise she didn't care much about herself because all of her care went to me. She did that for us kids. But now that she's gone, I can't tell her. When it gets too much I scream out my apology to the sky and pray that wherever she is she has heard my words.
LINDA, MOTHER OF ONE

The important news is that your mother knew that there would come a day when you'd "get it" – that you'd want to apologise and express your gratitude for all that she'd done – because the same thing happened to her with her mum! But she also knew (as you will) that it wasn't possible for you to have known these things any earlier. Being a mother makes you aware of the stages of life and the developing sense of self that cannot be learnt through anything other than experience. Know that your mother's love enabled her to *already* forgive you for all the ways you treated her – even when you were an absolute pain beyond measure. And you will forgive your own children in much the same way.

h. **The fear or sadness that our baby will never "know" our mother.** If we had a mother we considered pretty amazing, it's with great sadness that we contemplate our baby not knowing such a special person. Photos and videos are one thing, but being held in the arms of a grandmother who adores you is another.

Mum died the same year my first baby was born. It was like she held on to see me become a mother too. I am so glad she got to see Thomas. I cherish every video and photo I have of the two of them together. But my next baby won't have that. They will have nothing tangible to connect them with my mum. And neither child will truly know the richness of her mind, the warmth of her arms and the depths of her love. I can only try to pass on what I can through old photos and stories. It's not right. SALLY, MOTHER OF ONE

There simply isn't a way that we can ever compensate for all that our mothers would have brought into our baby's world, but that doesn't mean there aren't small things that can keep their influence and impact very much in the present. Reading books she liked, going to places she enjoyed, playing her songs and having photos around the house are all helpful ways to ensure our baby comes to know our mother. The author Allison Gilbert has launched the Keeping Their Memory Alive blog (www.allisongilbert.com), where she lists a range of other age-appropriate ideas to help keep the memory of our parents alive for our children.

So how do you cope?

I needed my mum to call at the end of a hard day full of crying and toddler tantrums – to have a cry and a tantrum of my own. I needed my mum to put her arms around me and tell me everything would be OK, just as I had done for my babies. TIFFANY, MOTHER OF THREE

My desire to learn more about helping women with grief led me to meet two truly extraordinary grief trainers and counsellors – Mal and Di McKissock (see www.bereavementcare.com.au for more information about their amazing work). They have both earned Order of Australia medals for their contribution to healthy and compassionate ways of understanding how we respond to loss.

Their work has greatly contributed to the way I work with mothers-without-mothers. Here is how I have made sense of their words of wisdom and how I help mothers understand what is going on for them:

- **There is no "right" way to grieve**. There is only *your* way. If that means churning over photo albums for hours on end to feel connected with your mother, then that is right for you. If it means wandering around in bushland because you did that with mum as a child, then that's OK too. Unless what you're choosing to do is harmful or destructive, don't let anybody lead you to believe that somehow what you're doing is "wrong".

- **No two people grieve the same way**. The way we express and experience our grief depends on many factors including: the way in which our mother died, what our relationship was like when she died, our personality, our previous life experiences, our experience with other deaths, our physical and emotional health; how we see other important people (such as our siblings) expressing their grief, and most importantly, the availability of support. No need to compare your coping style with anyone else's – no need to wonder if you're doing "better" or "worse" – two people couldn't ever possibly grieve in the same way.

- **You don't *have* to talk about your grief in order to cope**. The outdated notion that if you weren't talking about your sadness then you weren't *dealing* with it was widely held by "talking therapists" – who, you guessed it, were good at using verbal communication as their way of helping. Talking was the only way *they* knew to help others, but we now realise that people can work through their grief in many ways including drawing, creating, building, walking and meditating. I have one mother who places a new photo of her baby on the wall each month. She chooses it with the thought that her mother would like it too – as if they sort of select it together. It reminds her of what her mother would have done in her own home had she still been alive. It is her very healthy grieving ritual and it doesn't require any talking at all.

- **You will probably grieve as you have lived**. If you were an outspoken, highly verbal, larger-than-life person before your mother's death, you could well bring the same style to how you work through your grief. You will probably bring up examples of your mother whenever possible and want others to continue to remember who she was. If you were more introverted and tended to keep things to yourself, you'll probably grieve more quietly too – perhaps remembering her through photo albums, moments of quiet personal reflection or rereading her hand-written notes from the past.

- **There is no correct timeline for grief.** Don't let anyone lead you to believe that your grieving has "gone on long enough", or conversely that your grief response was "too short". How long you show outward grief is a choice only you need to make because it belongs to the relationship you had with your mother and *not anybody else*. There is no correct point at which you "should" stop crying each day, stop visiting her grave each week, stop holding onto her clothes, stop keeping all of her trinkets, or agree to sell her house or car.

- **Grief is not a mental illness.** It is a healthy response to a painful reality that our world is forever changed by our mother's absence. Absorbing this loss, and adapting to all the changes it unleashes follows a unique course for every one of us. It cannot be paused, reversed or stopped by some "quick fix". Death is a life-altering event, but grief is not a pathological condition. Be cautious of any well-meaning GP who is leaning toward treating your grief as a major depressive disorder requiring medication. Seek a second opinion.

- **At some point you *will* be able to put less emotional energy into your grieving and more into the people you are currently with.** This will be a genuine sign that you are starting to accept the loss of your mother. Acceptance neither means forgetting your mother nor remembering how much of a hole was left when she died. It only means that you have worked out how to go on living in a healthy way without her. For a while, the loss is all we can think about, but over time we can turn our thoughts not just to our loss, but to also what we still have. As one mother said:

It took me a long time to work through all that I had lost in not having a mother and to start focusing more on what Gemma needed. I know there were days when I was quite out of it – but I can't feel bad about that. I know I did my best for my baby every day, even though at times I know I just covered the basics. But now I can be more connected to Gemma as well as able to talk to her about my mum without falling apart. Hopefully Gemma will start to sense happiness about my mum, because Mum was a really happy person. It would be important to her that she could bring that happy feeling to Gemma. JULIE, MOTHER OF ONE

- **What comforts you, may not comfort another.** Just as our grief journey will differ to another mother's, so too will the needs for our support and comfort. Support groups may provide you the space you need to be with others who understand, but for another mother it could be too painful, or the ways in which her own mother left her life might differ too greatly for her to feel "connected". Never assume you know what another grieving mother needs. And never feel like you aren't "normal" if your comfort needs are different to others.

- **Be open to feedback.** Just as we can love other people in unhealthy ways, so too can we grieve in ways which place our physical or mental health at risk. By all means, feel confident in knowing you can grieve in the way that is right for you, but seek support and be prepared to listen if others suggest that the way you are grieving might be destructive. Your own physical and mental health must remain a priority if you are going to safely (and sanely) navigate this first year with baby.

- **There is no such thing as a substitute.** We are all unique.

The relationship with your mother was therefore unique and there simply won't be anyone else who will ever have that relationship with you again. But don't use this as a reason not to pursue any other potentially caring relationships. New relationships will have their own uniqueness too. And have positive aspects we might never have thought possible, so when you're ready, try to let new people get close to you again.

- **Grief doesn't end**. Nor should it. The depth at which our mother impacted our lives will mean her presence will always be missed. It's just that over time the pain is not so acute or so overwhelming and we learn that somehow we can still live without her by our side. The pain becomes more dull and more subtle over time, but there will be moments, sometimes predictable and sometimes not, where it will return in its acute form all over again. There will always be reminders of where your mother could have been. As there should. Your painful reaction is testament to how important she was in your life.

How can other people help you with your distress?

It can be hard work dealing with mothers without a mother. Whether the loss is recent, was a long time ago, or even due to estrangement, the emotional aspects and related behaviours can confuse, bewilder and generally freak out our unsuspecting partners or pals. So hand over this list (or photocopy it for them) to support others in supporting you.

WAYS TO SUPPORT A MOTHER WITHOUT HER MOTHER

1. **Listen**. She will talk about a range of feelings, emotions, memories, regrets and hopes. She doesn't need you to solve her problems or create solutions. Sometimes there just aren't any. Just offer a patient listening ear and an opportunity to share what she's feeling.

2. **Avoid the use of clichés**. In an attempt to be helpful, we can often say things we know we'd never want someone to say to us if our loved one died, such as: "Think of all the good times"". But sometimes these statements slip out before we have time to catch them and it can hurt. Don't beat yourself up about saying it, but do apologise if you think it's caused her distress.

3. **Talk about her mother**. Using her mother's name means you are continuing to respect her importance in your life. Death doesn't mean the end of her influence. Ask about how she would have felt about the baby (names, birthday parties, first smile, etc). If you know things her mother would have liked about her parenting then tell her. Talk to the baby about her mother to ensure everyone is comfortable with using her mother's name in conversation.

4. **But sometimes silence is golden**. It's a myth that your partner needs to *talk through every single part of her grief.* Sometimes she just needs to sit quietly, or *do* something with her grief – like look through photos. Don't force a conversation if she's not up for it. Sit with her and just look through the photos too.

5. **Don't set time limits**. There is no timeline for grief and sometimes it can get worse before it starts to get easier. Expecting the grief to end just because it has been "more than a few months" will only end up being destructive for everybody.

6. **Reassure her that she's not crazy**. Grief is normal. But it does bring with it a whole range of behaviours and feelings we don't expect. Remind her that the enormity of her feelings reflect the enormity of the loss. It doesn't mean she's "lost it".

7. **Try to remember important dates related to her mother**. Be aware of her mother's birthday and the date of her death. These are likely to be more emotional than other days in the calendar, so ask her what she might need. Some mothers prefer to be with their own children, whilst others want at least part of the day to attend cemeteries or other special places alone. As my friend Tiffany (mother of three) said: "*Words may not even be necessary, but an extra tight hug or other form of caring to show your emotional support to just let her know you remembered will definitely help. It is a sad and lonely day when no one else does.*"

8. **Know that everyone grieves differently**. If you've ever grieved for anyone then you'll only know your *own* grief response to *that* person at *that* particular time of your life. Avoid thinking she is "wrong" or "right" in how she grieves compared to how you grieved or how anyone else has. Allow her to do it in her own way and know that although it might not make sense to you, it will be making perfect sense to her.

9. **Know your own limits**. We can often feel capable of providing extraordinary amounts of support in the early stages of grief, but due to the long and convoluted nature of grieving, we can slowly become worn down and worn out. Take the time to care for yourself too. The last thing she needs is for her support system to "go under".

10. **Help her to get help**. Allow your partner her own unique way of dealing with grief, but if it interferes with her ability to care for herself or her baby, then it's time to get help. Go to your GP together if she won't go on her own.

Where can you get further help?

While I often despair at the overuse of technology in our homes, when it comes to linking up mothers with particular circumstances, it's certainly been a godsend. And mothers-without-mothers are one group of women who really use it to their advantage. Some use it to make connections so that they can meet up in person, others keep their relationships purely "cyber".

So if you want to connect with other mothers in a similar situation (or get inspired by what others have done to forge connections in their local area) get online and navigate your way to the relevant section on the following websites:

- http://community.babycenter.com
http://www.resourcingparents.nsw.gov.au
- http://www.meetup.com/Motherless-Mothers/
- http://community.babycentre.co.uk
- http://www.mumswithoutmothers.org

There are also some great websites for information about grief in general:

- The Bereavement Care Centre: www.bereavementcare.com. au
- The Australian Centre for Grief and Bereavement: www. grief.org.au
- Cruse bereavement care: www.cruse.org.uk

There are some great books to help mothers through their grief too:

- *Motherloss* by Lynn Davidman
- *Motherless Daughters: The Legacy of Loss* by Hope Edelman

- *Motherless Mothers: How Losing a Mother Shapes the Parent You Become* by Hope Edelman.
- *Letters from Motherless Daughters* by Hope Edelman
- *Parentless Parents: How the Loss of Our Mothers and Fathers Impacts the Way We Raise Our Children* by Allison Gilbert

When do you need professional help?

There is a great deal of misperception out there that grief counselling is "the answer" for healing the bereaved. Actually, most people just need a good support system and the fullness of time to process the enormous loss of their mother.

That being said, there are also some signs that additional help might be necessary, including:

1. If you can't get out of bed or just want to sleep all the time for days on end.
2. If you feel there is nobody you can talk to and you're completely alone with all that you're experiencing.
3. If you are neglecting yourself or your family, by not eating properly or not feeling like you can shower or bath yourself of your baby.
4. If you have any thoughts of not wanting to live any more without your mother (eg suicidal thoughts).
5. If your emotion is so intense that you can't be the mother you want to be.
6. If you're using unhealthy ways to cope with your pain such as consuming too much alcohol or harming yourself in any way.

> If these signs describe your current experience, then speak
> to your GP or child health nurse about a referral to a local
> counsellor or psychologist who is familiar with assisting
> people with grief.
>
> **But if you're experiencing any suicidal thoughts, please
> seek help immediately by calling 000 (Australia) or 999
> (UK).**

The websites listed above also outline a range of services that can support you during this vulnerable time in your life. And remember, getting help isn't a sign that you are weak, it's a sign you are taking responsibility for your own health and your baby's.

One last comment:

This chapter was written for the many mothers-without-mothers whose stories and experiences have inspired me with their courage, with their trust and with their hope. You are all very special women.

May you come to find some solace in the baby you hold in your arms and the supportive people in your life who hold you in theirs. May you always feel the love of the mother you have lost even when she cannot be felt. And may you know how loved you are by those of us who are here and are able to be by your side.

With the support of great friends and other family members I have found my own way as a mother, and I do the best with the skills

I have. I take the memories of my mum mothering me and relive them with my children...simple things that were a part of her, are a part of me and will be a part of my children.

I think of mum every day but I no longer yearn for her guidance or desire her reassurance. I am doing OK as a mother because I'm happy with the mum I've become. TIFFANY, MOTHER OF THREE

Chapter 10:

For the single mother. Keeping the pride and power in your parenting.

Truth is, I don't want a man in my life. Looking after one child is enough!

Partnerless and proud? Single and strong? Or more alone and angry? Whatever your reaction to your single parent status, it's safe to assume there'll be a bit of power behind it. Probably similar to the colossal level of feminine force required to survive this "little" baby's "mighty" workload.

But you'll find the strength. There isn't a single mother I know who doesn't. Extraordinary wisdom emerges in moments of misery. Unfathomable power surfaces in times of torment. Your baby will be both your toughest test and your most marvellous miracle. And the loyalty and love of those who support you through this journey will provide the reassurance that the world still yields both astonishing joy and incredible wonder. Well, most of the time.

Are you really alone in your single parent status?

Truth is that although there's many an isolated single mother, it's not even close to a solo situation. Approximately one in five babies born this year in America, Australia and the UK will be to single mothers. And don't be surprised if you find this figure, well, surprising: it represents an 80% increase since 1980, which means most of the western world (and the infrastructures within them) are behind the times when it comes to making sense of the escalating number of single modern mothers.

And the rising tide of single parent families is predicted to continue. In fact, one-parent families are the fastest growing type of family in Australia, with 823,300 single families recorded during the 2006 census. The Australian Government expects this number to reach 1.2 million by 2026[1].

But there has been some misinformed media hype sprouting nonexistent causations for such significant shifts. The idea of "the choice" single mother – highlighted by the media in both "Murphy Brown" and in Jennifer Aniston's movie *The Switch* – prolifically populating the planet has certainly raised the blood pressure of a few politicians and traditionalists. Fact is, there's just no evidence that this is a major causative factor for the increase[2]. Although there *are* some women who enter motherhood in this way, there still remains the vast proportion who don't.

So know that whichever way your situation led you to being single within your first year with baby, the numbers don't lie –

you are part of a HUGE social group. Any behind-the-times society leaders must let go of outdated ideas that single mothers are a minor "nuisance". As a community we must abandon any structure endorsing the notion that "women can be equal to men until they have children." We must embrace the fact that you are an integral, important, equal and powerful part of our social structure.

But what if our journey had a rocky start?

"So I want to feel empowered, but I'm already a bit shaky. That birth was *nothing* like what I'd imagined". If that's how you feel, then welcome to the motherhood mob – where whether we're partnerless or partnered up, we're all still a bit confused about the discrepancy between our almost fantasy-like expectations of birth and what our realistic version ended up being (episiotomy anyone?).

While your birth experience will be hugely impacted by your own individual pathway to becoming a single parent, there will be common themes you'll share with others. Themes that go above and beyond the typical confusion of what most mothers experience, including:

- Missing the person you most wanted to be there – whether because of death, divorce or unwanted departure – whatever the reason, birth without the baby's father can be tough. Well-meaning "others" can enthusiastically step in, but if the face you see when you pant and push isn't the one you planned, birth can be a grieving experience in its own right.
- Feeling scared – for those whose babies were fathered following rape or by an abusive ex-partner, birth can be a retraumatising experience in many ways. From triggers of

traumatic memories to the possibility the baby's features remind you of the abuser, it makes sense that you can feel very scared, very overwhelmed and possibly even very numb.

- Feeling unable to celebrate in the same way – because of multiple factors (grief, sense of being judged, or trauma), sometimes as single mothers we can feel unable to celebrate our baby's arrival like our partnered-up peers.

- Feeling judged by hospital staff – it's ironic that "educated" maternity professionals can have such dim-witted delusions that either:

  a. the woman alone created this pregnancy (so it's *her* fault the condom split or "the pill" didn't perform!? I'm sorry – I remember something about an egg *and* a sperm…);

  b. in choosing not to terminate the pregnancy the entire onus of responsibility must shift to us (oh, I see – because I morally struggle with abortion, *I'm* the bad guy!).

Whatever the story and whatever the experience, nothing can take away from the fact that your body produced a miracle beyond words:

- If the father of your baby decided to be absent from the birth by choice, it is he alone who must live with regret. Your baby only needed you to be present and to be graced by your love. Any man who does not honour your baby's arrival or existence does not deserve to be missed.

- If the father of your baby is deceased, know that he won't be – and never will be – completely absent from anything in your baby's life, because 50% of your baby's DNA will *always* be him.

- If your baby physically resembles an abusive father, know that appearances do not convey the soul, and that because of the way you raise your child their soul will be one of grace and beauty.

- Know that neither you nor your baby is under any obligation to ever see those judgmental hospital staff again. Strike them off the list. Redirect their toxic tendencies right back at them. From this day forward, commit to only considering the opinions of those people you admire and trust.

- And know that you deserve to celebrate with all the gusto of any new mother on the planet (perineal tears, caesarean stitches and bloated breasts accounted for). A man is not needed to determine when these celebrations begin or end – because you just performed a miracle that *no man* has ever achieved. So celebrate your heart out, sister – there'll never be anything else you create that will ever rival your little bundle.

So on this single parent pathway, what are you really in for?

Never tell a single mother you're tired.
Unless you're a masochist. STEPHANIE, MOTHER OF ONE

Just like any person on this planet there are many factors bearing on both the demands we face and our perceived capacity to meet them – including our personality, our early experiences, our social support and our genetics.

But there are some vulnerabilities that are unfairly allotted to single parents that need acknowledgement. Here are what the mothers I work with have shared with me:

- **Lack of in-house support**. Tired? I'll give you tired! Try being up five times a night with nobody to ever give you a break and then mustering the energy to look after the baby all day while also juggling some low-paying work! For those women who have partners – even those ones lousy on many a daddy dimension – at least they're actually there. At least they're able to mind the baby for half an hour while you catch those otherwise elusive moments to slumber or to shop or to shower. When you're solo parenting, even if there is family support or babysitting during the day, the nights can be tough.

I'm so tired. All the time. I get no break, EVER. I had no idea that in choosing to do this on my own I'd be choosing permanent and crippling exhaustion. LIBBY, MOTHER OF ONE

- **Lack of "adult-ness"**. When it comes to getting feedback to our daily baby news ("He rolled over. He puked twice"), we can often wonder whether a monosyllabic grunt might trump straight-out silence. The reason you've never had a conversation with yourself before is because other than a quick pep-talk, they're generally quite dull. Duller still when you're still stuck in solo conversations three months into baby's arrival. At the end of the day, it's just nice to revert back to your old voice (not the "goo-goo ga-ga" high-pitched version), to moan about a few things, to celebrate some others, and basically to have another adult talk back.
- **Lack of financial freedom**. It's no secret that single mothers are among the most financially disadvantaged members of our society. It's extraordinarily senseless that you have one of the hardest and yet most important jobs on this planet (raising the next generation of community members and leaders is still important, right?), yet aren't financially supported to do so. Without the benefits of a partner's

income, or inherited wealth, single mums are vulnerable to living within a financial status largely determined by the government of the day. And we're under no delusion about how these governments make their choices. In fact, there is yet to be a single country on earth where the single mother's child benefits get them anywhere near even middle-class status. Any person spruiking the "unfair" rights given to single mothers is correct – it really is "unfair" – for the mother and her baby. Both deserve a whole load more.

- **Limited choice.** Sure, a single mother can choose her baby's name, her preferred settling methods, her preferred parenting style. What she often can't do is choose the place where she lives, how long she'll stay home before returning to paid work, or the day-care (nursery) her child attends. These factors are hugely influenced by economics. So she'll probably live in a less desirable area, or be forced to share with boarders, return to work well before she'd hoped and will need to take the cheapest care options available. The lack of choice even extends down the supermarket aisle as she is compelled to opt for the cheapest products – you know – the ones that never appear in any "what's best for baby" campaign.

Has your single parent situation left you with all sorts of negative feelings?

He said he couldn't sacrifice his happiness (when he left). We now have a six- and an eight-year-old still struggling to adjust (and I feel I do most of the comforting)…He left me solo, lonely and with a battered self-esteem. He was not even interested in making any effort with our baby. He saw our baby boy for a total of three hours in the last month and that was on Christmas day. I'm so glad he's *happy…* SARAH, MOTHER OF THREE

- **Being "left out"**. Your girlfriends love you. You're invited to heaps of coffee dates. But when it comes to the fancy dinner-party festivities, the invitations are strangely scarce. "We thought you'd feel awkward" is a PC line for "We thought you'd steal our husbands" and you both know it. Or maybe it was more as my client Kylie (mother of one) said: "I actually wondered if it was really the wives who weren't inviting me to all the couples-type events or whether it was their husbands. I guess it would have been threatening for them to see a single woman with it all together and maybe they feared their own wives would prefer to be that way!"

- **Anger**. He left you in the lurch. He didn't pull his weight. He couldn't care less about the baby. His behaviour makes you want to scream – and you probably do – lots. Anger is a positive emotion when it's harnessed in the right direction. It gives us the power to make changes and take charge. But if your baby's father has chosen to be absent or behaved in objectionable ways, then there's no person to take this anger out on. Well, at least not the *right* person to take this anger out on. And because your lioness mother instincts will stop you venting anger on your baby – that kinda just leaves the anger to be taken out on…well…yourself.

  In her extraordinary book on mothers (*Naked Motherhood*, Random House, 1999), researcher and author Wendy LeBlanc wrote of the single mothers she had interviewed: "They were infuriated at the men who dumped them and with society for expecting so much from them while giving so little help and support. In every case, their anger was not

293

so much for the hardships they themselves were suffering, but because the hardships limited the lives and opportunities of their children."

- **Fear**. Can I do this on my own? Will we make it through? What will our future hold? The journey into parenthood fills most mothers with a sense of panic, especially for those whose travel plans contain predominantly solo missions. And then there's the fear that being "with child" dramatically reduces the chances of being "with man" and an apprehension of lifetime loneliness sets in.

I go over and over in my head how different I'd be as a mum if I had a partner to help. I created this fantasy that I'd be amazing and perfect and not the crazy psycho I felt I was.
NAME WITHHELD, MOTHER OF ONE

- **Loss of a dream**. I've yet to hear any little girl fantasising about solo parenting. It just doesn't enter into our heads. It's not until we're adults that raising our baby alone is either something we want to do or have to do. But as "grown ups", if our childhood dreams are too hard to let go, we can get forever stuck in a fantasy and avoid making the necessary steps to deal with our reality. Result – our coping capacity takes a gigantic nosedive.

I fantasise about Mike turning up at the door with roses and saying, "It's OK. I'm back. I've realised I was an idiot for leaving and I want to dedicate the rest of my life to being the best dad possible." But it won't happen. I've learned – very, very slowly – that he's too selfish to ever commit to anyone but himself. Still, I often find myself hoping he will. TINA, MOTHER OF TWO

- **Guilt**. So *you* walked out. Or you kicked him out. Or you initially thought single parenting was going to be a piece of cake and found it's more like a slice of cement. Maybe you should take him back? Maybe you should forgive him? For most mothers, guilt is the common side-effect of childbirth and lasts until you die, but knowing when to stay and when to go is one of the most difficult choices any mother can make. You can feel like it's a lose-lose situation whichever way you turn – the baby gains a dad, but he's an aggressive kind and you know you'll slowly shut down or get hurt. Or you leave – then your baby doesn't really get to know his dad and you do this whole parenting thing solo-style, slowly collapsing with exhaustion.

Sometimes I question whether I should have left. Maybe living with my alcoholic ex-partner would have been easier than doing this alone. I always have to remind myself I did it for Blake. That he didn't deserve to see the effects of alcoholism on a daily basis. But I've questioned it so many times. Now I understand for the first time why so many mothers stay in unhealthy relationships.
ROWENA, MOTHER OF ONE

- **Loneliness**. Weird that now there's virtually the two of you permanently together that you could feel so lonely. But you do. Even when you go out, it's you who returns to the empty house. In the best and worst moments, you can feel that there's nobody really to share it. As Wendy LeBlanc suggests (*Naked Motherhood*. Random House, 1999): "I do not know whether there is anyone who has not lived through it who can begin to comprehend the sheer loneliness of a mother who is trapped in isolation with only her children for company."

- **Overwhelmingly responsible**. The sleep routine that didn't work – my fault. The nappy rash – my fault too. Who else could I blame? Which means the big choices like "how long I should breastfeed?" are all down to me, too – and I'm over it. Many single mothers are only too acutely aware that while there are many well-meaning friends, family and family-doctors to support big decisions, ultimately choices regarding their child-rearing are up to them. As one client said to me: "I just want somebody to step in and tell me what to do. I'm over being responsible for every apparently life-changing decision. My head feels as though it's going to explode."

What if it's all sounding too negative?

I'm a single mother: What's your superpower? FACEBOOK POST, 2013

So far, you'd be right. It was important to get those bits out of the way. Being a mother is hard, and doing it on your own can be even tougher – but it can be amazing, too. So, now that we've covered the hard stuff, time now for the positive possibilities of single parenting:

- **I get to decide**. Yes indeed. No arguments, no tantrums, no "coming from different worlds". Unless there's a controlling father in the wings, mostly it's you making the decisions about how to raise your child – from breastfeeding (or not), attachment parenting, swimming lessons, circumcision and introducing solids.
- **I don't have to compromise**. So your friend wanted to go back to her old work. Her partner felt it was too soon. They

met half-way and now she's going back next month instead of this month. Not in your world. While there are plenty of life's stressors forcing you to make decisions you may not otherwise make, it's not your partner who inflicts this pressure. Wherever it's possible, you get to do it your way.

- **I don't have to feel less important in the relationship because I'm not bringing in the "big bucks"**. Sadly, many mothers with partners are treated almost second-rate once the money stops flowing in. Not you. The financial pressure is tougher than Bear Grylls, but at least what you *do* have is 100% yours.

- **I don't have to put up with toxic influences**. Physical violence? Not in this house. Emotional manipulation? Not in my backyard. If you've left due to a partner's harmful or abusive behaviour, then enjoy your new-found serenity and safety. If you're searching for new romance, know that toxic qualities can remain taboo on your tick list. Then enjoy the knowledge that in making this decision, your baby's psychological state is headed in a healthy direction.

- **I can choose someone who *likes* my baby**. Many new mothers have a fantasy of how their partner will care for their baby once it's born. The reality often fails to live up. Not for you. If a potential new beau doesn't seem interested, doesn't want to put in the effort, or has unrealistic expectations about a baby's capacities, then the relationship stops. No holding on for the sake of the family. Adiós. Moved on already. Ready to reassess the next one. You only need to settle once "Mr Right" actually behaves, well, right.

- **I can remind myself daily (or hourly) that I have one of the hardest jobs on the planet...and I'm succeeding** (in the best-I-can-be standard to which all reasonable mothers aspire). And it's all done without much support from broader society, with very little praise and with only a few people who truly understand or value the extent of your exertions. Which basically means – you rock!!

What if you're all right, but the daddy's the drama?

Single parenting is tough. And while there are some pretty dedicated and devoted dads out there, times can get even tougher still if the baby's father is kinda "tricky". Perhaps his behaviour is reflected in one of these "male modes":

- **Mr Man-Child**. Responsibility? What's that? Meeting my obligations? Are you kidding? They're all for, well, others. Yes, this type of father can leave you wondering whether he's moved beyond childhood himself. He'll want to be there for the good times – baby's christening or baby's first steps. But the hard times – expect more like a hasty Houdini. Don't go counting on him handling a screaming baby or dealing with a dirty nappy. Don't go expecting him on time for meet-ups, or for even those meet-ups to be regular. That type of behaviour is for, umm, grown-ups.

- **Mr Important**. Babies? Beneath me. Looking after them? Woman's work. Yes, this "man variety" is all delight and wonder of the egotistical kind. Usually he'll be far too busy, far too important and just all together too amazing to have time for you or your baby. If you're lucky, you'll get little windows of his time – but he'll remind you how blessed you are while he's there ("I should have been in 100 other places right now"). Don't expect him to be on time, or to make regular times for catching up to see the baby either. Last minute changes, running late, cancelling altogether are more his scene – and don't get upset about it — because, don't you know, he's just doing so many extraordinarily important things. Unlike you. What you do with the baby and all the extraordinary effort it requires, is just well, umm…totally less amazing.

- **Mr Missing in Action**. Hello? Anybody there? Nope. This type of father forgot it was *his* sperm that colluded – with your egg that is – in your baby's creation. Somehow it was *your* choice, and so now it's *your* responsibility. Make sense? Not at all. But he's running with it. In his deluded state, he'll honestly believe requests for child support are overtly outrageous and suggestions to "know his child" are equally absurd. Taking responsibility for bringing a baby into this world, that's for, umm…anybody but me.

- **Mr Punitive**. Happy? Let me put an end to that. Confident? Not in my lifetime. Yes, this type of ex-partner seems determined to ensure you never experience joy or ever get the chance to like yourself. The baby? Not even thought about, because this type of man couldn't care less about a child – unless he can use the child as a way to control you. No doubt he thought you'd never leave him and would always put up with his controlling behaviour. He'd love to have you back in the same place too. So he'll use meet-ups, phone calls and any communication really to put you down or cause you distress. Don't expect encouragement, support or positive reinforcement from this punitive ex-partner; that sort of crap's for, umm…the birds.

- **Mr Carrot Dangler:** Like me? Then you can't have me. Moved on? Then I want you back. This type of ex-partner gives mixed messages to rival any political party. Basically because it's all about how *you* meet *his* ego needs – it's not about how you feel – duh. So, when *you're* chasing *him* for regular meet-ups or to share baby's news, he'll be infuriatingly elusive. But when he thinks you've moved on to a more healthy relationship – you'll find he's amazingly attentive: baby and you will suddenly be centre stage. You'll think he's finally come to his senses and you can rejoice that your relationship is back on track, and just as you turn to hug him, he's, umm, gone...again.

If your ex-partner is any of these "man models' then be grateful that there *is* an "ex" before the "partner". While living *without* them no doubt creates some headaches, living *with* them would tip you into migraine territory. Quite frankly, a man with these characteristics doesn't deserve you. While you might have been in a space or place where it was OK in your past, stand your ground. It's not OK now. You deserve better. Your baby deserves better.

Does that mean you can cut him out of your life?

Unfortunately (for you) you can't. Because while *he* may not be focused on your baby – *you* thankfully are. And despite his delusions about his donor (of the sperm variety) status, your baby is and always will be part of his creation. And despite any other delusions of grandeur or his child-like choices, our kids will fare better off if they at least get the chance to know their father. As humans, we *are* hardwired to want to know both parents. I haven't met a kid yet who isn't.

And the research backs this up. It's a pretty clear-cut case that regardless of any other economic or cultural factors, the benefit of fathers being positively engaged with their kids includes better adjustment and increased resilience in the face of risks and vulnerabilities[3].

There is also evidence that when dads are able to stay active in their baby's life (ie not side-lined because *we've* stopped liking him anymore), the hormonal and brain changes that occur support a dad's ongoing parenting and co-parenting competence[4].

So unless – and this is an important "unless" – there is ongoing *unhealthy* behaviour by your baby's father, it is generally accepted that our kids benefit from both parents working together. In the professional world we call this "co-parenting". It should look like this[5].

My baby's needs are best met when we:

a. strive to agree on who our child is and what their needs are;

b. expressly and implicitly value the importance of the other parent's contribution to raising our child;

c. recognise the gender differences that lead each partner to think, feel and behave in distinctly different ways with respect to child-rearing;

d. allow our child's needs (and not our own) to dictate how conflicts get resolved;

e. create a "team" that commits to backing each other up when our child isn't faring so well.

So beware of tendencies to "gate-keep" (prevent dad's access to the children) if doing so results from your own issues – anger, disappointment, etc – or to "punish" him, rather than looking at contact from your baby's perspective.

So what sort of father-baby relationship should be encouraged?

Should I try to get him to meet up with the baby once a week? Should it be daily? And what do I say if he wants our baby to stay overnight at his place? Knowing the right amount of contact for a good relationship to develop and knowing what's best for baby is far from being a precise science.

Despite significant efforts by some pretty clever researchers, as yet they've been unable to quantify a solution. And realistically, this is understandable, because like any relationship, it depends on a complex interplay of infinite factors including health, personality, previous experiences, attitude and current stressors.

Several attempts have been made to place more rigid "rules" around parental contact during the early years. You'll probably find some evidence that taking under-twos and two- to three-year-olds away from their primary carer overnight, or providing shared care-arrangements for children under four, may result in an adverse effect on the children.

But this approach is not without its critics. In fact, the only things that the researchers really *can* agree on that are necessary for our infants, in addition to the sound parenting suggestions above, are:
- a high level of warmth and responsiveness from both parents;
- a high level of communication and cooperation between parents;
- low levels of hostility between the parents, particularly in front of the child;
- continuity and consistency of the care arrangements, preferably in a routine and preferably with the child not

being away from any one parent for more than a few days at a time[6].

If you want to make some decisions and put a contact arrangement in place, however, your general guide is this: the younger the child, the more frequent is the contact required to form a connection.

So for younger babies, aim for short periods of contact – a couple of hours every few days – working around baby's sleeps/breastfeeding/bottle feeding (whatever your situation). As your baby develops, extend the amount of time.

As hard as it might be for you, *as long as the father is a healthy influence*, this really is important for your baby.

Keep in mind though that as babies become more aware of their most important attachment figure (ie you) at around eight months, their separation response also becomes stronger. Which means:

a. **Everyone can be rejected!** They can protest at being with granny (who they see four times a week), with their day-care worker (who they see all day twice a week) and also with a father *who resides with them*, so it makes sense they would do the same for a father who doesn't. It does not mean that they don't "like" him or want to be with him.

b. **They will adjust.** If there have been sufficient opportunities to build a relationship then the distress is usually short-lived and settles quickly once you leave (just as it would at a day-care centre or with your own mum).

c. **But we need to help them.** How quickly your baby settles will be impacted by your attitude to the father's contact – so

303

despite all that you feel *inside* do what's best for baby on the *outside*. Settling times are also obviously quicker with a dad who's sensitively attuned to his baby's distress. Consoling, cuddling and reassurance from him will obviously help.

But I do understand that in separating from your very precious baby, to a man who's possibly less than amazing in your eyes, it can be tough. And possibly with an emotional impact big enough to rival a tsunami. As one single mother said to me about contact with her baby's father: *"I know he has some good parenting elements, but it's sooo hard to hand my baby over. I feel instinctively protective of him (my baby). And I'm the one who did all the hard yards in the early months when he walked away. The salt to the wound is that 'the new girlfriend' is there too and she has done nothing to deserve enjoyment with my baby. I just want to swipe a big sharp mumma lion claw at her!"* NAME WITHHELD, MOTHER OF THREE

Back to you now. So what do you do for those days where you feel less "rock star" and more "rock bottom"?

A single mother has only two choices. To spend her life regretting and feeling "less than" because she hasn't got a male attached. Or she rises up and claims her own power. AUTHOR UNKNOWN

Many of the tips in chapter three for managing new parent status will stand up and help sort you out, regardless of whether you're in a relationship or not. But there are important additions for the single mother to ensure persistency in her parenting power.

• **Know your rights and entitlements**. This is no time for quietly wondering what you might deserve. This is the time to demand it. And there are services that have done all the hard work for you. Before you decide you've reached the limit for obtaining financial, social and practical support, make sure you've spoken with the organisations listed at the end of this chapter.

- **Create your village**. The old saying "it takes a village to raise a child" is notable in the absence of the word "man" (or even "woman" for that matter) because it's not about one person. It's about a team. No woman can parent without support – whether it be family, friends, adopted aunts, free voluntary services or paid professionals. So if you're finding yourself increasingly socially isolated, use one of the recommended websites below to vamp up your village. A woman without support is placing both herself and her baby at risk.

- **Be choosy in your tribe membership**. Supporters in, but sad sacks, happy sappers and doomsdayers out. Or at least restricted to the village outskirts. Sometimes you'll find it's a whole range of mothers from around the world who share your interests or hobbies, other times it will make more sense to partner up with local partnerless pals, as these mums share with me:

I'm so sick of every other woman who has a partner. I can't bear to hear any of them complain. It's always at the tip of my tongue to say, "Try doing it on your own!" But I don't. It's just easier to hang out with my single parent buddies. They just get it. KERRIE, MOTHER OF TWO

I couldn't cope with mothers group. Everyone timetabled the catch-ups around their partners – always leaving at 4:30pm to get home and sort out the dinner. There were never offers to stay beyond a

certain time and never on weekends – that was their family time.
On some days I wondered if I was just a "fill-in" friend to amuse
them in-between their partner's presence. So I sought out single
mothers and felt far more supported and valued. JANINE, MOTHER
OF ONE

- **Seek out supportive men**. Whatever the reason you don't
  have your baby's dad living with you, it's important to
  prioritise seeking out male influences for your baby. The
  research is fairly clear that while babies don't *need* both a
  mother and father to develop in healthy ways, they certainly
  greatly *benefit* from the complementary approach of the
  male and female style. Richard Bowlby (son of John Bowlby,
  noted for his pioneering research into children's attachment
  issues) promotes the idea that there are often two primary
  attachment figures who serve two complementary and
  necessary functions, one for "love and security," and the other
  "to engage in exciting and challenging experiences"[7]. So where
  mothers tend to offer a more soothing, careful approach to
  parenting, the male tends to develop the baby's sense of self
  related to a more play-oriented and adventurous style of
  interaction. Having important men around will ensure this
  complementary role can still be a positive influence on your
  baby.
- **Develop a routine**. Routines are a hot topic in baby blogs
  and family forums alike. Ever seen the blood pressure rise
  in your mothers groups if you dared to suggest that your
  routine trumps another's. Turn to chapter two for some
  suggestions on making the best decision about routines for
  you and your baby, however I do tend to suggest that single
  mothers (or mothers with partners who are absent for long

periods due to work, etc) benefit from erring on the side of being more routined than not. It can help us create more predictability and with that, the possibility of a greater sense of control over what is otherwise a rather chaotic period in our lives. It can also help ex-partners know what times to safely have contact with baby without fear of it being sleep time or breastfeeding time.

- **Find your "time-savers".** Heard of online grocery shopping? Learned about a chemist that home delivers? What about just always making sure you never cook one meal at a time –make enough to freeze for the next day or more! The busy single mother needs to be super savvy in the time-saving stakes. Check out the websites below for further tips and ideas from other single mums who've made every second count (including the ones to rest-up!).

- **Stay the "parent".** "What other choice have I got?" you might ask, but experience tells me there's many a single parent who's wanted to be their child's best friend, partying pal and closest confidante all in one. "That's years away," you say. Actually, it often starts at this age with parenting choices such as co-sleeping. See chapter two for more details, but basically keep in mind this: as single parents, our need to feel connected to another human in the loneliness of the night can lead to sleeping habits with our baby that are more about helping us than them. And apart from the inherent safety risks of co-sleeping in the same bed, when it's about our needs and not the baby's I can safely predict problems in paradise, if not now then later. Try to find similar alternate sleeping arrangement that still match your parenting values.

- **Model self-care.** Me? Important? In my own life? Whatever! Actually, how we care for ourselves has a huge bearing on how much energy we have to care for others, particularly in the long term. No point burning out when baby's only three-months old. This parenting journey requires the stamina of a Kenyan marathon runner, not the brief explosive power of a sprinter. So turn to the exercises in chapter three to make sure you've got all that you can in place to go the distance.

She has to have four arms, four legs, two hearts and double the love. There is nothing single about a single mother. MANDY HALE, AUTHOR OF *THE SINGLE WOMAN: LIFE, LOVE, AND A DASH OF SASS* (THOMAS NELSON, 2013)

- **Hang up the hero outfit.** Many single mothers joke that the mere fact that they *are* single mothers makes them an automatic qualifier for superhero status. I couldn't agree more. So long as it's the less-than-perfect-vomit-stained-outfit kind. Otherwise, ditch it. This is no time to pressure yourself with perfectionist parenting. Be realistic. *You* know you've done your absolute best every day. If that "best" is a sink half-full of dishes, a floor unswept and cupcakes bought (ie not fancily home-made) for the mothers group get-together, then cheers to you. Parenting is not about point-scoring – nobody's tallying up the number of beds made in the morning or the number of washing piles in your laundry, except you. Set the tone for other mothers – both single and those with partners – because "perfect parent posers" really produce nothing that's actually "best for babies".

- **Harness your anger and make peace with your past.** "I caaan't," I hear you wail. "He's ruining my life!" Can I disagree just slightly? He could well be a moron of the man variety, making your life diabolically difficult, but unless he's rocking up to your home 24/7 with life-threatening intent, I'd say (in the kindest possible way) it's more likely to be *you* who's messing with your life. Think for a minute – as you peer down on the angelic face of your baby feeding – do you focus on this idyllic picture or find yourself replaying a past argument with your ex over and over and over again ? As you lay down at the end of another weary day, do you picture the inspirational women in your life and all that you've learned from them – or another blow-by-blow account of what you'd wished you'd said, when he'd said, etc etc?

Remember –your brain is your headspace. You choose what goes in there. So if he causes your blood to boil why would you want to think about him when he's not anywhere near you? Why choose to focus on scenarios and scenes that make you sad or seething with anger? Instead, think about him only as you need to – perhaps to make decisions about him visiting the baby or to query a child support payment. Then stop. Refocus on what inspires you. Channel your thoughts into visions of happiness, love, laughter and respectful relationships.

When one door of happiness closes, another opens; but often we look so long at the closed door that we do not see which one has been opened for us. HELEN KELLER, AMERICAN AUTHOR, 1880- 1968

- **Ditch the guilt**. Well, as much as you can. Guilt and motherhood kinda go hand in hand. Remember though, guilt is a feeling that's meant to help us. It's so we realise *we've* done something *wrong* so we can fix it and avoid doing it again. As mothers we're prone to confusion on this guilt issue. We can apply it to situations that are out of our control and by definition could then hardly be attributed to our "wrongdoing". So, if you can't spend as much time with your baby as you'd like, ask yourself: have I done the best I can, given all that I had to do today and how over-tired and worn out I'm feeling? Ditch the question: have I done my best today compared to someone with 10 arms, $1 million in the bank, and who adores sleep deprivation? It's not you. Your only obligation to your baby is to do the best that you can.

- **Dump the green-eyed monster**. Jealousy *is* a curse – on you that is. It's sooo hard not to think that the women with the hands-on-husbands and picture-perfect partners haven't got it better than you do. They might. Right now. But there'll also be millions of mothers around the world who'd give their right arm to have your situation. Safe home. Healthy baby. Access to health care. No civil war. OK, enough. Point made.

  Think, too, that when you compare yourself to these "flawless fantasy couples" you see only a moment in time – not their ten year struggle to fall pregnant, not that one's mother died when she was nine, not that one was abused as a child, etc. Enough already. Again, point made. Jealousy isn't an easy one to harness, but if you can focus on what you *have* rather than what you don't, chances are you'll find there's a whole load of positives you've inadvertently overlooked.

- **Plan ahead for emergencies**. Ever experienced these crazy scenes at midnight?
  - your baby's temperature is above 39 degrees and you're out of panadol.
  - you're sick yourself, and you're too busy dealing with bodily fluid emissions to get to your baby.

310

When there isn't another adult in the house to provide back-up, planning ahead is essential to deal with these stressful scenarios. So make sure you know of any emergency babysitting service in your area – they'll be expensive, but worth it in the long run. You'll also need your list of emergency contacts – friends and family members willing to be called on at a moment's notice to help you out.

- **Get creative about child-care**: Don't let outdated and traditional models of child-care put you off getting support. The world is very 18th-century when it comes to meeting the powerful presence of the 21st-century single mum. So take matters into your own hands, partner up with some pals, and see whether any of these would work for you:
  - trade-offs – I have your baby on Tuesday, you have mine on Wednesdays.
  - exchanges – you go to the gym and I mind the babies then we'll swap and I'll have my workout.
  - house-sharing – offer a room at home to a teaching student or child-care worker and have them care for your baby in exchange for rent.
  - bartering – I'll do your hair for free (if you're a hairdresser! Mechanics, change your offers accordingly) if you help out with my baby's care.
  - job sharing – you work Mondays and Tuesdays and I'll care for the babies, then I'll work Wednesdays and Fridays while you do the child care.
- **Set realistic goals**. The single mother has every right to dream. Big style. University degrees, returning to work, a bigger house, a secure future and sharing life with a positive partner – all possible. But every dream stays just that – a dream – unless you take the steps to make it a reality. So

get out a sheet of paper. Draw it into three columns. Insert headings above each column: Today – One month – A year. Start writing down your thoughts. You need to make sure your goals are realistic and they should also be connected: ie at some point, your "today" goal will need to contain a step to achieve your monthly or yearly goal or you simply won't achieve it. But in saying this, remember two important factors:

a. The younger your baby, the harder it is to make long term plans – purely on the basis that getting through each day can often be a major achievement in itself. If you're still counting your baby's age in weeks not months, perhaps limit "long-term" planning to a month ahead until the post-baby fog lifts a little.

b. Remember the importance of sanity saving goals, including much-needed "me time". Schedule in a phone call to a friend to organise a child-care arrangement such as those suggested above.

- **Guide your own life**. What are you waiting for? Who are you waiting for? And are you stuck in the "I'm going to do that when…" rut. When we stay where we are because we're waiting for some*one* or some*thing* to change, it's only us who's responsible for our predicament. Because at the end of the day, although it would be nice if everyone changed according to how we'd like, the only person we're in control of changing is *ourselves*. So, write down the top five people who inspire you then do the "House and Garden" exercise in chapter eleven. What is it that you could be doing today and every day that ensures your life reflects the person you want to be and the things you want to be doing?

- **Cast away caustic cognitions**. Caught yourself saying, "I

312

can't do this"? Noticed the thoughts "I've screwed up" or "I'm an idiot" recurring on a regular basis? Take a moment to notice whether these statements, in any way, shape or form help you to deal with your situation. How we talk to ourselves has an enormous impact on our capacity to deal with the situations we face and how we feel about ourselves. It's essential, for you and your baby, that you address any toxic talk inside your brain. So turn to chapter three and address the verbal self-abuse that's sabotaging your chances of sanity.

- **Back your judgment**. Chances are the decision to end a relationship or to raise a child on your own wasn't an easy one. No doubt it took considerable thought and much debate in your own head, if not with many supportive others. While your *current* experience about being a single mother may or may not have led you to the same decision, life cannot be lived stuck in "should haves", "could haves" and "wish I hads". Life is about backing yourself to make the best decision at any given moment *based on the information you have at that time*. That is all we can ever expect of ourselves. No more. No less. So remind yourself that you did make the best decision you could have when you made it. Then encourage yourself to do the same with your decisions today, ie to make the best ones you can today for you and your baby based on what information is in front of you right now.

- **Prioritise play**. Kids can get nearly all of their social, developmental and emotional learning needs met through play. Games of peek-a-boo, blowing raspberries and grabbing mobiles (that's play mobiles not mobile phones!) are so important for your baby (see chapter five for more information). But play is a crucial part of being an adult

313

too, as well as one of the most important dynamics in your mother-child relationship.

- **Allow yourself to grieve**. While your single parent status resulted from a possible myriad of reasons, many of these reasons involved loss of some kind. Loss of a loved one through death, loss through divorce, loss through estrangement, loss of a dream. In order to make yourself available to your baby today, you need to grieve your loss. That doesn't mean falling in a heap. Nor does it mean there's a day when the grief should "all be over". It means working through at your own pace what you miss and then planning to get through today without it in your life.

- **Roll out the role models**. Role models provide us with our much-needed maps in otherwise unchartered territory. If we haven't been somewhere before, or done something before – how do we know what to do or how we should behave? Role models provide us with the direction. They can also inspire us on our toughest of days, knowing that others found the strength and resilience in difficult times. So write down the people who inspire you – some may be single parents, some may not. Some may be celebrities, some may be "ordinary" mums. Write down what it is about that person you want to bring into your own life and how you can start doing that today. And if you need more inspiration, try reading the book *Holding Her Head High: 12 Single Mothers Who Championed Their Children and Changed History* by Janine Turner. It's quite spiritual in nature, but if that's OK with you, you'll love the stories of some amazing single mums dating back to the Middle Ages.

- **Let go of unhelpful habits**. I hear lots of excuses from people, but the one I find the most confusing is justifying an unhelpful behaviour simply on the basis it's always been done that way. Could you imagine your reaction to your baby saying (in later life!), "I'll continue being bullied by other kids in the playground because I've been putting up with it for years"? What? No chance. If it stops being helpful it stops being an option. So let go of any habits that don't bring you health or healing – such as avoiding exercise, arguing with family, turning to smoking or alcohol. Ditch the "I've always done it that way" and embrace the "I can choose the way I behave. And I choose to behave in ways that are best for me and my baby".

- **Lead with your head.** Cupid really has a weird sense of humour. The people we fall in love with can *feel* sooo right even though we know they're really all types of "wrong". And we stay with them, or want to be with them, even when the relationship is bitter, twisted, hurtful, harmful, abusive, disrespectful and sometimes, well, delusional. Because we looove them…And you probably do. But being an adult is about knowing what your heart tells you, and then using your head to figure out whether it's a wise choice. Try therapy, enrol in couples workshops. But even if you know that you might always love an ex-partner, be sensible enough to know when it's time to end the relationship anyway.

Stop holding onto the person who has let you go. TRENT SHELTON, FOUNDER OF REHABTIME AND HUGE SUPPORTER OF SINGLE MUMS

- **Fall in love again.** With yourself. The preciousness of a new baby requires we make a commitment to giving them the best we can provide: the best of us (which can still be of the half-exhausted, pyjama-wearing type) and the best of others

315

we bring into baby's life. But if we haven't yet decided we are the best we can be, we can fall into a new adult romantic relationship that either:

a. reinforces our poor opinion of ourselves – and is therefore abusive in some way, perhaps verbally, physically or emotionally.

b. requires the other person to compensate for all of our perceived inadequacies – a kind of hero if you like – which only serves to reinforce that we are some kind of "victim".

By all means, dream for a hero. So long as you see yourself as an equal counterpart – a sort of wonderwoman meets superman scenario. And go ahead, use your sense of superhero status to empower you – to only accept others who treat you with respect, dignity and kindness – or else face your kung-fu kick or robust right-hook. Well, at the very least, the absolute power to walk away.

- **Celebrate**. By far the most important factor of all. When you live alone with your baby, there aren't important others lurking behind the curtains ready to jump out and pat you on the back when you get through the toughest of times, or teach your baby the coolest of tricks. You know what you achieved. You know it was awesome. Make sure you tell yourself. Then post it on Facebook, or upload it to Instagram, and let others know too about your amazing achievement.

TEN PROMISES I MAKE TO MY BABY

1. I will only knowingly bring people into our life who are caring and responsible.
2. I will support you in having relationships with people who are caring and responsible too (even if I choose not to have relationships with these people myself).
3. I will love you to the moon and back. But I will also take a stand to ensure you behave like a caring and responsible person too.
4. I will remember that I am your mum not your friend. I will be friendly, but you will have many friends in your life. You will only have one mum.
5. I will make sure I keep my adult issues with my adult friends. You are my child, not my confidante, not my counsellor and not my rock to cry on.
6. I will seek help when needed to ensure I stay on top of things.
7. I will take care of myself physically and psychologically so you have a good role model for doing the same.
8. I will help you know that some men can be kind and good and to develop healthy relationships with those men that are.
9. I acknowledge that you are my child but not my property. I do not own the opinions and ideas you have. I will encourage you to be your own person.
10. We will rise to any challenge. We will cope in the face of any adversity. My courage and determination will always come from the love I have for you.

Increasing your knowledge and expanding your tribe – women unite on the worldwide web

Screens – whether they be on phones, ipods, computers or TVs – annoy me. They're often intrusive and anti-social. Bizarre then that I'm suggesting you get better acquainted with them to feel socially supported, but they really do offer some awesome opportunities for community connections if used in the right way.

So here are some recommendations for mounting the mummy cyberhighway to expand your knowledge, your social network and your self-confidence.

In Australia:

The Child Support Agency. This government organisation established in 1988 administers the assessment and collection of child support under the Australian Government's Child Support Scheme (phone: 131272; website: www.csa.gov.au).

Council of Single Mothers and Their Children. This organisation has been devoted to supporting single mothers since its inception in the early 1970s. It is dedicated to women empowering themselves through access to information and support (ph: 0396540622/ country toll free: 1300 552 511; website: www.csmc.org.au).

The Women's Information and Referral Exchange (WIRE). This service provides support, information and free legal advice on any women's issue for women across Victoria (see www.wire.org.au or call **1300 134 130**).

Single Parenting Successfully. SPS is a self-funded organisation, aiming to support parents during times of separation or those dealing with the Family Law system (www.singleparentingsuccessfully.com.au).

SingleMum. A website and directory for numerous financial, legal, social and community resources for single mothers (www.singlemum.com.au).

Parents Without Partners. An organisation designed to increase community resources to assist single parents and to increase their social networking (www.pwpaustralia.net; phone: 1300 797 842 (Victoria Head office)).

In the UK:
The Child Maintenance Service. This statutory child maintenance service works out how much should be paid, and can also collect the payments (www.gov.uk/child-maintenance).

Gingerbread. With single mother advocacy services dating back to the early 1900s this national charity is an extraordinary example of the power of bringing together single mothers and giving them a voice. The organisation provides free expert advice, practical support and campaigns with gusto for single parents (www.gingerbread.org.uk; phone: 0808 802 0925).

OnlyMums. Established in 2007, this UK-registered not-for-profit Community Interest Company offers on-line support and signposting service for parents who are going through or have been through separation or divorce. It includes free advice on key issues including: housing, family law, benefits and welfare, drugs and alcohol, and debt (www.onlymums.org; phone: 07794 848103).

One Space. An online community for single parents with support from experienced parenting facilitators. It brings together essential information, interactive learning games, multi-media content, links to other support organisations and news. The online groups also act as a support group, where people can gain information and support from others who have been through similar experiences (www.onespace.org.uk).

There are a few good reads out there too:
- Cassandra Mack – *The Single Mom's Little Book of Wisdom* (iUniverse, Inc)
- Sandy Chalkoun – *Single Mother in Charge* (Praeger)
- Orit Sutton – *How to Be a Happy Single Mother* (Eloquent Books)
- Janis Adams – *A Complete Guide for Single Moms* (Atlantic Publishing)

One last comment:

At times I've been flippant, but I do get it…It's no joke. Single parenting is hard. In fact, it could well rank within the hardest jobs on the planet. And the praise is whisper-quiet – sometimes inaudible – from the politicians, the governing bodies and the general powers on earth. If it wasn't for the extraordinary love we have for our babies, this job might well be considered near impossible. Which is why so many of those fancy-pants self-appointed VIPs of the world aren't doing it – I don't think they could.

So summon your supporters – those people who "get it". Ignore the delusional do-gooders, the people who are up-tight and uninformed, those who fear your power and those who adopt an 18th-century position. Leave them behind and in your past, just like their attitude.

Remember – one life. One opportunity to embrace who you are. And you are absolutely 100%, fundamentally and at all levels, deserving of standing as proud (perhaps prouder!) and as tall (perhaps taller!) as any other person who has ever walked the earth.

I am woman. I am strong. I am me. My baby is my energy, my reason for balance and my purpose to improve I am her lifeline. I am her guide. Together we are powerful. JEAN, MOTHER OF ONE.

Chapter 11:

Where did I go and who am I? Rediscovering yourself in motherhood.

On Tuesday, Amy had a wonderful dream.
She was important in her own life.

Then she woke up, fed the baby,
cleaned the house and took
care of everyone and
everything other
than herself.

Another mother once asked me how I found myself again after the first year with my baby. All I could say was, "I don't know. I'm still looking"! ROSIE, MOTHER OF TWO

Forgotten who you are? Wondering whether the real you still exists? Many mothers in their first year post-baby consider hiring a private detective…to locate the whereabouts of their capacity to think, hold intelligent conversations or even their entire identity (what's my name again?…Oh, that's right…

it's just "mum" now…). Other mothers are less hopeful and give up. They've just accepted they'll be "missing in action" in their own lives until their kids hit their 30s.

And for those who know who you are – do you even like yourself? Or have you morphed into a mother stereotype you swore in your adolescence you'd *never* become? You know the type – moany, whiney, sad, overanxious, boring, bossy, or unshowered! Well…the upside of this type of downturn is that at least you're a "somebody", that there is some definite identity lurking beneath the mounds of used nappies and sterilising equipment. It's a small step up from those mothers with an unknown identity well into middle-age.

Realistically, whether we've lost ourselves or found a bizarre and unwanted version of ourselves, neither option is particularly exciting. Nor is it good for our psychological health. So this chapter is aimed at halting the tide of both the missing in action (MIA) and the miserably-morphed mother.

As mothers, we are our children's role models – whether we want to be or not. We are the ones who help our children know who they are and who they want to be. It's not just about what we say. We have to show them how it's done, too. JUDY, MOTHER OF FOUR

SO…What type of mother are you? And do you want to admit it…? Sit back. Get a cup of tea (the left-over, cold dregs variety that most mothers come to appreciate) and take a moment to see whether any of these categories resemble your own sense of being a mother:

The Martyr Mother

Tired? Worn out? Living in some type of mothering hell? Don't you know it! And so does anybody else who stands still long enough to hear it. You know you're in this category if you find yourself equally torn by loudly declaring your woes whilst adamantly fending off any offers to ease your situation. "No," you sigh. "It's a mother's lot…" Deep down you want to enjoy mothering, but fear that unless you portray it as some really energy-sucking job, people won't appreciate your enormous capacities and life-giving sacrifices.

How you might relate to others:

- Generally your mind is set on avoiding even the faintest of possibilities that there's *anyone* on this planet who could have it harder than you. That other mother who declared she hadn't slept for days – ha! You've gone weeks without your eyelids closing.

- Oh, and woe betide any mother who seems happy with her lot – she clearly has a live-in nanny with a housekeeper on the side – not like you – had to do it all on your own because of your useless partner whilst also suffering from influenza, norovirus or limb amputation.

- In case you hadn't guessed it, this approach can pretty well annoy most people, eventually. Their initial concern with your incredibly awful predicaments will soon be replaced with bewilderment at your apparent desire to stay firmly lodged in the pity pit.

- Here's a hint: if most people's first comment to you becomes "I know. You've had the worst/hardest/crappiest day ever…",maybe it's time to negate the negativity. Although you'd probably prefer to moan that people don't listen anymore…

324

The Gold Medal Mother

Smiling? She did it at birth. Crawling? Virtually walked at three months. Switching to solids? Did it in a day! Who'd have known you'd have the world's most talented, intelligent, funny and beautiful baby on the planet. Yes, you'll know you're in this category if you feel a deep urge to compete with every other mother on every other mothering subject under the sun. But unlike the Martyr Mother, you don't want things to look bad – you want everyone to think you've got a world champion child on your hands. Deep down you might harbour some doubts (like if your baby hasn't rolled over by the time they're 12 months of age) but Lord knows you won't be letting any of those negatives out of the vault. Nope. Full steam ahead to successful station – Nobel Peace prizes and Olympic Gold medals here we come!

How you might relate to others:

- On the whole, other mothers and their babies become mere competitors in your race called "life".

- Usually you'll be most comfortable with those who seem to be achieving less (on the Baby Olympics front that is) than you.

- Your main interactions relate to identifying another baby's achievements – "Is little Archie holding his own bottle yet?" – with a hope the answer will be "no" (your baby has been self-feeding for a week! Yeah!).

- Your mummy blogs are filled with your baby's extraordinary exploits – "I think she'll be a supermodel before she's 12 months of age".

- Texts to friends aren't about an explosive poo (unless you think it's the biggest one in history) or all-night-cry-a-thons (she *never* cries!), the focus is on everyone knowing baby's latest superhero-like skills – "she rolled over by herself which makes her three weeks ahead of expected developmental targets. Again!".

- Your partner's reactions will depend on his related degree of competitiveness. Some will fuel the fire (eg baby's random kick in the air evokes "I always knew I'd be the father of a world champion footballer"). Others ponder on treatment options for your semi-delusional state ("Are you nuts? He can't walk – he's three weeks old!").

- In case you hadn't guessed it, you'll soon wear out your welcome with most mothers. You see, it's quite rare to find friends amongst women whose babies you've deemed ugly, unintelligent, delayed or generally non-fabulous compared to your own. Just saying…

The Perfect Vision Mother

Hair? Check. Makeup? Check. Fabulous frock? Check. Baby looking perfect? Check. Yes, you'll know you're this type of mother if your obsession with fashion far outweighs your focus on feelings. In the past, you've probably suffered pinched toes, backaches and hip displacement all in the name of stilettos. When you found out you were pregnant, you didn't enrol in baby classes – boring! You called your stylist (on speed-dial) to whip-up a killer maternity wardrobe. You lay awake at night, not because your baby's unsettled, but because you're thinking about where to buy the right pram, the right clothes and the right coloured cushions for baby's cot. Any gifts or toys that don't match the nursery colour scheme quickly find their way to the bin (or Vinnies). Yep, you've got your vision of motherhood so perfectly arranged that even on your worst days *emotionally*, you can still leave the house with you and baby *looking* just sensational!

How you might relate to others:

- Generally interactions with others will revolve around their knowledge of fashion, furnishings or food (of the perfect-biscuit-for-mothers-group kind) – or what I call the "three Fs".

- If you meet someone who doesn't seem interested in the "three Fs" you'll usually let them know what you think about their choice to buy non-fashionable items: "I've decided not to use a Dora the Explorer or other branded toys or furnishings. They're tacky". (Message – you have no taste. And quite frankly, it's not about what my baby might *like*, it's about what coordinates, duh).

- You'll also tend to find your main friendship group looks remarkably similar to you – ie perfect looking. Mothers with unruly hair, outdated clothes and babies in non-matching outfits are (un)surprisingly absent at your nicely-catered morning teas.

The Research Scientist Mother

Instinct? No way! Mothering is about statistics – far more helpful. Yes, you'll know you're this type of mother if your love affair with facts about babies registered an exponential growth from the positive sign on your pregnancy test. Your chosen "expert" to provide these facts can vary, but essentially you're a great believer in the "truth" being out there if you simply obtain enough information. You might read every book on parenting (if this book was one of 20 you bought recently, you can bet you're in this category). You spend many hours researching "Google" before considering even trying a new technique or purchasing a new item. And you'll have your "chosen one" – the local GP, paediatrician or distant family relative with nursing qualifications – as your go-to person for advice on every minor ailment or baby concern. Until, that is, you decide you have absorbed this knowledge. Then you'll carry out your own graduation ceremony, proudly declaring yourself a recipient of the "parenting wisdom" diploma, and disperse your knowledge to anyone silly enough to stand still long enough to hear.

How you might relate to others:

- Generally it will depend on how "wise" you think the other person is on parenting issues.
  - The "uneducated" will either be ignored or the focus of your teachings (eg "Let me show you how to wrap the baby sooo much better…").
  - The "informed" will be held much higher in your esteem and will be sought out for lengthy discussions on various parenting topics.
- In general, you'll start most sentences with "Well, the doctor/ nurse/scientist/guru (insert other chosen expert name here) thinks the best way is…" Which, perhaps, can end up driving your friends absolutely nuts. Use their repeated eye-rolling as a sign to lay-off sharing your wisdom or risk being vetoed from your local mummy mob.

The Scared Mother

Baby's scary?…No!…Actually, yes. Big time. You'll know you're in this category if anxiety and fear moved in just after baby came home. You worry that at any moment you will do something that will harm the baby, neglect the baby or otherwise screw up this whole mothering thing. You have local hospitals, the poisons information line and every GP in town on speed dial. You have trouble deciding on whether to feed or not to feed the baby, to put to them bed or to keep them awake, whether to wake the baby to change their nappy or leave them to sleep. They're simply questions of too great a magnitude to decide on your own. You yearn to have someone else with you at all times to help make the right decisions. At night you lay awake going through anything you stuffed up that day and planning how to deal with any possible emergency tomorrow. Deep down there is a burning question that invades your thinking on a regular basis:"How on earth did I ever think I was up for this mummy mayhem?"

How you might relate to others:

- Basically you'll be manoeuvring life so as to avoid being alone with your baby – with related behaviours ranging from gentle requests for your mother's help to threatening and hysterical phone calls to your partner ("Come home now. I mean NOW. I don't care if you lose your job or we lose the house or we have to live in our car forever. I just can't deal with this on my own!").

- You'll also be the one who organises the mothers group on a regular basis and turns up at every mother-baby class so that you can be *with* people.

- You're probably not surprised that others might be starting to describe you as a little, well…needy…which might work well if you have friends or relatives desperate to be *needed*, but could well wear down your support networks fast.

- If you start to notice that nobody returns your calls and people run away from you in shopping centres, you know you've taken your neediness a step too far.

The Laid-Back Mother

What's the fuss? Why all the drama? You'll know you're this type of mother if parenting has just been one long day on the couch after another! Does it really matter if you haven't washed your bedsheets for a few weeks or that the dirty dishes have piled up in the kitchen? Who cares if you shower? Sitting on the couch with Tim Tams and a cuppa is an ideal way to connect with baby, right? Sterilising is a good idea, but really…every time? Surely not in a first world country? Cooking, well that's for fools who don't know the number of the local takeaway Chinese restaurant.

How you might relate to others:

- Usually it's everyone else around you that's more worried than you are, so generally you're quite happy to sit back and let them stress out.
- However, the chances of you getting a mother or mother-in-law who shares your approach is pretty slim (remembering most of them came from a time where routines and a tidy home were touted as the answer to most parenting issues).
- You'll probably be a nice balance for the more anxious mother (if you can stand being in each other's company – she probably sees you as a slob).
- If people don't agree with your approach, you might let them know either:
  - directly: "It doesn't matter that the house isn't tidy, my main focus is the relationship I have with my baby." (Message: the fact that you want me to keep a tidy house means you don't really know how to prioritise relationships.)
  - indirectly: "I think a cleaner would really makes things run more smoothly." (Message: if you're going to keep raving on about the house, someone else has got to take the cleaning responsibility on, because I have other more important things to do.)

The Entitled Mother

Somebody do something! Fast! Sort this baby out! You'll know you're this type of mother if you feel like the world should be geared around helping you, usually as a priority over all others. You probably won't like to admit you're this type, but perhaps you'll recognise these characteristics: you can't stand waiting in queues, you insist on only the best of everything, you don't understand why mother or mother-in-law (or friends) aren't more available to help with the baby. Your partner should be 100% hands-on and never take a break (doesn't he know how much support you need. His needs? Whatever!). When it comes to the daily grind of baby needs – consistent waking in the night for feeding and settling, lots of dirty nappy changes, etc – you might be feeling ripped off ("my baby is the *worst* sleeper *ever*!!) and wondering who (night nannies, partners, neighbours, far-distant relatives, the kid next door) can do this job for you so you can get a good night's sleep (oh, and be refreshed for a day of getting your nails and hair done tomorrow).

How you might relate to others:

- Depending on whether things in your world are up to your standards at any time, you can greatly vary in what you say to others.
  - When things are going your way (ie you have the best pram, you're getting eight hours' sleep, you have a regular babysitter, your husband is earning a whole lot of money) you're really easy to get along with.
  - When they're not, you will be upset and overwhelmed, feeling as though you've got it tougher than anyone else and demanding that people support you.
- When things go wrong, you might handle it in either :
  - subtle ways: "Honey, why don't we make a little roster for

your mother and my mother so we make sure they babysit at least three hours a day."

- Less subtle ways: "I can't believe the baby has not stopped crying. We need a holiday. To the Maldives. With 24/7 nannies. For at least a month. It's the only way I can continue this parenting job. Sort it out or I'll **never** be happy *again*."

The Over-Connected Mother

Self-soothing? Hiring a baby-sitter? How ridiculous! You know you're this type of mother if the thought of your baby being out of arm's reach produces panic-like symptoms. You've probably been co-sleeping since the first night (ignoring the inherent risks) because it just feels better to have your baby *permanently* attached to your breast (or at least skin-to-skin). You fend off all offers to hold the baby (including your partner's – that would break the attachment, duh). You use the toilet with baby latched onto your breast because you simply can't bear her crying and not being there to pick her up immediately. You think education needs are best met by home schooling and plan to breastfeed until your child is at least in their 20s.

How you might relate to others:

- Often you'll seek out mothers of the same kind to reinforce that this parenting approach is "best for baby".
- When less "attached" mothers mention their difficulty taking a shower and momentarily leaving an unsettled baby, you proudly announce you've gone seven days without a wash to avoid such baby distress.
- Your relationship with your partner will depend on how long this behaviour has continued and whether he's a fan of your style.

- If he's not, life will get super tricky (not that you'll probably notice – your life is all about the *baby* now!).
- If he is, hours of family time are probably spent all bunked down in a co-sleeping in the same bed arrangement either feeding or settling the baby.

• Grandmothers are unlikely to have much sympathy for this approach though. They probably think your lack of routine and feeding-on-demand for hours on end is nothing short of absurd.

• Brace yourself and think like a rhino (skin-wise, that is) because while you'll attract some great fans of this type of parenting, you'll find you'll spend plenty of time defending it too. Oh, and you might find you get a bit worn out and smelly. Just saying…

The Well-Rounded Mother

Bits of some of these types but not others? Caught yourself out with these behaviours and then changed? Most well-rounded mothers have had a day or two in the lives of these other types. It's normal. A baby's arrival is as messy on our brains as it is on our uterus.

But if you're in this category, you've probably figured out that being a mother is about being patient, wise, humble and healthy (well, most of the time…On your good days anyway…). You'll know that leaving the washing and ironing will just have to happen sometimes, but that the home cannot be a breeding ground for chaos because everybody needs some structure and some level of organisation to feel safe and in control of their life. You'll know that every baby needs to be loved and nurtured but that from the time the umbilical cord was cut our baby needs to gradually learn how to help herself. And you'll know that

333

while looking good is part of a good self-care regime, it can never replace the importance of emotional connection and *real* relationships.

How you might relate to others:

- Most days you'll stand true to your conviction that nobody owes you anything and you are not beholden to anyone either.
- You'll know that your baby needs you to step up to meet her needs, but that you have the right to seek help and support when you need it – not just because you can't be bothered.
- You know you need to take advice from many sources – including "experts", mothers and mothers-in-law – but that sometimes you'll have to rely on your own natural instinct with your baby.
- You'll know that your responsibility is to be a role model for your baby – both now and when she grows up – who strikes the delicate balance of taking care of both others and yourself.

So what if you didn't like your mother category?

If you were able to allocate yourself into one of these categories (even if you didn't like it), or perhaps a combination of a few, the good news is you still believe you exist – or, in other words, haven't become a complete "nobody" since the baby was born. But I'd bet a few hours of precious sleep that unless you decided you were the "well-rounded mother" this has hardly left you jumping for joy (pelvic floor muscle-braced, of course).

The reason for this lack of excitement is probably that other than seeing ourselves as a "mother category" we've often lost every other connection with who we are. And, unless you're an "entitled" or "too easy" mother, you've probably fallen into the trap of prioritising *everyone* over yourself. You've probably forgotten what pleases *you*, or what *you* really want out of life (other than a nap!) Message to self – on the list of the world's priorities, you sooooo slipped off the last page!

So how do we change this around? It takes a few changes and reprioritisations, but using the few exercises I've outlined below usually gets most mothers I work with back to a place where they at least can remember their own name.

EXERCISE 1: The Circles Of Love And Care

Step one: how good's your throwing arm? Imagine yourself hurling a pebble into a pond. Compare the size of the ripples between an enthusiastic non-sleep-deprived throw and a post-labour exhausted attempt. No prizes for guessing which version had the wider ripple effect.

In the same way, our relationships are like a pond too: the more enthusiasm we give to *our* own existence, the wider the ripples of energy go out for *other* people in our lives. So it's good news all round really. If you want to give out more support to those you care about or lavish your love on a cast of thousands, permission granted to give more to yourself as well.

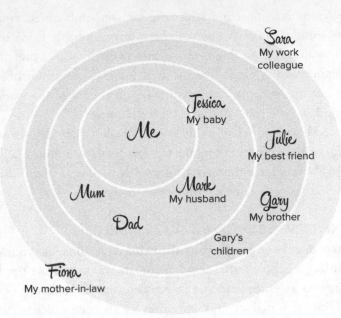

CASE EXAMPLE

The Circles of Love and Care example outlined above was from a mother named Cathy I worked with. When we did this exercise, she quickly realised she caught up far more with Sara (her work colleague) than with her best friend, simply because Sara kept nagging at her to meet up.

It also dawned on her that her daily 30-minute- phone calls to her mother-in-law were only because she felt obliged to, even though this precious energy (and all the things should could be doing instead of talking to her) could be used for her husband and home. It quickly made sense to her why she was so exhausted (yet feeling she achieved so little) and constantly battling her guilt about how she cared for the people closest to her.

Step two: it's about pecking order! Imagine each layer of the ripples in the pond represents a layer of importance. The people most important to you get the VIP positioning in the inner circle, then as the layers go out, the importance of the person you name gets less. Take a look at the example opposite to see how this might look and then draw this for yourself.

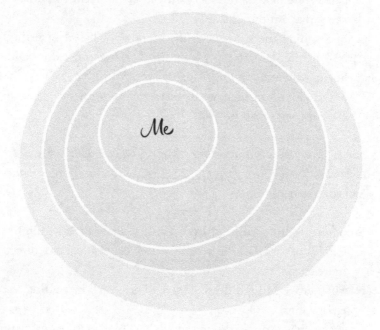

Step three: reality check time. Be honest with yourself. Are your VIP circles (the two inner layers) really getting the most of your energy, or are your best efforts being misdirected to the outer circles? If you find there's a problem with your prioritisation, then you've discovered a major clue as to why you're struggling with your role (and energy) in motherhood.

You see, our brain's feel-good centres crave the joyful happy chemicals we generate when we give priority to people in our closest circle. This means two things:

a. When we give people on the outer circle more energy than our inner circle – because they demand it or we feel it's the "right thing" to do – we might briefly feel good – but it will pass very quickly and our brain will be left feeling confused and sad about our choice.

b. In avoiding the short-term discomfort you'll feel in saying NO to the demanding people (or because you can't stand hurting anyone's feelings – except your own), you're actually doing long-term damage to relationships with people who are most important to you.

Say no. Even if it's just sometimes. You can't do everything you did before because life isn't the same as before. It's totally different now.
Sharon, mother of two

Step four: redirection required. This has a few steps within it:

a. Circle the names of the people you are determined to redirect more energy to.

b. Put a cross through those names where you'll be putting *less* energy into.

c. Write down three things you'll be doing with your new energy for your close circle (eg enjoying a romantic meal, paying closer attention when they talk, making a phone call every second day, giving a kiss goodbye each morning, etc).

d. Write down three things you'll be saying NO to or that you'll stop doing for those people you put a cross against (eg coming over only once a week, only calling once a week instead of three times, etc).

> But...if you're lacking the assertiveness skills to say no or step back from people in the outer circles who demand your time and energy then you need to do the assertiveness exercise outlined in chapter three.

It's hard not to feel guilty about not having time for everyone, so I accepted guilt was part of mothering and just worked out my priorities based on how much guilt I felt. That's how I worked out I needed to devote more time to my husband and my baby and less to my sister and boss at work. EMILY, MOTHER OF TWO

Step five: putting it into practice. There's no point making any decision to change, if it isn't matched by actually doing the things we decided. So:

a. Take a moment to choose one of the items you just wrote down and commit to doing it *today*.

b. If you're able to, put your list of changes on the fridge or another place where you'll see them and decide when you're going to start those changes, too.

c. Keep in mind that it doesn't all have to be done at once, but remember that the mother who makes small changes is the mother who reaps big rewards (of the sane-parent variety, that is).

EXERCISE TWO: Looking After Your "Well" Being

> Do this exercise today and it will be a tool you use for life. In the future, wherever you are and whatever you're doing, you'll be able to do a quick "well check" to keep yourself on track.

339

Now that you've redirected your energy to your VIPs, the next step is to master the art of throwing that pebble into your own pond with great gusto. Or in other words – looking after your "well" being. Yes, understanding "self-care" is really about seeing yourself like a well…Odd, but trust me.

Let's start by stating the obvious about this: a working well includes a bucket being wound down and bringing up water. It's considered a dud well when there's no water supply and nobody's getting a drink.

In the same way, *we're* often seen (sometimes mainly in our own eyes) as a "good mum" if we've got a constant supply of support for others, and a "dud mum" if we use the words "I can't" or "I'm too busy" or generally the word "no" to requests we deep-down know are stretching our coping capacity.

But it's unhealthy for us and our babies if we pretend to be the superhero mother who can "do it all" but meanwhile fall apart every time we're in our own bat cave. So to be a true superhero of the every-day, not-so-perfect, baby-puke-wearing kind, here's what to do.

Step one: draw a line on your well. How full is it? Half-way, three-quarters, or close to empty? Are you living on a high, or close to being as drained as your hooters after some breast-pump action? This is a simple and quick self-check that can be done each day to know your level of wellbeing.

Step two: if it's low, start looking for your "water source". In other words, work out your IN-FLOW by determining who (the people) and what (the activities) give you energy, support and enthusiasm for life? Then do as follows:

- Commit to increasing the amount of resources in the well by calling in the people and the activities that boost your feel-good factor. Even a five-minute foot massage by a partner is a great reboost for some mums. Helpful self-statements such as "you're doing the best job you can as a mum today" are another quick boost.
- See the list below to find out what quick and easy refuels (I call them the "rebooters") you can fit into your day – remember it's not about having a whole morning at a day spa (although if you can fit it in, that's great).
- And before you get too excited that I've just endorsed a love affair with the Mint Slices (what a rebooster, huh!?), food can't be your *only* well-filler…Its effects are too brief (except for on your hips). Same goes for alcohol – if it's the *only* thing you're using to get through, you'll find yourself in more trouble than you bargained for. Look at what other well-fillers you could choose before you reach for the second (or third) glass of chardonnay.

My husband and I did this exercise together and he desperately tried to convince me that sex would be a great "rebooter" for me. He seemed genuinely shocked when I told him sex had always seemed more of a drain! Men…
MARGIE, MOTHER OF THREE

Step three: if it's still low, limit the water going out of the well. In other words, reduce your OUT-FLOW by letting friends, family and demanding others know (always do it in the order of your "circles of love") that you're running near empty. And then assertively and politely tell them what you can't do that day as a result (such as not picking up a friend's shopping, or spending an hour on the phone to your mother-in-law for the third time that week).

Step four: learn your warning signs to prevent you "drying up" in the future. We all have signs we're starting to crack, whether it be:
- emotional warning signs (eg losing your cool with your baby or snapping at your husband big time); or
- physical warning signs (eg constantly wanting sleep even when you've actually had a good rest, ongoing illnesses, headaches, etc).

Use these indicators as big red flashing warning signs that you need to either limit what's going out of your well or increase what's coming in.

If you're brave enough to ask friends and family what they think your warning signs are, their comments can be really useful. But beware, you might not like what you hear!

I have a great girlfriend who always knew when I was overwhelmed. She said if I hadn't returned a text within 48 hours, it was a good bet I was having a hard time. She'd then arrive on my doorstep at 6:30pm with a tub of ice-cream and an old DVD we both loved. She'd help me settle the baby to bed and then we'd have our time to catch up. Gotta love a friend like that! SONIA, MOTHER OF ONE

The Rebooters

Foot massage by your partner	Paint your toenails
Picking a flower in your garden and putting it in a vase	Play a favourite song in the car while driving to the shops
Making a healthy snack	Write down an inspirational saying and pin it on your fridge
Putting on lipstick and a bit of mascara	Make yourself a favourite mocktail
Reading a magazine for two minutes	Pour yourself a cup of tea
A quick text to a much-loved friend	Read affirmations you've written about yourself, eg "you're doing the best job you can with what resources you've got", "you can do it, think about how many tough days you've managed already"
A shower with some super nice shower gel	
Phone your mum or other loved relative	Print out a favourite photo of you and baby and put it on your wall.
Invite your BFF for afternoon tea	

My favourites:-

_____

_____

_____

_____

EXERCISE 3: Your House And Garden

> Do this exercise today and you'll never wonder who you "really are" again. You'll be happier, able to be more assertive, and a great role model for your baby in the future too.

Mums need to remember that life is a matter of balance and that baby is only part of it – you need your friends, time with your partner and rest. Change your "hats" depending on your role, but don't ever see yourself as only a mother. CATHY, MOTHER OF THREE

Understanding your own values is crucial to steering your life where you want it to go. If you don't know your own values, it's hard to know who you are or what you want out of life.

A great book to read if you want to know more about this area is *An Intelligent Life* by Dr Julian Short. But in the whirlwind of baby bedlam, I'm guessing getting through this book is a big deal, so another would be just too much. So I've adapted some of his ideas for new mothers, summarised his ideas and made them tangible (I hope) for you to actually apply to your own life.

Your very own "House and Garden" is based on these four key factors:

1. We have two MAJOR values (what I refer to as our "house"): to care for and protect (a) ourselves, and (b) the people we love.
2. We have a number of MINOR values (what I refer to as our "garden"). These further define who we are and how we behave (eg creativity).
3. Our MAJOR values must always come before our MINOR ones, or else we'll feel like crap in the long term. It would

be like prioritising the state of your garden over the state of your house. Take, for example, the typical mother's trip to her baby's swimming lessons. Her MINOR value is "being on time", but if she drives like a Senseless Susie, the moment of satisfaction for being punctual is soon lost as the guilt sets in for ignoring her MAJOR values, namely failing to care and protect those people she loved – her baby and herself on the road!

4. If we don't know our values or don't live by our values we have a very sad-looking "house and land package" which is ultimately our cause for feeling miserable, depressed and baby-blues-like. Once we know our values and start living by them, we start to feel "ourselves" again.

Step one: working on your major values (your house). Let's start with your MAJOR values. If you're like most mothers, you have heaps of behaviours that involve "protecting and caring for *others*". However, the other essential part of the home is the behaviours that involve "protecting and caring for *yourself*". We need to ensure our house always looks balanced if we want our sanity to stick around. To do this:

a. On a piece of paper, going width-ways, divide it into three equal parts.

b. In the top one-third draw a picture of a house with a line down the middle of it.

c. Label one half – "protecting and caring for the people I love".

d. Label the other half – "protecting and caring for myself".

e. Look at how you care for yourself by using the table below. Put a tick next to the ones you're already doing and a circle around the ones you want to change in the future.

f. Write what behaviours reflect your MAJOR values (or which ones you *want* to reflect your values) onto your own drawing of a house. See Sally's example below for some guidance.

My **physical needs**, for example:

☐ Is my diet healthy and well-balanced and am I eating regularly?

☐ Am I exercising, even if it's just 10 minutes a day? (Pushing a pram to get a baby to sleep can count, but you could throw some squats or lunges in just to be sure, and it might even assist baby's sleep!)

☐ Am I getting sleep when I can?

☐ Am I using some yoga breathing or slow breathing whenever I get a moment (you can do this while you feed your baby).

☐ Other:

My **social needs**, for example:

☐ Am I catching up with friends and/or family that FILL my emotional cup (and not further drain it).

☐ How is my relationship with my partner – does it need more time, energy and/or effort?

☐ Am I lonely and feeling house-bound? Could I be linking in with other mums at mothers group or on the internet?

☐ Do I want to be at work?

☐ Other:

My **psychological needs**, for example:

☐ Am I kind and compassionate to myself about my strengths and my weaknesses?

☐ Do I talk to myself in helpful ways or am I critical and demeaning?

☐ Do I tell myself I can change or am I helpless about my ability to make things different?

☐ Can I be assertive with friends and family when needed?

☐	Do I keep going over and over things in my mind until I feel like I'm going crazy?
☐	Am I able to "switch off" when it's time for sleep?
☐	Other

CASE EXAMPLE

Sally was a client who came to see me when her baby was around six months old. She was miserable and she was lost. She adored her baby, Ellie, but felt she had nothing much else going on in her life.

When I asked her what she wanted to bring into her life and how she could best act in ways to reflect who she really was, she stared at me blankly. "I have no idea," she said.

We worked on these concepts together over six weeks and I've presented below her "house". I'll include the "garden" in the next section and finish with her entire "house and garden" at the end.

Step two: working on your minor values (your garden). This requires multiple actions:

a. Under your house, draw a line across the bottom third of the page.

b. Look at the values in the table below. Choose 10 that you think most reflect who you are or who you'd like to be in the future.

c. Write these 10 values under the line.

d. Write the behaviours that reflect these values ABOVE the line, as if they were the trees within your garden, growing from your "root values".

....

Accomplishment	Faith
Adventure	Freedom
Beauty	Friendship
Calm (inner peace)	Fun
Challenge	Hard work
Change	Harmony
Cleanliness	Honesty
Commitment	Honour
Communication	Independence
Community	Innovation
Competence	Integrity
Competition	Justice
Courteousness	Knowledge
Creativity	Leadership
Discovery	Love or romance
Efficiency	Loyalty
Equality	Money
Excellence	Non-violence
Fairness	Orderliness

Patience	Strength
Patriotism	Success
Persistence	Teamwork
Power	Tolerance
Punctuality	Tradition
Quality of work	Tranquility
Safety	Trust
Security	Truth
Speed	Wealth
Spirituality	
Status	

I've given you an example of what part of Sally's garden looked like. I've included just three of her values here.

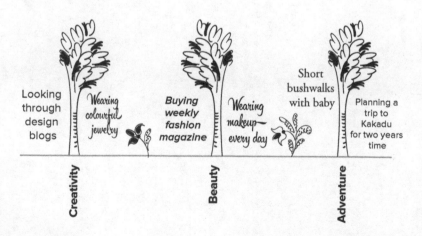

Draw Your Entire House and Garden Here.

Step three: putting it into practice. If we want great ideas to become a reality, we don't need to call on any superhero, we just need to draw on our own parent power. Here are some tips to keep up a determined attitude despite sleep deprivation, cracked nipples and other mummy-chaos contributors:

- Don't do it all at once. You can focus on one value for a while and allow the others to develop more slowly. Some mothers like to make their most important values the bigger plants. Sometimes they "tag" the plants they want to focus on developing over the next few months.

- Work within the timeframe you've got. Don't get stuck by choosing behaviours that take hours (we all know mums usually have no more than five minutes – keep referring back to my "rebooters").

- Stay focused. Keep your house and garden picture somewhere easy to see. In all the mothering mayhem, unless your plan is within regular eyesight you can get off course pretty quick.

- Be patient. No house and garden emerges overnight (even the makeover shows demand a 48-hour window). It will take time to get to know yourself all over again. Be patient, kind and tolerant of yourself in this important process.

CASE EXAMPLE

I still remember the change in Sally when she walked in wheeling Ellie in the pram, wearing her red scarf, red ring and matching red shoes. In those few brief moments to put her outfit together she had honoured her value of "creativity". It was a small step in terms of time and effort, but a great leap for her sense of self-worth. And I'm pleased to report that she's gone on to make many other changes that echo this same sentiment. This is what she said to me at her last session:

Being ME isn't about being selfish. And it's not about neglecting Ellie either. I am a better mother for cherishing myself and living by my own values. But until I knew what they were I was sort of just drifting. Now I now what they are, it helps me to enjoy Ellie more than I ever have before.

One last comment:

Well, hello there! If this chapter has been helpful, I guess I'm greeting a new, or at least an "improved" (in your eyes most importantly), version of who you were before. And I know you'll like your "new and improved model" – because it was generated by caring about *your* needs as well as *your* important values.

And a big thanks! From your baby that is. For having the determination and the courage to dig deep and become a future role model for her too. As Joyce Maynard, author and mother of three, wrote:

It's not only children who grow. Parents do too. As we watch to see what our children are doing with their lives, they are watching us to see what we will do with ours. I can't tell my children to reach for the sun. All I can do is reach for it myself.

Endnotes

from the Reasons to be Grateful Box

[1] Save the Children is an international organisation working in 120 countries to bring immediate and lasting improvements to children's lives through the realisation of their rights. It highlights all that has been done and all that there is still to do to improve both mothers' and children's lives across the world.

Chapter 1

[1] Beck, C., "Birth trauma: in the eye of the beholder", *Nursing Research*, 53 (1), 2004.

[2] Kim, P., Leckman, J., Feldman, R., Wang, X., Swain, J., "The Plasticity of Human Maternal Brain: Longitudinal Changes in Brain Anatomy During the Early Postpartum Period", *Behavioral Neuroscience*, 124 (5), 2010.

[3] Eastwood, J., Phung, H., and Barnett, B., "Postnatal depression and socio-demographic risk: factors associated with Edinburgh Depression Scale scores in a metropolitan area of New South Wales, Australia, *Australian and New Zealand Journal of Psychiatry*, 45(12), pp 1040-1046, 2011.

Chapter 2

[1] Books like *Baby Love* by Robin Barker are awesome, and the classic book *What to Expect the First Year* by Heidi Murkoff and Sharon Mazel has sold 10 million copies for good reason. *Baby on Board* by Dr Howard Chilton also gives extremely helpful practical parenting and sound medical advice.

[2] Source: Raising Children Network, raisingchildren.net.au, supported by the Australian Government.

[3] Canada Research Chair in Community Child Health Research at the University of British Columbia, Professor of Pediatrics in the Faculty of Medicine at UBC, and Head of Developmental Neurosciences and Child Health at the Child and Family Research Institute at BC Children's Hospital. Barr is also a Fellow of the Experience-based Brain and Biological Development Program of the Canadian Institute of Advanced Research.

[4] *Caring for your Baby and Young Child, Birth to Age 5* (5th Edition), The American Academy of Pediatrics, Bantam Books, 2009.

[5] Dr Karp is a board-certified pediatrician, associate professor of pediatrics at UCLA School of Medicine and the author of the book and video, *The Happiest Baby on the Block*. What's great about his ideas is that you can also check out a load of YouTube videos of him performing the techniques, and they make a heap more sense once you've seen these ideas in action.

[6] Authors of *Helping Baby Sleep*, Finch Publishing, 2009. They bring a great deal of commonsense to their very sensible application of the attachment methods of parenting in helping babies settle. This is a delightful read!

[7] Douglas, P., and Hill, P., "The crying baby: what approach?", *Current Opinion in Pediatrics*, 3 (5) 523–529, 2011.

[8] Burnham, M., Goodlin-Jones, B., Gaylor, E., Anders, T., "Night time sleep-wake patterns and self-soothing from birth to one year of age: a longitudinal intervention study", *Journal of Child Psychology and Psychiatry*, 43(6):713-725, 2002.

CHAPTER 3

[1] A) Salmon, P., "Effects of Physical Exercise on Anxiety, Depression, and Sensitivity to Stress", *Clinical Psychology Review*, 21 (1): 33-61, 2001.

B) Sidhu, K. S., Vandana, P., and Balon, R., "Exercise prescription: A practical effective therapy for depression", *Current Psychiatry*, 8(6), 39–51, 2009.

C) Mutrie N., "The relationship between physical activity and clinically defined depression", in S.J.H. Biddle, K.R. Fox and S.H. Boutcher, Editors, *Physical activity and psychological well-being*, Routledge, London, 46–62, 2000.

[2] Armstrong, A., and Edwards, H., "The effectiveness of a pram walking exercise program in reducing depressive symptomatology for postnatal women", *International Journal of Nursing Practice*, (10) 177–194, 2004.

[3] University of Warwick , "Fruits and vegetables: Seven-a-day for happiness and mental health", *ScienceDaily*. Retrieved October 19, 2012, from http://www.sciencedaily.com/releases/2012/10/121009102003.htm.

[4] Jacka, F.N., Pasco, J.A., Mykletun, A., Williams, L.J., Hodge, A.M.,

O'Reilly, S.L., Nicholson, G.C., Kotowicz, M.A., Berk, M., (2010), "Association of Western and traditional diets with depression and anxiety in women", *American Journal of Psychiatry* 167(3):305-11. Epub 2010 Jan 4.

[5] Beyondblue: factsheet on sleep (see www.beyondblue.org.au).

[6] Linde K., Berner M.M., Kriston L., "St. John's wort for treating depression", published online October 7, 2009 at www.summaries. cochrane.org/CD000448/st.-johns-wort-for-treating-depression.

[7] McGee, M., "Meditation and psychiatry", *Psychiatry*, 5, 28–40, 2008.

[8] Grossman, P., Niemann, L., Schmidt, S., and Walach, H., "Mindfulness-based stress reduction and health benefits. A meta-analysis", *Journal of Psychosomatic Research, 57,* 35–43.

CHAPTER 4

[1] "Preventing Shaken Baby Syndrome: A Guide for Health Departments and Community-Based Organizations", *A part of CDC's "Heads Up" Series*, U.S. Department of Health and Human Services Centers for Disease Control and Prevention.

[2] Cox, J., Holden, J., Sagovsky, R., *British Journal of Psychiatry*, 150, 782-6, 1987.

[3] Gilley, T., *Access for Growth: Services for Mothers and Babies*, Brotherhood of St Laurence, Melbourne, 1993.

[4] Milgrom, J., Martin., P. and Negri, L, *Treating Postnatal Depression: A Psychological Approach for Health Care Practitioners*, John Wiley and Sons, 2006.

CHAPTER 5

[1] Brockington, I.F., Oates, J., Turner, D., Vostanis, P., Loh C., and Murdoch C, "A screening questionnaire for mother-infant bonding disorders", *Archives of Women's Mental Health*, 3, 133-140, 2001.

[2] Bussel, J.C., Spitz, B. and Demyttenaere, K., "Three self-report questionnaires of the early mother-to-infant bond: reliability and validity of the Dutch version of the MPAS, PBQ and MIBS", *Archives of Women's Mental Health*, 1,: 373-384, 2010.

[3] Simpson, J. A., "Attachment theory in modern evolutionary context", in: J. Cassidy and P. R. Shaver, (Eds.). *Handbook of attachment: theory, research, and clinical applications*, The Guilford Press, 2002.

[4] Ditto.

[5] Costello, V., "Five Ways To Create a Secure Attachment with Your Baby, Without Sharing Your Bed", *Psychology Central*. Retrieved on February 28, 2012, from http://psychcentral.com/lib/2011/five-ways-to-create-a-secure-attachment-with-your-baby-without-sharing-your-bed/.

[6] Nugent, K., Keefer, C.H., Minear, S., Johnson, L.C., Blanchard, Y., *Understanding newborn behavior and early relationships: The Newborn Behavioral Observations (NBO) system handbook*, Paul H. Brookes Publishing Co, Baltimore, 2007.

[7] Forman, D.R., O'Hara, M.W., Stuart, S., Gorman, L.L., Larsen, K.E., Coy, K.C., "Effective treatment for postpartum depression is not sufficient to improve the developing mother-child relationship", *Development and Psychopathology*, 19, 585–602, 2007.

[8] Zealey, C., "The benefits of infant massage: a critical review", *Community Practitioner*, 78(3) 98-102, 2005.

[9] Cited at http://www.med.wisc.edu/news-events/unique-observation-system-provides-support-to-parents-with-newborns/28868.

[10] Dr Michael Zilibowitz presented this programme and research on its effectiveness at the 2006 World Association of Infant Mental Health Conference in Paris, at the Queen Elizabeth Centre Fourth Biennial International Conference in Melbourne in November 2006, and at numerous local seminars and meetings in Australia, as well as in the United Kingdom and South Africa.

[11] Tedder, J., "H.U.G. Your Baby – Help, understanding, guidance for young families", retrieved April 13, 2013, from http://www.hugyourbaby.com mother-infant bonding disorders", *Archives of Women's Mental Health*, 3, 133-140, 2001.

CHAPTER 6

[1] The research was carried out by CLIC Sargent, the UK children's cancer charity for marking the launch of the Yummy Mummy Week fundraising campaign.

2   Ford, J., Nassar, N., Sullivan, E.A., Chambers, G. and Lancaster, P., "Reproductive health indicators Australia 2002", Cat. no. PER 20, Canberra: AIHW, 2002.

3   Ditto at (i).

CHAPTER 7

1   Milgrom, J., Gemmill, A., Bilszta, J., Hayes, B., Barnett, B., Brooks, J., Ericksen, J., Ellwood, D., and Buist. A., "Antenatal risk factors for postnatal depression: A large prospective study", *Journal of Affective Disorders*, 108 (1), 147-157, 2008.

2   Twenge, J., Campbell, W. and Foster, C, "Parenthood and Marital Satisfaction: A Meta-Analytic Review", *Journal of Marriage and Family* 65 (3), 574–583, 2003.

3   Ditto.

4   Schulz, M., Cowan, C. and Cowan, P., "Promoting healthy beginnings: A randomized controlled trial of a preventive intervention to preserve marital quality during the transition to parenthood", *Journal of Consulting and Clinical Psychology* 74(1), 20–31, 2006.

5   Ditto at (iii).

6   Shapiro, A., Gottman, S. and Carrere, S., "The baby and the marriage: identifying factors that buffer against decline in marital satisfaction after the first baby arrives", *Journal of Family Psychology*, 14(1):59-70, 2000.

7   Rowe, H., Fisher, J., "The contribution of Australian residential early parenting centres to comprehensive mental health care for mothers of infants: evidence from a prospective study", *International Journal of Mental Health Systems*, 4, 6, 2010.

8   For more information see www.gottman.com/about-the-bringing-baby-home-program.

9   McDonald, E., and Brown, S., "Does method of birth make a difference to when women resume sex after childbirth?", *BJOG: An International Journal of Obstetrics & Gynaecology*, 120 (7) 823–830, 2013.

Chapter 8

[1] Dr Terri Apter, author of *What Do You Really Want From Me?: Learning to Get Along With In-laws,* Norton and Company, 2010.

[2] *The Changing Face of Motherhood,* The Social Issues Research Centre, commissioned by P & G, 2011.

[3] Bureau of Labor Statistics, U.S. Department of Labor, *The Editor's Desk,* "Changes in women's labor force participation in the 20th century", see http://www.bls.gov/opub/ted/2000/feb/wk3/art03.htm (visited January 09, 2014).

[4] Source: The National Bureau of Economic Research, see www.nber.org/digest/jan07/w12139.html.

Chapter 10

[1] From raisingchildren.net.au, obtained December 17, 2013.

[2] Hayford, S., Guzzo, K., "The Myth Of The Middle-Class Single Mother: Decomposing Demographic Change In Nonmarital Fertility, 1988-2008", The Center for Family and Demographic Research, 2011.

[3] Pruett, M., Cowan, C., Cowan, P. and Diamond, J., "Supporting father involvement in the context of separation and divorce", in K. Kuehnle and L. Drozd, *Parenting Plan Evaluations: Applied Research for the Family Court,* Oxford University Press, 2012.

[4] Hayford, S., Guzzo, K., at ii above.

[5] Ebling, R., Pruett, M.K., and Pruett, K.D., "'Get Over It': Perspectives on Divorce from Young Children", *Family Court Review,* 47, 665-681, 2009.

[6] Cashmore, J., and Parkinson, P., "Judicial Conversations with Children in Parenting Disputes: The Views of Australian Judges" 21(1) *International Journal of Law, Policy and The Family* 160-189, 2007.

[7] Bowlby, R., & McIntosh, J., "John Bowlby's legacy and meanings for the family law field: In conversation with Sir Richard Bowlby", *Family Court Review,* 49, 549–556, 2011.